Other books
by Richard Wheeler

Sherman's March

The Siege of Vicksburg

Voices of the Civil War

Voices of 1776

IWO

Richard Wheeler

Naval Institute Press
Annapolis, Maryland

To my sister
Margery Wheeler Mattox
who lived through
the home-front adventures

Originally published by Lippincott & Crowell, Publishers.

ISBN 1-55750-922-0

Designed by Ginger Legato

Printed in the United States of America

CONTENTS

	List of Illustrations	vi
	Preface	viii
	Prologue	1
1.	Birth of a Fortress	5
2.	The Spirit of *Bushido*	20
3.	Against a Rising Fury	30
4.	The Landing Force	44
5.	Toward the Objective	58
6.	The Assault Begins	73
7.	A Violent Afternoon	92
8.	The First Night	109
9.	Carnage on Two Fronts	116
10.	To the Base of Suribachi	132
11.	The Flag Raising	147
12.	Pressing the Main Attack	165
13.	Heartless Iron	179
14.	Battles in the Darkness	197
15.	On to the Bitter End	214
	Epilogue	235
	Bibliography	237
	Index	239

LIST OF ILLUSTRATIONS

(Map) The assault on Iwo Jima xii

(Map) Strategic situation, February, 1945 2–3

Lieutenant General Tadamichi Kuribayashi 9

Major Yoshitaka Horie 14

Rear Admiral Toshinosuke Ichimaru 24

General Kuribayashi and his staff 27

Aerial view of *Salt Lake City* 32

General Kuribayashi supervising buildup 38

Japanese officers studying map 39

Bird's-eye view of Marines off Tinian 63

Casualty being removed from LCI 69

American carrier plane strike 76

Scene on board landing craft 78

Iwo obscured by smoke and dust 79

Fifth Division Marines start inland 81

Aid station on beach 83

Machine gunner near Suribachi 91

Litter accumulates at shoreline 95

Jeep in sand during unloading 96

Wrecked Sherman tank 97

Fourth Division Marines pour from landing craft 101

Blasted tank and amphibian tractors 117

(Map) Progress of attack to north 119

Communications team moving inland 120

Iwo Jima phone booth 120

Fifth Division Marines being briefed 123

Fourth Division Marines at grenade distance 124

A 155-millimeter howitzer 127

Shattered Japanese emplacement 128

Attacking through the brush 133

Flamethrower in operation 139

Japanese soldiers shot while running 143

Destroyer standing off Suribachi 145

Crew of *Saratoga* fighting flames 146

Japanese flamethrower victim 148

Interpreter questioning prisoner 149

Rocket unit launching barrage 151

Unloading operations seen from LCI 153

Beach scene on February 23 154

Patrol passing Japanese corpse 156

First flag raising 158

Marine examining Japanese body 160

First flag comes down 162

Second flag raising 164

Poncho being used as stretcher 172

Marine officers in dugout 174

Major General Sadasue Senda 174

Helping a disabled comrade 180

Fourth Division post office 184

Stretcher team evacuating casualty 190

Fifth Division Marine and dead Japanese 198

Group of prisoners 200

Evacuation of casualties by air 202

General Erskine discussing attack 206

Terrain on way to Kitano Point 210

Marines urging Japanese to surrender 217

Front-line scene on March 11 219

Fifth Division cemetery 233

PREFACE

I served with the Marines on Iwo Jima, being an enlisted man with a rifle, a member of the company that raised the flag on Mount Suribachi, and one of the battle's more serious casualties. For the most part, I have kept myself out of the book. This is not a personal account but the story of Iwo Jima. However, considerable attention has been given to my "Easy" Company comrades, whose unique and especially dramatic role in the struggle resulted in the most famous combat photograph ever taken and inspired one of the largest bronze statues ever cast.

Much of the material in the book came directly from participants in the assault, many veterans responding to my request for information. Some gave it in interviews, others provided cassettes, and still others went to the trouble of writing long memoirs. These obliging men also made available letters they had written home, maps used on the battlefield, reports, unit rosters, casualty lists, newspaper clippings, and other items they had saved through the years. I am deeply grateful to all of these veterans and want to offer a special thanks to four who went "above and beyond the call of duty": Colonel Dave E. Severance, Arthur J. Stanton, Frank L. Crowe, and Robert D. Sinclair.

Some very useful contacts with participants were arranged by Virginia K. Stassen, ever a booster of the 5th Marine Division. And valuable aid with both research and correspondence was given by my longtime friend and assistant Kathleen Bross, who was also a constant source of support and encouragement.

Frequently consulted for the purpose of gleaning the Japanese side of the story was the manuscript account "Fighting Spirit: Iwo Jima," by Major Yoshitaka Horie of General Tadamichi Kuribayashi's staff. Also especially helpful was the material from Japanese sources used in publications by the Historical Division, Marine Corps Headquarters, and the books *Iwo Jima* by Richard Newcomb and *The Rising Sun* by John Toland.

The majority of the illustrations are official Marine Corps and Navy photographs, many of them obtained from the History and Museums Division of Marine Corps Headquarters. Others were provided by Louis R. Lowery, who took them while serving as a photographer for *Leatherneck* magazine. Major Horie supplied those from Japan, securing the Kuribayashi items from the general's widow.

Iwo was first published in 1980, the battle's thirty-fifth anniversary year. This edition is intended to help mark the fiftieth.

IWO

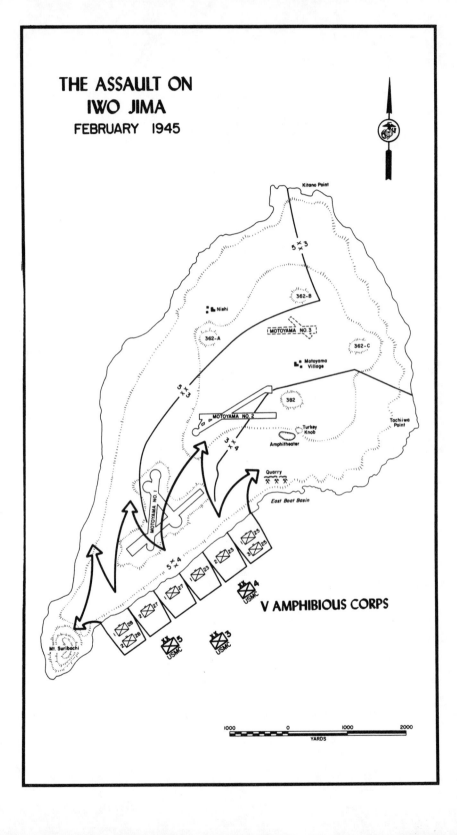

THE ASSAULT ON
IWO JIMA
FEBRUARY 1945

Kitano Point

5 X 3

362-B

Nishi

MOTOYAMA NO. 3

362-A

362-C

Motoyama
Village

5 X 3

382

MOTOYAMA NO. 2

Turkey
Knob

Tachiiwa
Point

3 X 4

Amphitheater

Quarry

East Boat Basin

5 X 4

3 25

2 23

3 25

1 23

2 4

USMC

V AMPHIBIOUS CORPS

2 27

1 23

1 27

1 28

1 5

3

2 28

USMC

USMC

Mt. Suribachi

1000   0   1000   2000
YARDS

PROLOGUE

It was the dawn of February 19, 1945. The waters of the western Pacific took on a silvery shimmer, and Iwo Jima was revealed to the Marines of the 5th Amphibious Corps—standing in full combat gear on the weather decks of their transports—as a gray silhouette with faint green tracings. The Marines were several miles east of the Japanese island, and this was their first view of it, their transports having eased up during the night and merged with the great assemblage of warships that had been bombarding the enemy's defenses for the past seventy-two hours.

It was D day, and the bombardment's pre-H-hour phase was opening. H hour, the time the first wave would hit the beach, was nine o'clock. The big guns of the battleships and cruisers flashed a vivid orange as they boomed their projectiles toward their assigned target areas. Also in action were rocket ships whose missiles left long white backblasts as they whooshed from their launchers. Destroyers, destroyer escorts, and mortar ships were moving into positions from which their weight could be added to the effort. Spotter planes wheeled overhead. The island sparkled with shellbursts, and a steady rumble issued back across the water. Smoke and dust billowed skyward.

A formation of heavy bombers from an Army base in the Marianas Islands was droning its way toward Iwo, its object to deliver a last-minute strike at an altitude of about 5,000 feet. And roaring from the decks of carriers in the waters about a hundred miles northwest of the island came Navy and Marine fighters and bombers equipped to assail the enemy with bullets, rockets, and napalm.

Iwo's defenders did not reply with fire of their own, but waited out the bombardment huddled in the dim light of an elaborate system of blockhouses, bunkers, pillboxes, caves, tunnels, and underground

1

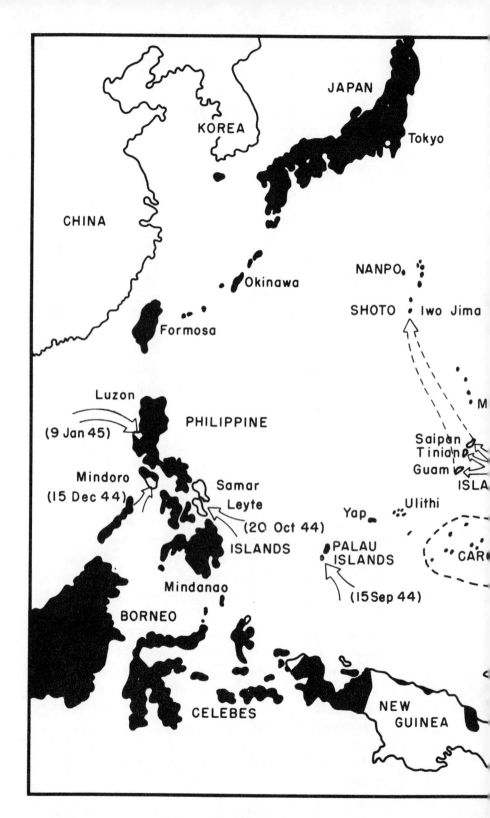

STRATEGIC SITUATION
FEBRUARY 1945

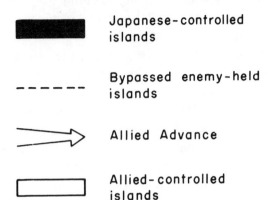

Japanese-controlled islands

Bypassed enemy-held islands

Allied Advance

Allied-controlled islands

us Island

Wake Island

Jun-10 Aug 44)

MARSHALL

Eniwetok

Kwajalein

ISLANDS

LANDS

NEW
IRELAND
Bougainville
SOLOMON
AIN   ISLANDS

rooms. Many of the men tried to shut out the noise by covering their ears with their hands. The island trembled as though in the grip of a major earthquake. Bits of concrete, volcanic rock, and dirt were shaken from shadowy ceilings and came pattering down on anxious heads. In sandy areas on Iwo, new craters were blasted in rapid succession, while those areas made up chiefly of craggy rocks underwent radical topographical changes. The sparse green brushwood was slashed and splintered. Direct hits collapsed cave entrances and damaged bunkers and pillboxes. But thousands of defenses remained fully operational, and the great majority of the defenders were unharmed.

Now, as the warships and aircraft prepared to bring the pre-H-hour bombardment to a furious conclusion, orders were shouted for the Marines on the transports to board their landing craft. One of the bloodiest invasions in the history of warfare was about to begin.

1
BIRTH OF A FORTRESS

In the mid-1930s, with World War II imminent, Iwo Jima, or Sulphur Island, was dreamily quiet under the subtropical sun. It was an obscure place, and seemed destined to remain so. Even the people of Japan, whose leaders had held dominion over the island for seventy years, were mostly unaware it existed. It lay in the Nanpo Shoto, an island chain that began at the entrance of Tokyo Bay and extended in a southerly direction for 750 miles. The chain, which was governed as part of the Japanese homeland, was made up of island groups, Iwo being in the southernmost, or Volcano group. The Bonin Islands lay immediately to the north. Iwo was about 700 miles south of Tokyo.

The island had an area of only seven and a half square miles. Viewed from the air it resembled a pork chop, with the shank extending toward the southwest. At the tip of the shank was Suribachi, a name that translates as "cone-shaped mountain." It was an extinct volcano. Composed chiefly of rocks, sand, sulphur, and patches of scraggy vegetation, Iwo lacked natural sources of fresh water. Its inhabitants—about 1,100 civilians, all of Japanese descent—had to rely on cisterns that held rainwater, distilled salt water, and water provided by visiting tankers. Ships came to this out-of-the-way place only six times a year. There was no harbor, and the vessels had to anchor well at sea, conducting their business with the beach by means of small boats. This was hazardous work when the surf was high, as it often was.

The islanders lived in typical one-story Japanese cottages, their livelihood depending on a sulphur refinery, a plant that processed medicinal herbs, fishing, and small-scale agriculture. The sandy soil yielded vegetables, grains, sugar cane, pineapples, bananas, and papayas. Iwo had a small inn used chiefly by visiting government officials, a bar serviced by young women, the necessary stores, and both a grade school and a high school. There was no motion picture theater. Communication with the mainland was maintained by radio.

It was through radio bulletins from Tokyo that the islanders followed the series of crises that brought on the war in Europe. In 1940 a civilian construction company from the Japanese mainland began building Iwo's first airport. The purpose was military, and in the spring of 1941 a naval detachment arrived and set up a few guns. But Iwo's ultimate military role was still unsuspected. These early preparations did nothing more than bring an element of excitement to the island.

Along with most of the rest of the Japanese people, the islanders were surprised when Japan entered the war on the side of Germany and Italy with a stunning air strike on the American naval forces at Pearl Harbor in the Hawaiian Islands on December 7, 1941. Surprise turned to elation as the Imperial Army and Navy pressed ahead with a promising campaign of conquest in the Pacific and in Southeast Asia, an extension of adventures begun in Manchuria and China a few years earlier.

News came quickly of the capture of the American islands of Guam and Wake, and January and February, 1942, brought the announcement of great victories over the Americans in the Philippines and over the British at Hong Kong and Singapore. The news in March and April was equally stirring: The conquering forces occupied the Netherlands East Indies, New Guinea, New Ireland, New Britain, the Solomons, the Admiralties, the Bismarcks, and the Gilberts.

To the majority of the Japanese people, this expansionism seemed wholly justified. They were the proud and sensitive products of a venerable culture, and they felt that Japan had been denied her rightful role of leadership in the Eastern world. The Western powers had long been dominating the region and exploiting it economically, while treating its people as inferiors. The Japanese believed they were striking now in self-defense. They dreamed of creating a rich and powerful empire, one of benefit to all people of their color, and one safe not only from Western exploitation but also from Russian communism. Many Japanese viewed the war as a holy crusade. This feeling was reinforced by the Shinto religion, which taught that the Japanese were of divine origin and was construed as prophesying their domination of the world.

The great dream had a short life. In May the Japanese fleet was checked by American carrier planes in the Coral Sea, northeast of Australia. And in June occurred the Battle of Midway, in the central Pacific, in which the fleet was badly diminished. In August the Americans took the offensive by invading the southernmost island in Japan's new empire, Guadalcanal in the Solomons. This was the starting point of a two-pronged advance toward the Japanese mainland. The plan, set in motion in 1943, called for the Army's General Douglas MacArthur to command on the left, moving by way of the Bismarcks, New Guinea, and the Philippines, while the Navy, under Admiral Chester W. Nimitz, proceeded on the right through the Gilberts and the Marshalls to the Marianas.

With the war's tide having turned also in Europe, Japan could expect no help from Germany and Italy. She fought stubbornly, but, one by one, her outposts were overrun. At the same time her naval and air forces sustained crippling blows, and her merchant shipping, equally vital to her defense, was devastated by planes and submarines.

The spring of 1944 found MacArthur on the northern coast of New Guinea looking toward the islands that led to the Philippines, while Nimitz, having taken the Gilberts and the Marshalls, was preparing to assault the Marianas. The Navy's route toward Japan was the more direct and the objectives were all relatively small islands, easier of conquest than the large islands in MacArthur's path. Therefore, the campaign for the Marianas—Guam, Saipan, and Tinian—was given priority. The Marianas, suitable as bases for America's newest long-range bomber, the B-29 Superfort, were less than 1,500 miles south of Tokyo. Once the islands were captured and the bases established, the B-29s could conduct regular strikes against Japan.

On a line between the Marianas and Tokyo, close to the halfway point, lay tiny Iwo Jima. Its medial location, coupled with the fact that it was the only spot in the Nanpo Shoto capable of supporting airfields with long runways, transformed Iwo, after ages of insignificance, into one of the islands of the hour.

Even as the American forces prepared for their invasion of the Marianas, Japan marked Iwo for a major buildup. The first ships carrying reinforcements—both army and naval units—reached the island in March and April, 1944, and the men were welcomed at the beaches by Iwo's civilians, few of whom could have suspected how drastically their lives were about to change.

Officers informed the troops that "those who want to return home alive must build fortifications." Also undertaken was the construction of a second airfield. By the end of May, the island held 7,000 soldiers, sailors, and airmen, about 200 aircraft (fighters, bombers, and patrol planes), and a burgeoning arsenal of weapons, including coast defense guns, antiaircraft guns, artillery pieces, machine guns, and rifles.

Initially, the garrison's top commander was Captain Tsuenezo Wachi of the Imperial Navy. At the outbreak of hostilities he had been a highly successful spy, operating against the United States from Mexico City, where he was deputy naval attaché at the Japanese embassy. Wachi was destined to survive the war, after which he exchanged his cloak and dagger and his naval sword for the trappings of a Buddhist priest. At present, the captain was troubled by growing rivalry and dissension between Iwo's army and navy units. He warned that "on this narrow island where water and other necessities of life are very scarce" a proper fighting strength could be maintained only if "the army and navy are especially careful to act as one harmonious unit."

Wachi issued his warning on May 31. A day or two earlier, Tokyo was the scene of an event that would lift the burden of Iwo's top command from the captain's shoulders. Lieutenant General Tadamichi Kuribayashi, in charge of Tokyo's Imperial Guards, was summoned to the office of the Prime Minister, General Hideki Tojo, and informed that the Iwo command was his.

"The eyes of the entire nation will be focused on the defense of this island," said Tojo. "Among all our generals, you are best qualified for the task."

Kuribayashi replied that he was honored to be chosen. But privately he suspected that his name had come to the fore because of a regrettable incident that had occurred in a Tokyo barracks under his command. A rambunctious cadet had set it on fire. Kuribayashi had also heard a rumor that another general had been picked for the Iwo job but had talked himself out of it.

It was true, however, that Kuribayashi was well qualified for this vital and difficult assignment. In the first place he was a *samurai*, a

Lieutenant General Tadamichi Kuribayashi.

member of Japan's warrior caste. Although the caste was no longer recognized by the government, it was still a strong part of the nation's traditions. Kuribayashi's male ancestors had been warriors for generations, and he had been in the army for thirty years. In his early fifties, he was tall for a Japanese, nearly five feet nine inches, and was well proportioned, though he had a small potbelly that Radio Tokyo later described as being "filled with strong fighting spirit." He had confidence and a firm will. In his high school days he had led a strike against the school authorities and narrowly escaped expulsion, doubtless surviving because of his scholastic record. A classmate described him as "a young literary enthusiast" who excelled at "speech-making, composition, and poem-making."

Kuribayashi's many military assignments included tours in both the United States and Canada. In the late 1920s he served in Washington, D.C., as a deputy attaché. Taught to drive by an American officer, he bought a car and toured the nation. He was fascinated by the tall buildings on Broadway in New York City, and in Buffalo stayed at a rooming house run by a tattooed woman he found to be "bigger than a *sumo* wrestler." She helped him practice his English.

Kuribayashi was especially impressed by America's industrial strength, as evidenced in Detroit. He decided that the nation's great peacetime economy could be turned into a powerful war machine by a single telegram from Washington. The American people, he noted, were "energetic and versatile," and he was sure that in an emergency they would show real fighting ability.

"The United States," he said in a letter home, "is the last country in the world that Japan should fight."

Kuribayashi studied cavalry tactics under American officers, one of whom, Brigadier General George V. H. Mosely, gave him an autographed picture of himself as a token of friendship and esteem. Following his years in the United States and Canada, Kuribayashi served in his own country's cavalry, seeing combat in China. After Pearl Harbor, by this time a general, he took part in the occupation of Hong Kong as Chief of Staff of the 23rd Army. In 1943 he was summoned to Tokyo to take command of the Guards, one of his duties being to protect the Imperial Palace. During these days he was accorded the singular honor of an audience with Emperor Hirohito. Then came the incident of the blazing barracks and his session with Tojo.

As he prepared to leave home for Iwo Jima in early June, 1944, the general decided not to take his *samurai* sword. He said nothing pessimistic to his wife, Yoshii, and the children, but told his brother, "I may not return alive from this assignment." He vowed to fight like a true *samurai*.

It was the *samurai* caste that, hundreds of years before, in connection with the Shinto religion, had developed the *Bushido* code. This stressed courage, honor, loyalty, stoicism during suffering and pain, self-sacrifice, and a contempt for death. To become a prisoner of war was a disgrace; it was far better to commit suicide than to live in shame. The Emperor was venerated, for Shinto taught that he had a divine origin. Also revered were heroic ancestors, and the *samurai* sought to perform deeds that would earn him a place among these legendary figures. The *Bushido* code eventually spread beyond its *samurai* origins to become an integral part of Japan's ideology.

On arrival at Iwo Jima, Kuribayashi was greeted by a delegation of officers and a hundred schoolchildren waving small Japanese flags and singing patriotic songs. He liked children, and the demonstration pleased him, but a conference with the officers and an inspection of the island put him in a sober mood. The troops were disorganized and too few in number, and the defenses were still far too weak to withstand even a minor assault. There was a staggering amount of work to be done. Would American plans, the general wondered, allow him time enough to do it?

During the night of June 13 a sleepy radioman at the Iwo station was startled into alertness. A large American naval force was bombarding the Marianas island of Saipan, apparently preliminary to an invasion. The excitement this caused among Iwo's troops was accompanied by uncertainty. What was intended for them? The most likely development—if Saipan was truly about to be invaded—was a covering attack by carrier planes. Since Iwo lay only 700 miles north of Saipan, her aircraft were a threat to the landing.

Seven carriers under Rear Admiral Joseph J. Clark approached to within 135 miles of Iwo's east coast on June 15. Even as the island set "Condition 1" and the troops and civilians were running toward their air raid shelters, Clark's planes swarmed over the horizon like so many hornets. A series of fighters roared off Iwo's runways, and antiaircraft crews rushed into action. Some of the American planes met the Japanese in dogfights, while others dive-bombed the airfields, and still others took intelligence photos.

Hundreds of the people running for shelter stopped to watch the show, which was over in minutes as the Americans took control of the sky. Ten Japanese planes were shot down, and a number of others were destroyed on the ground. Two American planes were lost. The attackers winged away to their carriers, and that evening a Japanese soldier wrote in his diary: "Somehow my faith in our naval air groups has been somewhat shaken."

The photos of the island secured that day were to prove remarkably helpful to the intelligence personnel whose job it was to keep tabs on the defenses. Taken while the buildup was still in its infancy, these pictures would be used for comparison with sets snapped during ensuing months. The enemy's progress would always be a known factor.

Clark's planes returned to Iwo, through thick gray skies, the following day. With no Japanese planes rising to meet them, they attacked those on the ground, destroying many before departing.

These raids did not keep Iwo Jima from sending groups of bombers and torpedo planes to the Marianas to contest the American landing. The missions were flown at night. But the power against them was overwhelming, and few of the planes returned. Most of the fliers met their ends in the dark sea.

On June 24, a week after his second strike at Iwo, the American admiral sent his aircraft toward the island a third time. The Japanese were alerted early, and eighty planes rose to intercept. Many of the pilots were students still in training, and a veteran who survived the day said later that it was very disheartening to see "our inexperienced pilots falling in flames, one after the other, as the Hellcats blasted our outmoded Zeroes out of the sky." About thirty were lost. In addition, two more waves, a total of about sixty planes, were sent aloft, and nearly two-thirds became casualties. In all, the losses numbered sixty-six.

The mood was dismal in the airmen's quarters on Iwo that night. In the light of a few weak bulbs, men sat on their bunks smoking and discussing the day in subdued tones, acutely aware of the empty bunks in the shadows about them.

Events of the past ten days had come as a shock to Iwo's 1,100 civilians. Heretofore, they had taken for granted that Japan, in spite of the fall of her Pacific outposts, was amply able to defend her inner circle. Now, when they looked to Iwo's officers for reassurance, none was forthcoming. Instead, they were told they would have to evacuate to the home islands, with the exception of healthy men under forty, who were to be drafted.

General Kuribayashi now began writing letters home that spoke of the probability of his death. He warned his wife, Yoshii: "You must not expect my survival." To his youngest daughter, Takako, who was ten, he wrote that she was his chief concern: "Let me pray that you will grow up fast and in health, so that you will be able to help your mother."

Although Iwo Jima was directly under the authority of Imperial General Headquarters in Tokyo, Kuribayashi was permitted to defend Iwo Jima as he thought best. Previously, it had been Headquarters practice to dictate to island commanders, but this had gained nothing and perhaps had lost much. While pushing his defense and organizational plans, the general issued calls for additional troops, arms, and supplies. It was not easy to get them, for Japan's supply routes were being harassed by American planes and submarines. Nor was unloading at the island a simple task, due to the lack of harborage and the frequent high seas. Moreover, at any moment those punishing planes might appear.

Kuribayashi had one clear advantage. The beach areas where an enemy might land were limited to the southwestern half of the island, the most likely beach being on the east. The defense could be planned around this knowledge. Since it was obvious that Iwo would be heavily pounded by planes and warships, most installations would have to be moved underground, a task facilitated by the fact that the island's volcanic rock was honeycombed with caves.

At about this time in the United States, high-ranking Americans were secretly pondering the possibility of subduing the island with gas. Neither the United States nor Japan had signed that part of the Geneva Convention outlawing gas warfare. The plan under consideration was for Iwo to be covered with gas by means of naval shells, the ships standing off at a safe distance; the gunners would be unaware they were firing gas, especially since a few high-explosive shells would be mixed in. The job done, a short wait was to follow, while the island became safe through natural decontamination. Then the Americans were to step ashore, having won the objective without receiving a single casualty. The idea seemed to be on its way toward implementation, but when the time came for the White House to make its final decision, the secret paper was marked: "All prior endorsements denied—Franklin D. Roosevelt, Commander in Chief."

The President was not, it appears, governed so much by the fear of gas retaliation as by the recollection of American outrage, expressed internationally, when the Germans launched gas warfare during World War I. To use gas against Iwo Jima would be to fly in the face of America's own propaganda.

It was now late June, 1944. A young major in Tokyo was about to become a member of General Kuribayashi's staff. He was Yoshitaka Horie, first commissioned in 1936 upon graduating from the Military Academy, Imperial Japanese Army. As a first lieutenant in China in 1938, Horie had been badly wounded by machine gun fire, one of the bullets entering his head and grazing the motor nerves controlling his legs. He called himself "a crippled person," but had remained a first-rate officer.

For the past year Major Horie had been working as a liaison officer between the army and the navy, and this gave him access to many telegrams and much other information regarding the progress of the war. His perspective being broader than that of most officers, he was among the few who realized how badly things were going, and he had begun carrying a packet of potassium cyanide against the day—which he was certain would come—when he would have to take

Major Yoshitaka Horie.

the honorable way out. He had barely missed being sent to Saipan, where many Japanese were presently dying.

The major was destined to survive and to become one of the chroniclers of the Iwo campaign. Before leaving Japan for the island, he went home for a brief visit. "My wife and I," he says in his manuscript account "Fighting Spirit: Iwo Jima," "exchanged cups of water for everlasting separation." She was pregnant with their second child.

Horie's plane took off on June 29, into a fine blue sky. After raising himself in his seat for a last wistful look at Japan's coastal scenery, the major settled down and went to sleep. When he awoke, the plane was banking over Iwo Jima. "What a tiny island!" he exclaimed to himself, and as the plane landed he added, "Sink this island to the bottom of the sea!"

That evening Horie talked with Kuribayashi over supper and whiskey. The general still had his headquarters in a private home, and the pair sat on *tatamis*, or straw mats, at a low table. Kuribayashi expressed bitter regret that, before the war, no one had listened to him and the other officers who had served in America and understood the nation's power. But the general revealed a spark of optimism about Iwo, suggesting that a battle there might result in a great containing operation, especially since Japan's Combined Fleet would undoubtedly participate.

Horie informed him that Japan's Combined Fleet no longer existed and that no such operation would develop.

"You're drunk!" said the general. "This island belongs to Tokyo City."

The major explained that the Combined Fleet had been devastated in a battle in the Philippine Sea ten days earlier, and that Japan now had only a few scattered naval forces. Kuribayashi remained incredulous. The discussion was interrupted by an air raid siren, and the officers went to a shelter. When the "all clear" sounded, they bid each other good night. Horie retired to a room with some other officers, but he did not sleep well. He was annoyed that Kuribayashi had questioned his word. As if this was not enough, one of his roommates was a heavy snorer.

The next morning, with the sky again a bright blue, Kuribayashi called for his car, "a poor old one," and took Horie to the eastern beach, near the base of Mount Suribachi. Looking out over the cobalt sea, which was sparkling in the sun, the general said, "The enemy must land here. He has no alternative." Then the general surprised the major by throwing himself down on the dark volcanic sand as though he had just stormed ashore.

Next they drove to the first airfield, on a plateau just to the north. This time the major was required to become the enemy, the general giving such commands as "Lie down, Horie!" "Make yourself lower, Horie!" and "Stand up, Horie!" With Kuribayashi pretending that his swagger stick was a rifle, the major was repeatedly "shot." Horie began to believe a complaint he had heard about the general— that he paid too much attention to minor details.

The major thought that some attention should be given to the possibility of blowing up and sinking at least a part of the island, thus making it useless to the enemy as an air station. Weeks later, Kuribayashi was to give this idea a hearing, then drop it as impossible.

That afternoon Horie slipped away to the island's north coast to seek a hot spring that was said to be fine for bathing. As he was taking off his shirt, the air raid siren sounded. Instead of trying to make for a shelter, Horie went into the sea and hid under a cliff. When the planes were gone, he returned to the spring, and found its waters just right for comfort. As he lolled there, he mused that this sort of thing would be a real delight in peacetime.

In the evening Horie again dined and drank with the general. Once more Horie brought up the state of Japan's defenses, citing in particular naval setbacks that were not generally known to army men. At first Kuribayashi tried to disparage the major, calling him "a walking encyclopedia," but soon the general began to realize that he was hearing the truth. He stopped eating and drinking to listen in earnest. Horie closed his sad recital, his eyes brimming, by repeating the story of the recent disaster in the Philippine Sea. He called this "the death day of Japan."

"Ah," said Kuribayashi, "I did not know these things."

Horie went on to say that, under the old traditions, their only choice as Japanese officers seemed to be to try to kill as many Americans as they could before they themselves died. To dramatize his point, the major displayed his packet of potassium cyanide. For a time after this, the two men sat in silence.

It was decided that Major Horie would not stay on Iwo Jima, but would join the garrison at Chichi Jima, an island about 150 miles to the north. This had become Iwo's staging area. Most of the troops, arms, and supplies coming from the home islands stopped first at Chichi, and were sent on to Iwo as they were called for, or as the hazardous conditions permitted. Horie was to take charge of these important activities, his designation "emergency supply officer," and he was flown from Iwo to Chichi on July 1. Chichi had both seaplane accommodations and a small airport.

Although Chichi, about twelve square miles in area, was ruggedly hilly, it was a pleasant island, having fresh water, scenic vegetation, and a sheltered harbor. The major decided it was the kind of place where a man might be happy when he grew old.

Living on Chichi when Horie arrived was a family with American blood, descendants of Nathanial Savory, a whaler from Massachusetts who had settled there more than a hundred years earlier. During their decades on the island the Savorys had retained some American customs, celebrating the Fourth of July and Washington's Birthday each year, for example, by displaying the Stars and Stripes. They were astonished when they and their small, out-of-the-way island were caught up in a war in which that flag was involved. The family was about to be evacuated to Japan but would return at the close of hostilities.

On Iwo Jima, the evening of July 2 brought a new alarm. Radio monitors detected a sudden increase in American messages. The code was undecipherable, but the strength of the signals indicated that a large naval force was somewhere nearby. Dawn brought another raid by carrier planes, both Hellcats and Avengers, the latter being torpedo bombers carrying three-man crews. The dwindling garrison of Japanese fighters—about forty Zeroes—tried valiantly to intercept, but within a short time twenty crashed into the sea, some of them in flames. During the dogfights, the American bombers attacked the island in five waves, and had everything their own way as they pounded the installations and grounded planes. The next day, July 4, the attack was resumed. Eleven more Zeroes fell to the Hellcats, and the bombers struck again.

That day, at earliest dawn, Chichi Jima also was hit. Major Horie was still in bed. "It was very shameful that I could not find my trousers for a while. The bombing continued the whole morning. We could not do anything."

Also busy on the fourth was the U. S. Army's 28th Photo Reconnaissance Squadron, which came from Saipan. Making sixteen low-altitude passes over Iwo, these planes took pictures of excellent scope and clarity.

When the last group of aircraft vanished over the horizon and quiet came to Iwo, it was discovered that only seventeen planes— nine Zeroes and eight Jills, or torpedo bombers—remained operational, and even some of these were damaged. The airstrips were cratered, and numerous surface installations were shattered.

Instead of giving up in despair, the air commanders called a meeting to determine how they might carry on, and they decided to plan a suicide mission. This was probably the first organized suicide mission of the war. All prior crash-attacks on American vessels were apparently made by pilots acting on their own.

Captain Kanzo Miura called together the men of the seventeen operational planes. Solemnly he told them he was about to send them on a mission they would not survive; that they were to seek out the American carrier force and crash their planes into it. They might be met by hundreds of fighter planes, but they were to decline battle, flying wing to wing to their objective. "No obstacle," the captain concluded, "is to stop you from completing your mission. Every plane will plunge directly into a carrier."

The fliers had their orders, but no one shouted, "*Banzai!*" Voluntary suicide for Japan was a glorious thing, but to have the choice made for you was something else. After a few moments of silence, however, the mandate was accepted and the fliers began preparing at once for their departure from both Iwo Jima and the earth. The other airmen presented them with small gifts—objects from among their personal belongings—as tokens of admiration and affection.

The seventeen planes took off on July 5, information having come that the American force was about 500 miles south of Iwo. While the little squadron was still some 60 miles from the objective, American fighters suddenly began pouring from the clouds on all sides. The Japanese tightened their formation and obeyed their orders not to fight back. But within minutes two of the torpedo bombers were careening toward the sea. It became impossible for the rest of the planes to continue in formation, and they broke and began to return the fire. But this accomplished little. One by one, the Jills and Zeroes began going down in smoke and flames.

At last the survivors found cover in a cloud formation. Here they encountered violent turbulence and blinding rain, but after a long struggle they broke out of the storm into an area that was calm and clear. The American planes were nowhere in sight, nor did the long expanse of rippling blue sea reveal any carriers. They searched until twilight without success. What should they do? Trying to find the ships in the dark would only exhaust their fuel and send them into the sea, which seemed senseless. After some anguished soul-searching they decided to return to Iwo, despite their fear that this would be construed as a dishonorable act.

The darkness on Iwo was deep when they found the airstrip markers and landed, the surviving planes numbering four Zeroes and one Jill. The fliers told their story of failure with bowed heads, expecting at the very least to be severely reprimanded. Instead, they received the warmest sympathy.

These men hoped to be able to take their planes up again, but the chance never came. The next day an array of American warships moved in close to the island and began to shell it furiously. Soon four of the five surviving planes were flaming junk. Elsewhere, tent camps were blown away, and buildings went up in splinters. "For two days," one soldier wrote later, "we cowered like rats, trying to dig ourselves deeper into the acrid volcanic ash and dust. Never have I felt so helpless, so puny." He noted that "men screamed and cursed and shouted; they shook their fists and swore revenge." Casualties were frequent and bloody. Some of the men were blown to pieces.

For several days after the task force withdrew, the Japanese were in a state of taut apprehension. An invasion seemed imminent. Calls went out to Tokyo to rush all available reinforcements, and lookouts were posted atop Mount Suribachi to scan the ocean for signs of the invasion fleet. False alarms brought periods of confusion. One day several Japanese transports appeared on the horizon, and elation swept the island. Some of the men rushed to high spots and waved and shouted. Then the ships sank before their eyes, victims of torpedoes from American submarines.

Actually, the invasion was still more than seven months away. The United States, in fact, was not yet certain what it intended to do about Iwo. Most of the operations against the island up to this time were meant only as cover for the assault on the Marianas.

2

THE SPIRIT OF *BUSHIDO*

One of Major Horie's earliest jobs on Chichi Jima was to see to it that the civilians evacuated from Iwo, and those living on Chichi, were sent to Japan. Some of these unhappy people, reluctant to journey so far from their homes, asked permission to stay on Chichi for a while to watch the situation, and Horie permitted this. His kindness soon got the major into trouble with General Kuribayashi, who telegraphed from Iwo: "According to some rumors, there have remained some civilians at Chichi Jima. Don't you know that they become an encumbrance to the armed forces in the case of battle?" Horie sent back a telegram apologizing for his "carelessness," and the tarrying civilians were booked for passage to Japan on the first available ship.

Most of the reinforcements and supplies intended for Iwo came from Japan to Chichi by means of organized convoys, which included armed escort vessels. Japan's escort service, however, was inadequate. Planned around a limited number of vessels in the first place, it had been made still smaller by American submarines. The vessels were spread very thinly now, and their overworked commanders had announced, "We have stopped rescuing floating personnel." This sometimes made for calamitous casualties when submarines struck.

Japan had her own submarines, but, as Horie lamented, they had "a poor level of science." This weakness was characteristic of the navy in general. Moreover, many officers viewed modern technology with skepticism. Some ship captains spurned their radar systems, preferring to fight entirely "with inherited eyes."

Horie, though bound by the ancient *Bushido* code, was a progressive thinker. He was astonished to find the commander of the

Chichi Jima garrison, Lieutenant General Yosio Tachibana, studying Japanese military tactics of preceding centuries, as far back as the 1500s, and insisting that if Japan applied these tactics now she could win the war. This was consistent with what Horie had heard from some of the people back in Japan, who believed that if the enemy ever managed to hit the home islands with its fire bombs the emergency could be handled by bucket brigades.

As for General Tachibana, it was his destiny to be hanged as a war criminal when Japan surrendered. He allowed—possibly ordered—the Chichi garrison to kill, over a period of some months, a dozen American fliers who were shot down in the area and captured. Most of the men were tied to a stake and beheaded or bayoneted, and at least one was beaten to death. Bizarre to the point of seeming untrue is that, at the instigation of an infantry major who believed that eating an enemy's flesh boosted morale and that human liver was good for ulcers, pieces of some of the slain were eaten at *sake* parties. One of the bodies had been buried for a day before the major decided to have it exhumed and its liver taken. From a fresher corpse came both the liver and a six-pound piece of thigh.

To run his reinforcement and supply operation, Major Horie had the aid of about 3,000 troops of the Chichi garrison. He had gathered about fifty small vessels, mostly fishing craft and sailboats, to make the stealthy trips to Iwo. Vessels this size, it was hoped, might go unnoticed by planes and submarines.

The bigger ships that reached Chichi from Japan were unloaded at night, and the troops and supplies were trucked back into the hills. The supplies were simply dispersed to suitable spots in the woods, while the men were housed in the island's several long highway tunnels. They were obliged to huddle on mats placed beside the road and against the walls, and were often disturbed by trucks rumbling through. The next evening those supplies and troops slated for passage to Iwo were assembled at the harbor and loaded aboard Horie's vessels. During the first night these craft negotiated the dark waters to Haha Jima, a small island along the route to Iwo, and remained hidden there during the following day. On the second night they went on to Iwo, where they were unloaded in the darkness, menaced by the island's treacherous surf, with the garrison lending a hand.

Among the most important supplies arriving on Iwo were

thousands of bags of cement and many tons of reinforcement rods for building the fortifications. Obtaining sand for making good, hard concrete was no problem; the island abounded with it.

American submarine activity in Japanese waters was increasing, and the danger to Iwo's supply lines started where they left the home islands. On July 18 the USS *Cobia* sighted a convoy nearing Chichi and sent a torpedo crashing into the transport *Nishu Maru*. Only two men were lost, but twenty-eight tanks went down. They belonged to the 26th Tank Regiment, whose commander was Lieutenant Colonel Takeichi Nishi.

Nishi was a baron, the scion of an old and wealthy family. After graduating from Japan's elite cavalry school, the young baron—one of the best horsemen the school ever turned out—began to earn an international reputation. In 1930 he competed in horse shows all over Europe. A dashing figure very appealing to women, he was admired also by men, not only for his personal qualities and horsemanship but also for his remarkable drinking ability. While in Europe, Nishi bought a spirited horse he named Uranus, and in 1932 took the horse to Los Angeles to compete in the Olympics. A superb team, Nishi and Uranus gained for Japan the gold medal in the individual jumping event. The baron enjoyed his stay in California. He won a ready acceptance among the Hollywood people, was entertained by other well-known figures, and emerged the victor in many a drinking bout.

Nishi was in his early forties now, and Uranus was old and gray. Before leaving Tokyo, the baron had spent a long moment of farewell with the horse, and he carried a lock of its mane in his pocket.

Reaching Chichi Jima after the torpedo attack, Nishi went to Horie's office. The major had heard of the baron's unquenchable thirst, and hastened to present him with a bottle of beer. Horie's first impression of the celebrated horseman was that he was "an aristocratic gentleman" but tough, and that he had long legs. During their meeting the air raid siren sounded, and within moments a bullet splintered its way through Horie's table and into the floor. The baron hurried toward an air raid shelter, but Horie stopped just outside his office building. He was accustomed to these raids, and expected no further danger from this one. When the "all clear" sounded, the two men returned to their beer.

Nishi was sad over the loss of his tanks. He would have to apply for replacements through Tokyo. The baron admitted to Horie that he wasn't keen on being sent to Iwo. When he was transferred from the cavalry to the tank corps he had envisioned doing his fighting in an area large enough to allow him mobility. Iwo was too confined. He added that he regretted Japan's war with America. "I have some friends there, in connection with a horse. Everything is ironic. Well, let me go to Iwo Jima and talk with General Kuribayashi."

Kuribayashi greeted Nishi warmly, probably more because they were both former cavalry officers than because Nishi was a celebrity. They toured the island together and discussed defense plans. Nishi noted that fortifications were still sparse. Although the island's manpower was growing and arms and supplies were beginning to accumulate, the defense network was still largely in the planning stage.

Air transportation was being maintained between Iwo and the home islands, and at the end of July, Kuribayashi sent Nishi to Tokyo to obtain more tanks. A few days later Kuribayashi wrote his wife: "Open my army suitcase which I sent by Lt. Col. Nishi as soon as possible. Particularly, kill the insects of Iwo Jima. I am afraid of them growing in Tokyo." The island, he said, was full of flies "that come in our mouths and eyes"; also "many ants that climb up our bodies," and "many cockroaches that crawl around us." He explained that the suitcase, which held some of his personal effects, was only the beginning. "I am going to send back most of my belongings before I die."

Along with 2,300 naval reinforcements that arrived at Iwo in early August came Rear Admiral Toshinosuke Ichimaru, from then on to be the island's top naval officer. His was not the usual sort of naval command, for most of his sailors were destined to fight as ground troops, much of the time huddling in holes—the last situation in the world a respectable sailor would choose for himself.

The admiral was a serious, taciturn man, and a naval flier, one of Japan's best. But he had been hurt in the crash of an experimental plane in the mid-1920s and had been left with a serious limp. Thereafter, he was given mostly training commands, a fate he resented. Consequently, he was more than willing to go to Iwo. Like Kuribayashi, he had a talent for composing poetry, and penned an ode to his transfer. He was grateful for the chance "to fight on the foremost front." Regarding his death as inevitable, he wished to "fall like the flower petals" in his garden at home. "May enemy bombs aim at me," he wrote, "and enemy shells mark me as their target."

Ichimaru got his wish about enemy bombs very quickly, for the

Americans began raiding Iwo regularly, starting August 10. The admiral had the means to do at least a limited amount of striking back, for the navy's antiaircraft positions were well developed, and its shattered air groups had been replaced.

Iwo had a new enemy—the U. S. Army's Seventh Air Force, which had established itself in the Marianas, all three of the islands being now in American hands. The squadrons, composed of heavy B-24 bombers, or Liberators, did considerable damage, though a great many of their bombs were merely absorbed by Iwo's sand. Huge craters appeared where they struck.

The men of the Seventh found Iwo to be an unpredictable target. One day they would be met by only fitful and inaccurate antiaircraft fire, with no fighter planes coming up, and the big bombers would simply drop their loads and return to the Marianas. On the next visit, Iwo's ack-ack would be terrible, and Japanese fighters would be buzzing everywhere. The B-24s had no fighter escort (though a long-range escort service was being readied), and their security

Rear Admiral Toshinosuke Ichimaru.

depended on their own gunners. The ack-ack often made hits, and Iwo's fighters proved a real hazard to the relatively clumsy bombers.

On August 14, thirteen Liberators struck Iwo with 147 bombs, their target being the first airfield. The craters made a good bit of work for the island's repair crews, but the raiders paid a high price. Two of the big planes were hit. The first was penetrated by three exploding shells and took fire on its command deck. Sergeant Bernard Temple, a combat photographer, smothered the flames with his hands and torso. The craft was able to make it back to its base, but it had about 150 holes for its ground crew to work on. The second B-24 had just unleashed its load and was heading out when it was surrounded by Japanese planes. Three phosphorus bombs burst just ahead of it but did no damage. The Liberator's gunners were firing, and shortly one hollered, "I got the bastard!" A plane peeled off and plunged toward the sea.

Then a burst of machine gun bullets from another craft hit a set of the big bomber's control cables. At the same time a 20-millimeter shell exploded in the cockpit, killing the co-pilot and wounding the pilot in the right arm, body, and face. The damage to the manual controls caused the plane to zoom upward for several thousand feet. The attackers did not follow. The wounded pilot, Lieutenant James R. Mosher of Minneapolis, managed to switch to automatic pilot and use the trim tabs to level the plane. Three of her four engines were acting up alarmingly, but the resourceful Mosher managed to obtain a fairly even distribution of power by feathering one of the props and jockeying the throttles.

Mosher's flight jacket was cut off and he was given first aid. Captain Carey A. Stone, a flight surgeon who had come along as an observer and who had also been hurt, offered the pilot sulfanilamide tablets, but Mosher refused them, saying he did not want to risk impairing his sight or reflexes.

Two of the Liberators that had come through the raid safely moved in to fly cover, but their prop wash nearly sent the crippled plane out of control. They quickly withdrew. Makeshift repairs were made to the manual cables, but Mosher continued to use automatic pilot, wishing to save the repaired manuals for the landing at home.

The three-hour trip was an anxious eternity. Spirits rose when the Marianas were spotted, at first only tiny patches in the sea. Mosher headed the plane toward Saipan at 11,000 feet. He asked whether the men wanted to bail out or risk a crash landing. All elected to stay with the plane, but faces were grave as Mosher switched from automatic pilot to manual.

The repaired cables failed to do their job. The plane kept slipping off to one side or the other. Soon it slipped completely and went spiraling toward the water. As he fought to regain control, Mosher shouted, "You'd better get the hell out of here!"

Several of the men managed to jump, their chutes breaking white against the sky. The others held on and went down with the plane. When it hit the waves with a heavy splash, only Mosher and Private First Class Kealer Harbin, of Tulsa, Oklahoma, the crew's assistant radio operator, managed to swim clear and climb aboard one of the rubber rafts that inflated automatically. As the Liberator went under, the other men were nowhere in sight. Of those who chuted out, only one seems to have survived, the flight surgeon who had come along to observe combat conditions.

Air raids notwithstanding, the month of September saw the work on Iwo Jima's defenses undertaken in earnest. The island now held about 15,000 men, the basic army unit being the 109th Infantry Division. Chief components of this force were the 2nd Mixed Brigade, the 145th Infantry Regiment, and the 3rd Battalion, 17th Mixed Infantry Regiment. Attached were several independent tank battalions and an air group. The division's armaments included artillery, howitzers, rockets, mortars, and machine guns.

Navy personnel included air groups, a specially organized Iwo Jima Naval Guard Force, and the 204th Naval Construction Battalion, composed of Koreans and Japanese, 400 of whom were natives of the island. The navy manned the island's antiaircraft batteries and its huge coast defense guns. All navy men but the coast defense and antiaircraft crews were equipped and trained for infantry action.

The island's chain of command was complicated. Although the majority of the forces were army, General Kuribayashi was not in absolute control. Admiral Ichimaru maintained command of the naval forces. A certain autonomy was even kept by a portion of Kuribayashi's troops, the 2nd Mixed Brigade. Moreover, each defense sector held a mixture of army and navy units, and both services had their own headquarters. Although Kuribayashi and Ichimaru maintained a working relationship and directed their subordinates to cooperate with one another, the island naturally saw considerable confusion and argument.

General Kuribayashi and his staff.

Kuribayashi disagreed with some of his staff and some of the navy men on defense tactics. Many of Iwo's officers still believed that when the island was assaulted Japan would send out a powerful fleet and that, with this aid, the garrison would be able to annihilate the landing force in the surf. Kuribayashi knew that even if Japan had the fleet these men envisioned, the Americans would still get ashore. They always had. It was the Japanese troops at the water's edge who were annihilated.

The general proposed that the defenders keep under cover at inland points and not resist the Americans until after they had landed and were jammed up on the beaches. It wasn't that he believed his proposal would bring victory. He simply wanted to kill as many Americans as possible before his own troops were destroyed. If American casualties were high enough, Washington's war planners might think twice before they launched another invasion so close to Japan. The attack on the home islands might be at least delayed, and the chances made better for gaining an honorable peace.

Kuribayashi was preaching combat that was strictly defensive, whereas Japanese soldiers preferred offensive operations. The answer to an attack should be a counterattack. In these island battles, which the Japanese were losing, this method had an extra advantage: A prompt counterattack offered a quick death.

Said Kuribayashi: "We would all like to die quickly and easily, but that would not inflict heavy casualties. We must fight from cover as long as we possibly can."

This disagreement and many others—including how the dynamite and cement for building fortifications should be allocated among the army and the navy units—did not interfere substantially with progress. Fifteen thousand men can do a lot of work, even when time out for bickering is added to disruptions by air raids.

Among the specialists were draftsmen who drew the plans, stone masons who cut building blocks from the volcanic rock, authorities on cave formations, and demolitions experts. Built close to the surface were pillboxes, bunkers, and blockhouses. Their reinforced concrete walls were several feet thick, some of their ceilings as many as six. Sand was piled over them for added protection, and mingled among them were dummy positions intended to confuse the enemy. Camouflage was also employed.

Farther underground were living quarters, some of the chambers capable of holding only a few men, and others large enough to accommodate three or four hundred. Included were hospital wards with surgical instruments and operating tables. There was ample room for the storage of food, water cans, ammunition, and other supplies. The lighting ranged from electricity to fuel lamps and candles. To prevent entrapment, the chambers were provided with multiple entrances and exits. Those on levels one above the other were linked by stairways. Some of the chambers were made of block and concrete, while others were utilizations of the island's caves. This network was augmented with miles of tunnels, much of the system being interconnected. The surface openings were designed as fighting positions.

The second airport, begun earlier, was completed, and plans were drawn for a third. Crews composed of hundreds of men were assigned to filling the craters in the airstrips made by the B-24s. Using trucks, bulldozers, and rollers, they became so proficient at this that they could have the air facilities functional again within a few hours after the severest raid. The airfields, too, were equipped with subterranean installations.

The men of Iwo Jima soon began to call themselves "the

underground troops." Their work, especially that of the pick-and-shovel laborers, was difficult, hot, and tedious. In sulphurous areas, gas masks had to be worn, and the shifts kept short. Progress everywhere was well sustained, though occasionally a man would stop digging, mop his brow, and lament, "Why are we working so hard? We're all going to die anyway."

Death had become a much-mentioned topic in Kuribayashi's letters home. He wrote his son, Taro, who was nearly twenty, "The life of your father is just like a lamp before the wind." The missive went on to urge the boy to try to quit smoking. In a letter to his wife, Yoshii, the general said, "I am sorry to end my life here, fighting the United States of America. But I want to defend this island as long as I can." He told her on another day, "I am very sorry for you, because too many heavy duties will fall upon your shoulders." If it proved to be possible, he promised, he would protect her from his place in the other world. "Thank you," he closed, "for your kind care of me for such a long time."

3

AGAINST A RISING FURY

It was not until October, 1944, that the United States began to get definite about Iwo. The war planners decided that it had become necessary to capture, occupy, and defend the island in order for American forces to extend their control over the western Pacific and maintain unremitting pressure on the Japanese Empire. Specifically, the island had to be taken to eliminate its air threat to the Marianas, to use as a base to help cover naval operations in Japanese waters, to equip with a fighter escort service for the very long-range bombers, the new B-29 Superforts, that were soon to start bombing Japan from the Marianas bases, and to provide these bombers with an emergency landing place. After Iwo, Okinawa would be needed as a staging area for the planned invasion of Japan's home islands, but Iwo's capture was expected to put the seal on the empire's defeat.

Iwo received increased attention from the Marianas-based B-24s during October. The men working on the surface had to run for cover at least once a day, huddling there while the island boomed and trembled. The Liberators came also at night. Most of the men slept on the surface because of the discomfort below, and their rest was disrupted. When the siren sounded they struggled up and headed for cover, sometimes half asleep. Some of the sluggish, caught in their bedding, were maimed or killed.

The American bombers, along with the submarine service, began to pay greater attention also to the supply lines between Japan and Iwo. While the submarines stalked their victims in open waters, moving in a world of shadows, the planes struck again and again at Chichi Jima and Haha Jima. In the harbor at Chichi, both transports and small craft were blasted, and at Haha the toll was high among small craft trying to reach Iwo.

The reinforcement and supply operations were continued, but

morale sagged. Major Horie noted that when units of troops survived the hazardous trip from Japan to Chichi, only to learn that the trip from Chichi to Iwo would be even more hazardous, their faces became "pale with uncertainty and tension." Members of the Chichi garrison who, day after day, had to bend their backs to the inglorious and dangerous work of unloading the transports and placing the materials on the smaller craft, began to balk. Some of the older men—a number were past sixty—said they no longer cared very much what happened; their time on earth was short anyway. The younger men grumbled particularly about the work that had to be done in the hours past midnight, when they were tired and hungry and got no relief. Their attempts to quit working were countered by officers swinging clubs and rods. This practice was almost tearfully regretted by Major Horie, though he condoned it. He began to believe that the failure of the war was driving Japan's officers nearly insane.

On Iwo, October 21 saw an American B-24 meet its match in a single Japanese fighter plane. The bomber had just moved in over the target when the fighter dived into its tail assembly, tearing it away. Both the fighter and the B-24 plunged into the sea, the bomber exploding on impact. The encounter left no survivors.

Those bomber crews who got back to their base safely after this mission were cheered by the news that General MacArthur had established a beachhead in the Philippines, about 1,500 miles west of the Marianas. The campaign for Iwo was contingent upon MacArthur's successful "return." His new beachhead represented another step toward the Japanese mainland, one planned in conjunction with the Navy's Marianas campaign.

America's B-29 Superforts, the bombers capable of reaching Japan from the Marianas, were now well established in those islands and had begun making practice runs to nearer targets. Early in November they made two visits to Iwo. The strikes were ineffective, the crews being new to the prevailing conditions, but the Japanese were awed by the sight of the great planes, gleaming silver in the sun, apparently so sure of themselves that they had spurned the usual protective camouflage.

On November 12 the prevalent color displayed by the Americans was a dull gray, as a naval task force composed of cruisers and destroyers moved in to gather intelligence and lay down a bombardment. Some of the coast defense guns boomed in reply, but the ships were not intimidated. Seeing the island for the first time, First Lieutenant Robert K. West, of the Marine detachment aboard the heavy cruiser *Salt Lake City*, found it "bleak and ominous-looking."

Aerial view of the heavy cruiser Salt Lake City.

During all of the raiding—by bombers, naval task forces, and submarines—supplies and reinforcements kept making it through, and the work of creating the fortress continued. Moreover, time was also found for intensive training. Arriving at this time to help with the latter was Lieutenant Colonel Kaneji Nakane, known as "a god of infantry tactics." He had a composed and inspiring nature and became the focal point of determination and good morale. Back in Japan Nakane had a wife and two daughters, one nine years old and one only nine months. The colonel shared the plight of all of Iwo's family men. They were tied to the island when things seemed about to become perilous at home. All they could do to minimize their concern was to throw themselves into the job at hand.

The training consisted of sniper practice, particularly from the cave entrances and the bunker and pillbox apertures; night infiltration tactics; antitank operations; and artillery, rocket, and mortar practice. It was found that when the artillery pieces were fired they raised too much dust and that this could be taken care of by putting down straw matting or sprinkling the area with water. The water, of course, came from the sea, since fresh water was at a premium.

General Kuribayashi set an example among the officers for water discipline, using only a cup a day for his personal toilet, and often sharing even that with his adjutant. The enlisted men used water from the sea—all of the sticky stuff they wanted.

Kuribayashi issued a general order in which he informed the troops: "The Japanese spirit is based upon 3,000 years of history and a respect for God and our ancestors. We must purify our mental condition and increase this spirit, destroying the enemy that is trying to overrun it, and making the spirit known to the world. We are now in the front line of the national defense. We must do everything we can for the Emperor, for the personnel already perished in the war, and for the people of the homeland."

A set of "courageous battle vows" was mimeographed and posted in almost every cave, pillbox, and bunker: "Above all, we shall dedicate ourselves and our entire strength to the defense of this island; we shall grasp bombs, charge enemy tanks and destroy them; we shall infiltrate into the midst of the enemy and annihilate them; with every salvo we will, without fail, kill the enemy; each man will make it his duty to kill ten of the enemy before dying; until we are destroyed to the last man we shall harass the enemy with guerrilla tactics."

These vows were intended to be taken literally. Kuribayashi really expected these things of his men—or at least expected them to make the effort. More was required of the Japanese soldier than of any other in the world. And if he survived his heroism he couldn't even look for a medal. Decorations went only to the illustrious dead.

Although Iwo's unhealthful conditions caused many of the men to sicken, the garrison as a whole maintained the spirit Kuribayashi demanded. If complaints were heard about the shortage of *sake* and beer and the absence of women, there was also singing. A group of officers and men composed a patriotic piece they called "The Song of Iwo Jima." It became the garrison's theme song, and copies were sent to Japan.

Baron Nishi, wearing cavalry boots and carrying a riding whip as a swagger stick, strode about the island, and wherever he went he drew attention. The soldiers had grown up listening to tales of his horsemanship. Nishi was getting his tanks ready for the battle, and he wasn't pleased. He was to be allowed no mobility at all. The tanks were being buried, with only their turrets and guns in evidence. They were becoming metal pillboxes.

Sent to Japan a second time to secure more tanks and other weapons for the defense, Nishi was given a rare opportunity. He wasn't looking his usual vigorous and healthful self, and influential friends intimated that this could be used as a basis for pulling strings. He could secure orders to stay in Japan.

No, sighed the baron, he could not. His men were waiting for him. Seeing the pain in the faces of his wife and children as he prepared to leave, Nishi tried to cheer them by saying that he might not be required to die. "I will try as hard as I can to live."

On November 24 about a hundred silver B-29 Superforts flew from the Marianas to Japan, making their first raid on Tokyo. The bombers went over at 30,000 feet, pushed by a heavy tail wind, and because visibility was poor only light damage was inflicted on the target, the Nakajima airplane-engine plant at Musashino, ten miles northwest of the Imperial Palace. About 250 people were killed or wounded, and at least a hundred homes were smashed. This was the modest beginning of a wave of destruction, death, and misery on a scale the Japanese people had not imagined possible.

Two of the Superforts were lost to Japanese fighters, one being rammed over the target and the other ditching on its way home. It is not known whether American possession of Iwo Jima as an emergency base would have saved this particular plane, but the incident dramatized the fact that such a base was needed.

Three days later something else was dramatized: Iwo's air threat to the Marianas bases. Although the Japanese raids were often broken up, on November 27 two tries by twin-engine bombers were successful. Fifteen of the new B-29s were hit on the ground, some as they were loading bombs. The destruction was heavy. A subsequent raid demolished three of the Superforts, and twenty-three were damaged. These planes cost the United States half a million dollars each.

As the B-29 raids on Japan became regular, Iwo posed another threat. The bombers had to pass near the island, and not only did its radiomen warn Japan they were coming, but fighters rose to meet them, coming and going. This was particularly trying on the homeward trip, when the men were tired and were sometimes flying damaged planes.

At the end of November a secret visitor arrived off Iwo, the USS *Spearfish*, a submarine on reconnaissance. The vessel slipped about at periscope level, her commander gluing his eye to that instrument and giving a running account of what he saw: an armored car in motion, a variety of construction work, some completed blockhouses, numerous caves. Surveillance of a cave at the base of Mount Suribachi revealed "a dejected-looking individual sitting right in the entrance sunning himself."

Photos were made of the landing beach, and some of the island's sounds were recorded. The Japanese had been warned earlier that reconnaissance subs might come, and that they should keep their voices down, particularly when near the beach.

On December 1 an antiaircraft crew firing phosphorus shells gave a B-24 a bad moment. As the bombardier, Lieutenant Wilfred A. Bloom, was preparing to release his load, one of the shells burst about fifty feet from the plane. The lieutenant was sent reeling by the concussion, and a few fragments came inside. Glass splinters from the bombardier's window were thrown in his face, and a small fragment of phosphorus entered his left shoulder. Bloom collected himself and got his bombs away, watching them land on target before calling for aid. His shoulder pained him fiercely all the way back to Saipan, and he was rushed to the hospital for emergency treatment. When the fragment was removed it was still smoking.

On December 8 (December 7 in the United States) a great

assemblage of American forces made Iwo Jima the object of some noisy Pearl Harbor Day ceremonies. Around 10 A.M. twenty-eight P-38 fighters swooped in and strafed and bombed the island, the thunder of both their engines and their work reverberating from the slopes of Mount Suribachi. Soon afterward sixty-two B-29s appeared in all their silver majesty and rained down more than 600 tons of bombs, causing sand and volcanic rock to rise in huge funnels. After another fighter attack, about a hundred somber-looking B-24s droned over and added nearly 200 tons of bombs to the crush. In the afternoon the force of cruisers and destroyers that had been there on November 12 moved in and rocked the island with a seventy-minute bombardment. The whole thing went off as the carefully orchestrated demonstration it was intended to be.

If the target had been a town, it might have been leveled, but Iwo was already level and the damage was minimal. Two of Admiral Ichimaru's men who were caught in an open ditch during the B-24 attack counted forty bombs exploding about them and were terribly shaken up, but when it was over they noted that, aside from some damage to two antiaircraft positions, the chief result was a rearrangement of the sand. That evening an army private who kept a diary did not even mention the series of attacks. He recorded only that the day was the third anniversary of the war and that he and his comrades "had a ceremony of bowing to the Emperor."

The raids were nonetheless nerve-racking, and they were to worsen. The Seventh Air Force now began the longest sustained aerial offensive of the Pacific war. Some of the night flights were arranged so that the bombers assaulted Iwo singly, every forty-five minutes, all night long. Searchlights picked out the planes over the target, but there was little resistance. Many of the fliers, however, preferred the daylight work. According to one: "There was a terrific feeling of loneliness over the ocean in the darkness with no other planes around you. And there was no more naked feeling in the world than to be caught in those lights and not be able to evade them." The possibility of a strong antiaircraft response was always present.

In a letter to his wife, Baron Nishi called the American bombings "psychological warfare." The night attacks, he told her, interfered seriously with the garrison's sleep. But he believed the problem would be solved: "When we complete our underground rooms we will be able to sleep. We won't even have to worry about the enemy's one-ton bombs."

The cool and easygoing Colonel Nakane, Iwo's "god of infantry tactics," seemed undisturbed by the worst the Americans managed to deliver. In mid-December he wrote his wife that the big bombers were coming ten times each twenty-four hours, their schedule so regular that "if they don't come we miss them." For one thing, he said, when the bombs failed to hit the island and exploded in the water, many choice fish were washed up on the beach. He was raising a garden that promised "good squashes and eggplants," and had saved enough water to enjoy the luxury of a good bath. Everybody around him, he added, seemed to be very happy. "We are gladly waiting for the enemy."

At least a part of the good cheer radiated by the colonel's letter was doubtless intended for the benefit of his wife's morale. It might be easier for her to accept the fact of his death if she believed he approached it in high spirits, surrounded by equally spirited men. It was true that much spirit was in evidence, but behind it was a weight of serious thought.

General Kuribayashi was among the deeply troubled. Never had his family needed him more. He was thankful he had a son coming to adulthood but wondered whether he was ready to take over as the family's head. On Taro's birthday in November the general had written him that "willpower is the essence of manhood" and that he must develop his will in order to become "a trustworthy man for Japan and the foundation of our home."

Kuribayashi wrote Yoshii that he was very sad to know of the mounting B-29 raids on Tokyo. He listed ways for her to improve the air raid shelter in their yard. "Make the covering of earth thicker. Did Taro make a thick board door for the entrance?" Yes, it was all right for her to bury their important papers in a corner of the garden, but only until a better disposition could be made. Since Tokyo was now a kind of battlefield, she must be as strong as a warrior. But she should be sure to wear plenty of warm clothing, including her belly band, and she must dry her hands and feet carefully after her bath so they would not chap and crack. And she had better take a hot water bottle into the shelter during raids for extra heat.

Along with his comments about the children, Kuribayashi included a complaint about their daughter Yohko. Her last letter to him had shown poor penmanship and had "many wrong words and omitted words."

His schedule on the island, the general told Yoshii, was often interrupted by air raids, the fury of which defied description. The napalm bombs caused seas of fire even where there was nothing to burn, and the regular bombs caused the island to rumble and shake fearfully. Nonetheless, he said, the garrison's affairs were proceeding in an effective way. He himself rose early, first exercising with his wooden sword and then having breakfast. Most of the morning was spent working with his staff and touring the defenses, which were now approaching a fair state of readiness. After lunch he watched the troops go through their training exercises, then returned to his headquarters to do his paper work. He had his supper around five o'clock. Then, he wrote, "I sing some songs or recite poetry, and go to bed at six." The island, he added, was not getting enough rain to fill the garrison's freshwater needs. "Every day we look at the sky and sigh."

Kuribayashi now took an administrative step that was necessary to unify his command, replacing eighteen officers who disagreed with

General Kuribayashi supervising buildup of Iwo's defenses.

Japanese officers studying map of island. General Kuribayashi is second from left.

him on defense tactics or were otherwise abrasive to his machinery. Among the rest of the officers, Kuribayashi's concept of fighting the enemy from concealment after he had landed had gained a general, if not altogether enthusiastic, acceptance. Even the most optimistic had begun to realize that no Japanese fleet would be sent to help fight the enemy in the sea or at the shoreline. The garrison would be fighting in complete isolation.

In latter December news reached the island that the United States was assembling a huge fleet and thousands of Marines. Iwo's garrison had expected that the attacking troops would be the Marines, who had spearheaded several other assaults on Japanese islands, starting with Guadalcanal in 1942. The Marines always got the toughest jobs; Iwo was obviously being regarded with respect. Not that the garrison was at all intimidated by the Marines as fighting men. By Japanese standards, the Marines, in spite of their reputation, were rather cowardly. They had been known to choose surrender when the honorable choice was death. Their psychology, and that of all American fighting men, had been clearly explained in pamphlets published by the Japanese government. Americans did not fight for the glory of their ancestors, posterity, or their family name. They wanted "to be known as brave soldiers and to be given publicity. Their desires are very materialistic. They go into battle with no spiritual incentive, but rely on material superiority."

By this time many of the Japanese had memorized their "courageous battle vows." Some were seen wearing the *hachimaki*, the white headband that had served as a symbol of defiance and death-acceptance for Japanese warriors down through the centuries. Others wore the *sennimbari*, a cotton belly band of a thousand stitches made by the women at home, a charm to ward off enemy bullets.

A few of the enlisted men persisted in telling themselves that the garrison would gain a great victory and that they would see home again. In diary entries they conjured up visions of affectionate reunions with wives, children, other relatives, and friends. One man wrote his family that he hoped to return home soon, but that the actual time of his arrival was "really uncertain."

Many of the men used their ammunition boxes as tables to write their letters upon, and also as receptacles for their writing materials. One soldier who sought out his special box after an air raid found it had been penetrated by a bullet. His next letter home was on stationery with a hole in the center. "This made my mother aware of how serious things were on Iwo Jima."

The fortification of the island continued. The training exercises continued. The American attacks continued to worsen. Powerful naval forces came over the horizon more often now, brazenly approaching to close range and lobbing in their terrible shells, which they seemed to have in endless number. Marine Lieutenant Robert West, of the cruiser *Salt Lake City*, was later to explain: "We would cruise along the different sides of the island, trying to learn as much about it as we could. We had our spotter planes up, and also had some carrier plane coverage. Our fire knocked out some of their emplacements and put holes in their runways. We were shot at, but were never seriously hit."

Fighter planes were still getting off Iwo's airstrips to meet the B-24s and their escorts, and the island's antiaircraft positions were now numerous, but the damage inflicted was easily absorbed. The bombers kept coming—and coming—and coming. They destroyed grounded planes and blasted innumerable holes in the airstrips, keeping the repair crews perpetually busy, and changed the island's contours again and again. They struck antiaircraft positions and radio and radar installations, damaged cave entrances, and blew the covering sand from bunkers and pillboxes.

Almost by habit now, the troops ran for cover when the raid siren sounded, and returned to their work or training exercises at the "all clear." The nights remained a trial, with the matter of getting enough sleep still a problem. More and more of the men were showing the strain, some being only overtired, while others were genuinely sick. Deaths occurred from both illness and American missiles, and the bodies were quickly but solemnly buried.

The submarine and aerial damage to Iwo's supply lines, especially in the areas around Chichi Jima and Haha Jima, had become critical. Supply losses now numbered hundreds of tons, and 1,500 lives had been lost. Marine Corps fliers stationed in the Marianas had joined this effort. Making night flights in B-25 medium bombers, and using radar and rockets, they reported knocking out twenty-three vessels. To counter their losses, the Japanese had resorted to using air freight for many materials usually sent by ship. These included foodstuffs, automotive parts, and munitions. The trips required good timing. The planes had to arrive at hours when Iwo did not have hostile visitors.

These hours were getting fewer. On February 1, 1945, the Army assigned "every available aircraft in the Pacific" to the Iwo operation. It was now only eighteen days until the invasion of the "stinking pork chop," as it was called by airmen who had sniffed its sulphurous fumes. During the past six months, the fliers had taken thousands of photographs while over Iwo, and these had been studied assiduously by intelligence personnel. Repeated comparisons were made with earlier photos, and it was known all along that the island's strength was growing. The air raids and shellings were called "softening-up" activities, but Iwo had become "harder."

The garrison now numbered about 21,000 men, and the great labyrinth of fortifications was ready to receive the landing forces. The biggest weapons were the coast defense guns, their broad muzzles jutting from heavy concrete bunkers. Hundreds of other gun positions distributed in five defense sectors about the island were mutually supporting. Almost every square foot of the terrain could be brought under fire.

Artillery pieces of various weights were poised in cave entrances and bunkers, ammunition stacked about them. Rocket launchers and mortar tubes stood in scattered pits, and some of the mortar pits had concrete covers with firing apertures. The turrets of the buried tanks pointed their light cannon from commanding places. Many of the antiaircraft guns had been given new assignments, their long barrels cranked down so that they paralleled the ground.

Slender machine gun muzzles peered from apertures in pillboxes. Numberless cave entrances, tunnel openings, and other holes had been allotted to snipers, who were also armed with hand grenades. Antipersonnel mines had been prepared for shallow burial on the beaches, and heavier mines were concealed along the routes it was believed American tanks would travel. These routes were also lined with deep antitank ditches. For extra measure, the island had been provided with networks of trenches, and some of the ditches and trenches had been rigged with booby traps.

Working under enormous difficulties, the Japanese had succeeded in turning Iwo Jima, an obscure bit of volcanic rock and sand, into what was probably the most ingenious fortress the world has ever seen.

The general presiding over this somber arsenal had established his headquarters at its northern end, where he believed that, in accord with the dictates of tactics, the Americans would come last. Above the ground level was a huge communications blockhouse. Built of reinforced concrete, its walls were five feet thick, its roof ten. It held about twenty radios and the appropriate personnel, whose job was to maintain contact not only with the defense sectors on the island but also with Chichi Jima and Imperial Headquarters in Tokyo.

Seventy-five feet below the floor of the radio room was a system of caves and tunnels in which Kuribayashi and his staff had their personal quarters—small concrete rooms, lit by candles. Sitting in his dim cubicle, the general wrote his last letters to Yoshii, about whom his worries had increased. He was about to sacrifice his life in an attempt to help protect the people on the mainland, but already the effort had begun to seem futile. General MacArthur, with his strong hold on the Philippines, south of Japan, was getting too close. Moreover the B-29s from the Marianas were raiding Japan with increasing boldness and in growing numbers. The damage they inflicted, Kuribayashi knew, would soon be horrendous.

All the condemned general could do from his small cell to help Yoshii and the children was to write them and implore them to be careful of their health and safety. Yes, he said in answer to one of Yoshii's comments, he could understand that her mother could find comfort during the raids by reciting Buddhist *sutras*. It was good for her to have faith. "But, as you know, the bombs and incendiaries will drop at any time and at any place without regard to her faith." Yoshii should listen to radio reports and read the newspapers and base her actions on them. It might be a good idea if she left Tokyo. No, there was not the slightest possibility he would be transferred. Commanding officers were never transferred when a battle was imminent. He was soon to die, and she must accept the fact. Not even his remains would return home. But that did not matter. His soul would live on in her and the children.

In a letter written on February 3, 1945, he lamented that her letters hadn't been getting through. Was she all right? Had she left Tokyo? He reported that he was well, had even gained a few pounds. He needed nothing from Japan, and she should not trouble herself to send any gifts by the air transport service. She should be careful not to catch cold and should have herself massaged frequently to help combat her fatigue. And she should tell their son Taro to lead a punctual life. "The plane is about to leave. I must close this. Goodbye." The letter was the last Yoshii was to receive.

February 11 was a Japanese holiday, the birthday of the much-venerated Emperor Meiji, grandfather of Hirohito. The celebration was tied in with the 2,605 years of Japan's history as a nation. Between air raids, the men of Iwo, most of them showing fatigue after months of labor with insufficient sleep, conducted ceremonies honoring the present Emperor, and also tapped their dwindling supplies of beer and *sake*. The observance gave many an intense longing for home. This was a popular family holiday.

Then home was heard from in an unexpected way. Tokyo broadcast "The Song of Iwo Jima" in the garrison's honor. Listening over the island's loudspeakers, the men were seized with fervent patriotism. Eyes brimmed everywhere as the cry went up: *"Banzai! Banzai! Banzai!"*

That night a soldier wrote in his diary: "We are proud that we are going to fight to the end."

4

THE LANDING FORCE

The United States Marines in the Pacific were a confident lot. They believed themselves to be the greatest fighting men in the world, primarily because this had been drummed into their heads from the day they signed up. It was actually phrased as a kind of threat: They were the greatest fighting men in the world and they had better never do anything to discredit their standing!

The building of the Marine *esprit de corps* began with boot camp, which was painfully tough. No Marine ever forgot his boot camp hitch. It was common for Marines to split up after boot camp, go through several campaigns, then meet again and barely mention their campaigns in their eagerness to reminisce about boot camp.

"Wasn't that a son of a bitch!"

One of the hardest things about boot camp was the sudden adjustment a youth had to make. One day he was a civilian enjoying a life of comfort, security, and individuality—a life in which he was endowed with "certain unalienable rights." The next day he was just another clip-haired "boot," a drill instructor's puppet, an object of derision and harassment, an American with no rights at all. He was plunged into a frantically paced schedule of unfamiliar and highly demanding activities. His health was jeopardized. He was baited and humiliated. His adequacy was constantly questioned. Could he prove that he was a man and not just a sniveling boy? Had he the stamina and the guts to make it through the program without cracking?

"I am not here to teach you to fight for your country," a drill instructor would tell his platoon, "but to teach you to fight for your life!"

The platoon was subjected to long hours of calisthenics, hiking, and double-timing; to close order, extended order, and guard duty drill; to bayonet, hand grenade, and gas mask practice, and to a barrage of lectures on topics that ranged from weapons care to venereal disease. The boots also had to put in a hitch on the rifle range. This involved hiking several miles a day and doing contortions as they assumed the various firing positions, the "snapping in" leaving them with acutely complaining muscles. The hike back to camp in the afternoon, when the men were already weary, was grueling. The instructor found this a good time to hurl the old taunt: "Anybody who's tired of walking can start running!"

The men experienced many other discomforts and annoyances. They shivered during pre-dawn roll call and sweltered during later activities in the sun. Colds and mysterious fevers multiplied among them. Their aching muscles were further abused by vaccine injections. They were often deprived of sufficient sleep, and then disciplined for nodding during their lecture periods. When they responded too slowly to a command they were sometimes accelerated by a rap of the instructor's swagger stick, and they were occasionally even "handled" when they made him angry.

Penalties for failure and neglect were sternly administered. The victim might be made to double-time to the point of exhaustion, or be forced to stand and hold his rifle at arm's length until the tension and pain became unbearable. If a man let his whiskers become noticeable, he was ordered to shave "dry." Certain drill instructors imposed a particularly humiliating punishment for witless blunders. The offender was made to stand before the platoon with a bucket inverted over his head and obliged to shout until his ears rang, "I am a shit-head! I am a shit-head!"

A boot was not permitted to call his rifle a "gun." It was a rifle, a weapon, or a piece, but never a gun. A man who made this slip might be punished in one of two ways. The easier requirement was that he sleep with his rifle beside him beneath his blankets. The instructor did not check to see if the weapon was there. He knew it would be there. It had better be there! The other punishment was a public one. The offending boot was made to walk up and down the platoon street with his right hand holding his rifle and his left cupped around his genitals, all the while reciting a little poem: "This is my rifle, and this is my gun; the one is for work, and the other for fun."

After undergoing this punishment, one seventeen-year-old recruit was overheard saying: "I know well enough what my rifle is for, but I'm not really sure about my gun yet."

Rigorous as the training was, it had its bright spots. Much of it was interesting, and the men experienced a thrill of satisfaction each time they mastered one of its more difficult challenges. The lecture periods provided the breaks needed from physical activity. Mealtime was a special pleasure; appetites were sharp and the food was good. There were evenings when the platoon was granted two free hours to attend an outdoor motion picture. And the men could look forward to mail call once a day—though any man who received more than one or two letters was censured by the instructor for keeping his home ties too strong.

Not everyone in a platoon completed the program, but the great majority, being both physically and mentally sound, got through without any serious problems. And what had begun in deep anguish ended in high pride. The men had proved they could adjust to rigid discipline and stand up under severe physical and mental strain. They had mastered the military fundamentals, had become proficient with their weapons, and had learned some of the tricks of survival. They had qualified themselves for admission into a highly capable outfit with worthy traditions. They had become full-fledged United States Marines!

Chosen to make the landing on Iwo Jima were the Marines of the 5th Amphibious Corps (usually designated VAC). The corps was composed of the 3rd, 4th, and 5th Marine Divisions, and commanded by Major General Harry Schmidt, a fifty-eight-year-old Nebraskan who had played a leading role in the capture of the Marshalls and the Marianas.

Schmidt's immediate superior was Lieutenant General Holland M. "Howlin' Mad" Smith, a legendary Marine engaged in his final operation after a career that began in the clean green jungles of the Philippines in 1906 and burgeoned in the muddy trenches of France in 1917 and 1918. His campaigns had included Soissons, Champagne, and St. Mihiel. Smith was the number one Marine in the Pacific, his role in the war having started with Tarawa in November, 1943.

Combat correspondent Robert Sherrod, on seeing Smith for the first time, decided that he "looked and talked like Wallace Beery might in the role of a Marine general." Although irascible and profane, Smith had a gentler side, and he laughed often, the sound coming from deep down. A devout partisan of the Marines, the general was forever at odds with his naval counterparts and superiors. Nonetheless, he was respected by most, including Admiral Nimitz, the top naval commander in the Pacific, from whom his Iwo orders had come.

The 3rd Marine Division, which had fought at Bougainville in the Solomons and at Guam in the Marianas, was reorganizing in its camp on the latter island, still fighting the last pockets of Japanese resistance, when it received its orders to prepare for a new campaign. The division was commanded by Major General Graves B. Erskine, at forty-seven one of the youngest generals in the Corps. A lieutenant during World War I, Erskine had been hospitalized for nine months, the result of concussion from a German shell. The general's part in the drive across the Pacific had begun with his helping to plan the assault on Tarawa.

The 4th Marine Division got its new orders while in its camp on Maui in the Hawaiian Islands. Iwo Jima would be the division's fourth campaign in a little over a year. It had fought at Roi-Namur in the Marshalls and at Saipan and Tinian in the Marianas. The division's commander, Major General Clifton B. Cates, had seen heavy combat as a young officer in France. He was a daredevil with a cool contempt for the enemy, and was able to laugh when he lost his trousers in a shrapnel blast at Aisne-Marne. Wounded several times and gassed once, he came home with various decorations, including the Navy Cross. He began his Pacific service by leading one of the two assault regiments that landed on Guadalcanal.

The 5th Marine Division had seen no combat as a unit, but was formed around a forty-percent nucleus of Pacific veterans, most of them former Marine Raiders and Marine Paratroopers, both outfits having been disbanded. Major General Keller E. Rockey commanded, and he was another officer who had made a name for himself in World War I. At Château Thierry he won the Navy Cross "by bringing up supports and placing them in the front lines at great personal exposure, showing exceptional ability and extraordinary heroism." Iwo Jima would be his first World War II combat role.

The 5th Division had received its preliminary training on the California coast. An observer at one of its final amphibious exercises was the Commander in Chief, Franklin Roosevelt. Most of the men found this inspirational. Marines in general liked the President, even though they bore a grudge against his wife, Eleanor. She was reputed to have said that Marine Corps combat veterans, as they rotated from the Pacific to the States, should be put into a special camp that allowed them to reassociate with their fellow Americans only in easy stages. According to the Marines, Eleanor had no cause at all to say this. All they had done was smash up a few West Coast saloons.

Late in the summer of 1944 the 5th had sailed for the Hawaiian Islands, landing at Hilo on the island of Hawaii itself. The men were surprised by the warmth of the greeting they received from the islanders as they marched to the trains that were to take them to their camp on the great Parker Ranch. The people cheered, waved flags, and plucked fruit from the trees and tossed it among the marchers. A few dissidents may have been present, however, for a couple of men were hit by coconuts.

Tokyo Rose, Japan's famed radio propagandist, noted the arrival of the 5th in Hawaii and promised that when the division made its next landing on a Pacific island the reception would be even warmer.

Although Japan knew the 5th had come to Hilo, the men of the division were not allowed to tell where they were when they wrote to people in the States. There was a joke in camp that the censors would not even pass letters that began with "Hello, how are you?" because this sounded too much like "Hilo, Hawaii."

It was about four months before the Iwo landing that the 5th Amphibious Corps began preparing for it, and only the top officers were aware of what was going on. The men in the ranks noticed only that changes were made in their training. A greater emphasis was placed upon attacking fortified positions, and all of the large-scale field exercises began to include a mountain, a stand-in for Mount Suribachi.

Much of the training continued as it would have for any operation. The men hiked and bivouacked and worked with rifles, carbines, Browning Automatic Rifles (BARs), pistols, flamethrowers, machine guns, mortars, rockets, bazookas, hand grenades, and demolitions. Field problems often found the infantry cooperating with artillery and tank units. The training took on an added hazard when these support units used live ammunition.

The infantry's aptitude with entrenching tools was tested in a bizarre way, the men being ordered to dig deep foxholes and then sit in them while Sherman tanks rolled overhead. Officers reasoned that one day Japanese tanks might do this, and that foxholes should be well engineered. This exercise caused few casualties. A man whose foxhole crumbled experienced a moment of terror, but he was likely to be found unhurt when he was dug out.

During invasion rehearsals in coastal waters the men generally disembarked from their troop transport by going over its rail and climbing down a rope net into a landing craft waiting below. In a heavy sea, with the ship rolling and the landing craft dipping, this wasn't easy to do, particularly since the men were always bearing a full combat load. Often as they reached the bottom of the net and tried to step off, the landing craft would suddenly drop many feet or would leap up, sometimes bruising them painfully. Some rifles and other pieces of equipment were dropped into the waves.

Once on board, the men usually bobbed around in the sea for a couple of hours before heading for the beach or simply returning to their transports. These were miserable hours even for those who did not mind the motion, since the craft was confining, horridly noisy, and filled with oil fumes. A man subject to seasickness usually took the fiber liner out of his helmet, restored the liner to his head, and hung the metal shell by its strap over his elbow, where it served as a handy receptacle for vomit.

All of the mechanized equipment owned by the three divisions—the trucks, jeeps, tanks, and even the artillery pieces—had special names, often bestowed with little ceremonies. A jeep was apt to be named for its driver's wife or sweetheart. One driver changed the name of his jeep from "Frances" to "Ella Mae" and when asked why said simply, "Frances got married."

A novel part of the training was that done by a group of Navaho Indians. As communications personnel, their job was to transmit messages among each other—messages between aircraft and the ground, between ships and stations on shore, between front-line tanks or artillery and the rear, and among the various infantry command posts. Their language, known to only a few non-Navahos, was absolutely undecipherable to the Japanese. It amounted to a secret code.

All of the Marines were taught a few words of Japanese. *Koh-sahn seh yoh!* meant "Surrender!"; *Boo-kee oh steh roh!,* "Drop your weapons!"; *Koh-roh-sah-nah-ee-yoh!,* "We won't murder you!"; *Koh-chee koh-ee!,* "Come here!"; and *Dah-mah-reh!,* "Shut up!"

The Marines got along well together in spite of their constant shoulder-to-shoulder contact and their frequent exposure to field hardships and other vexations. They realized that their battlefield chances depended to a great degree on their capacity for teamwork, so instead of taking the edge off their nerves by snapping at each other they attacked the System. Obscenities and blasphemies filled the air with such an intensity they soon lost their power to shock.

Many Marines countered the strains of the training with beer and whiskey. A regular beer ration was issued, and whiskey, which the men were not supposed to have in camp, kept appearing in mysterious ways. Most of the serious drinking, however, was done during liberties in towns outside the camps. Not all of the men who drank really enjoyed it. There were those who drank because they had the curious notion that this was a necessary part of being a Marine. But perhaps the notion wasn't all that curious, for the non-drinkers were under considerable pressure from the drinkers, often in the name of manhood, to participate in the sprees.

Regular Christian religious services were conducted in the camps, but the worship was keyed to the needs of war, and much of it seemed strangely out of keeping with the Lord's teachings. Little was said about the universal brotherhood of man under a universally loving father. The supplications were addressed not so much to the Jesus of gentleness and compassion as to the Jesus who could be roused to "righteous indignation." The Lord was entreated to help defeat America's enemies. The Cross must precede the Marines into battle. Although it would be the same cross that symbolized salvation through faith and the milder virtues, it must double as a mace.

Each of the three divisions numbered between 20,000 and 25,000 men. Although made up basically of infantrymen, a division had many specialized troops, some an integral part of its makeup and some attached. These included a motor transport battalion, various heavy weapons units, Naval Construction Battalions, engineers and pioneers, ordnance and service and supply companies, intelligence personnel, military policemen, a signal company, a reconnaissance company, medical companies, a war dog platoon, and other units. Each division also had a team of Red Cross workers.

The Naval Construction Battalions, or Seabees (from the "C" and "B" in their official title), were something new in American military circles. Organized shortly after Pearl Harbor, these men, many of whom were older than the average serviceman, were the cream of the nation's construction industries, and their labors had become vital to the war effort. Often put ashore very early in an operation so they could begin critical construction jobs as soon as possible, they suffered a high casualty rate, and they liked to say that "the Army makes some of the landings and the Marines make others, but the

Seabees make them all." They called themselves "soldiers in sailors' uniforms who endure Marine training and do civilian work at WPA wages." They were also known to insist that the initials "C.B." really stood for "Confused Bastards."

These enterprising workers constructed everything from airports to bathroom facilities for visiting celebrities. On the island of Eniwetok stood a neat little portable toilet that had been used for only a few days and had then become a shrine. Above it hung a sign: "Hats off, mates! Betty Hutton sat here!"

A Marine division was made up of three infantry regiments. Each regiment had three battalions, and each battalion three companies. Because of the organization's vastness, a great many of the men were complete strangers to one another. At company level, however, things were different. A company held about 250 men, and these men not only knew each other but were in many cases close friends. This made the company the division's fundamental element. It was here that *esprit de corps* was bolstered by warm fellowship. The men in a company fought not only to take objectives and win battles but also to gain and hold each other's respect. They also strove to aid and protect each other. To let a company buddy down in combat was unthinkable.

The 5th Amphibious Corps had about eighty infantry companies—or, as they were called, rifle companies. Perhaps typical was E Company, 2nd Battalion, 28th Marines, 5th Marine Division. This was the unit that would raise the flag on Mount Suribachi. Of course, nothing was known of this in advance. "Easy" Company was simply one of the assemblage of rifle companies composed of a headquarters platoon, three rifle platoons, a machine gun platoon, and a mortar platoon.

Its commander was Captain Dave E. Severance, a former Marine Paratrooper. In his mid-twenties, the captain was tall and erect and managed to keep his military bearing under the most uncomfortable and trying field conditions. His face, endowed with good lines and clear blue eyes, showed little emotion. He never shouted or railed, but issued his orders in calm, even tones. He was an enigma to the men, who rarely glimpsed the inner workings of his mind. Years after the war Severance admitted that he had all the normal emotions and that his cool professional image was the product of careful cultivation.

The captain was an able company commander but nonetheless managed to fall into disfavor with the battalion commander, Lieutenant Colonel Chandler W. Johnson, a gruff, heavyset Annapolis graduate. The colonel had an explosive temper, and this kept everyone about him on edge. Both officers and men tried so hard to avoid his displeasure that they were sometimes tripped up by the intensity of their efforts. Happily, Johnson had not only a temper but also a sense of humor. It often happened that he had scarcely finished a tirade when he would see something funny in the situation and break into laughter.

Severance got into trouble with the colonel during a simulated landing exercise—a rehearsal conducted not at sea but on dry ground. The three companies of the battalion were in their respective assembly areas. Johnson, who had his command post up ahead, sent word back to Easy Company headquarters: "Dave Severance, come forward."

Dave hurried to the command post. As he arrived, Colonel Johnson asked, "Where is your company?"

Dave replied, "Back in the assembly area. I thought you wanted to see me alone."

The colonel's face reddened. "You are relieved of your command!" he bellowed, and sent word back for Easy Company's executive officer, First Lieutenant Harold G. Schrier, to bring the company forward.

As the exercise continued, Severance, not knowing what else to do, trailed along behind Johnson and his command post staff. It wasn't long before the colonel turned around and asked, "What are *you* doing here, Dave?"

"You relieved me of my command, sir."

"Get the hell back with your company!"

A development a few weeks later offered Captain Severance an opportunity to redeem himself and Easy Company with the colonel. Although it was still a carefully guarded secret that Iwo Jima was to be the 5th Amphibious Corps' objective, it was known that the island had a steep mountain that would have to be scaled. An enterprising group of men from Second Lieutenant George E. Stoddard's rifle platoon—Corporal Robert D. Sinclair, Pfc. George S. Scott, Jr., Pfc. Eugene J. Ehrenhaft, and Private Isadore J. Fuertsch—invented a scaling device. A grappling hook was welded to a rocket, and a long rope attached to the hook. The rocket's launching charge was adjusted so that it would carry the hook and rope about 150 feet into the air.

All of this took days of experimentation. Dave Severance gave the project his sanction and watched its progress. At last everything was working well, and the captain invited Colonel Johnson to a cliff area near camp to witness a demonstration. The colonel accepted the invitation but intimated he was a busy man. This had better be worth his while. The day was heavily overcast, and the top of the chosen hill was obscured from view. Visibility was ample, however, as far up as the rocket was adjusted to travel. Bob Sinclair, aided by the other young inventors, poised it on its launcher with the rope carefully coiled on the ground. At a signal from Severance, the rocket was ignited.

It was off with a whoosh. But the leaping rope was caught in the fiery backblast and was burnt through. Most of the great coil was left on the ground, with only a short tail accompanying the rocket and hook. Unrestrained by the weight of the rope, the rocket and hook shot upward at great speed and disappeared into the overcast, obviously headed for a passage entirely over the hill.

The captain and the young inventors watched this performance in stunned silence. Then, as one, their eyes turned to Colonel Johnson to determine his reaction. He looked at the disconnected pile of rope, and looked at them. Then he began to laugh, and he laughed so long and so hard that he nearly fell to the ground.

The day was not lost. Bob Sinclair and his group had another model of their invention on hand, and the second demonstration was successful. Johnson was satisfied. The grappling device was to be further refined, mass produced, and taken to Iwo Jima. But it was never used.

Among Easy Company's platoon leaders was First Lieutenant J. Keith Wells, a tall, dark-haired Texan. Like Dave Severance, Wells was a former Marine Paratrooper. He was twenty-three but looked older, having strong features that had matured early in the Southwestern sun and wind. His habit of mixing freely with the enlisted men made him popular, and among themselves the men referred to him as "J.K." or the inevitable "Tex." Although he liked to walk around camp in a casual manner, his overseas cap tilted so far forward its brim was near the bridge of his nose, he was serious about his job. He enjoyed discussing the art of warfare, and his approach to the subject was often dramatic. He once told his platoon, with a resolute expression and a raised fist: "Give me fifty men who aren't afraid to die, and I can take *any* position!"

Those men who intended to be careful with their lives didn't know what to make of this heroic pronouncement. Sergeant Kenneth D. "Katie" Midkiff, an easygoing West Virginian, admitted to his squad that the lieutenant's attitude had him a little worried.

"He wants fifty men who aren't afraid to die," Midkiff said ruefully. Then he pointed at a man he had picked at random and added, "And do you know what? *You're* one of the fifty!"

Wells once obtained a paperbound book that dealt with the sweep of the Mongols across Asia in the thirteenth century, and he carried it in his hip pocket and dipped into it during free moments. His comments about its strategic and tactical content prompted his men, for a time, to give him a new designation when talking among themselves. They converted his initials "J.K." to "Jenghiz Khan."

Wells was another Easy Company officer who got into trouble with Chandler Johnson. It was in connection with a USO show on the regiment's outdoor stage, the chief attraction being a troupe of hula girls. When the show started, about 2,000 Marines were seated on the grass of the long slope rising from the foot of the stage. Chandler Johnson and dozens of other officers, looking clean, neat, and proper, occupied camp chairs in a special section in front. Wells, however, was not present at the outset. He was at his tent in camp, enjoying his beer ration. The camp was only about a hundred yards from the side of the stage on the audience's right.

The girls were in the middle of their first number, swaying gracefully to a Hawaiian tune played by a band behind them, when a lone Marine was seen approaching the stage from the camp. His overseas cap was tilted far forward, his shirttail was hanging out in back, and he was carrying a can of beer. Hundreds of pairs of eyes were distracted from the girls to the man. Said someone in Easy Company's section: "My God, it's Wells!"

The lieutenant walked to the front of the stage and began toasting the girls with his beer can, drawing chuckles from the audience. Satisfied he had performed enough by the time the number ended, Wells turned and started back toward his tent. At that moment the girls began descending a stairway at the right of the stage in order to go to the tent they were using as a dressing room. Seeing Wells coming right behind, and getting the idea he was after them, they shrieked and began running. The enlisted men in the audience gave a guffaw, and the lieutenant, getting into the spirit of things, *did* begin chasing the girls. For the moment, the pursuit became the whole show, the audience cheering wildly. Wells never caught up with the girls, saying later, "Their chaperones diverted me, and I returned to my tent."

If Chandler Johnson shared the general amusement created by this episode, which he probably did, he kept it a secret. In the resulting interview between Johnson and Wells, the colonel used a great many harsh words and never smiled once.

Keith Wells was undeniably colorful and likeable, but he was also puzzling. He talked like a dedicated warrior, and his leadership on the training field was competent, but the men of Easy Company couldn't help but wonder what he'd be like when the shooting started.

The company's platoon sergeants included blond, curly-headed Ernest I. "Boots" Thomas, who was something of a phenomenon. A straight "A" student and all-around athlete during his high school days in Monticello, Florida, he was only twenty years old, one of the youngest platoon sergeants in the Corps. No one in Easy Company faulted him for being too young for his job. He handled it expertly. He was ordinarily soft-spoken, but when he issued orders on the drillfield he deepened his voice until it resembled a low growl. He was liked and admired by the men, who referred to him as "Thomas the Tiger."

Among the company's buck sergeants was twenty-five-year-old Michael Strank of Conemaugh, Pennsylvania, whose parents were immigrants from Czechoslovakia. Strikingly vital and sturdy, Strank had an attractive don't-give-a-damn manner, an irrepressible grin, and a playful sense of humor. "Don't you know," he would say to a young Marine he saw grooming himself to perfection, "that cleanliness is next to the devil?" Strank had seen action with the 3rd Marine Raider Battalion.

The corporals included Harold P. Keller of Brooklyn, Iowa, who had served with the 2nd Marine Raider Battalion in four Pacific engagements and had been wounded in the assault on Bougainville. The presence in the company of combat veterans like Strank and Keller was a comfort to those who had seen no action. The veterans were very capable and evinced the assurance of men who knew they had proved their courage. They seemed to be ideal figures to follow and emulate.

The majority of the company's men, of course, were privates and privates first class. There was Pfc. James C. Buchanan, who had scored 326 points out of a possible 340 on the rifle range in boot camp—a remarkable record. But was Jim made a sniper? No, that is not the way of the armed forces. He was put into Easy Company's mortar platoon.

Pfc. James A. Robeson bore the nickname "Chick." He was eighteen, but looked younger. His face was well favored, but in a sunny, boyish way. Chick was very popular, especially with the veterans, who regarded him with a kind of paternal affection. They advised him with particular care, and he was eager to learn from them. Chick's boyish features did not obscure his manly resolution.

The company had three full-blooded American Indians: Pfc. Louie Adrian, Pfc. Daniel Friday, and Pfc. Ira Hayes. Ira, called "Chief," was known for the unique way in which he removed the few hairs from his chin. He had a short piece of coil spring he used as tweezers.

Private Arthur J. Stanton, a fine-looking, dark-haired Texan with a ruddy complexion, who also had some Indian blood, was not really physically qualified to be a Marine. Although his eyes looked normal enough, the sight of the right one was seriously impaired. When Stanton was put before the eye chart during his preliminary physical, he managed to hold the blinder card in such a way that he read the letters twice with his good eye. The impairment was discovered during a second physical, but Stanton appealed so strongly to be allowed into the Corps that the doctor passed him. Stanton's left eye was extra sharp. The dimness of his right one in no way interfered with his effectiveness as a BAR man.

Pfc. Rolla E. Perry, a genial and good-natured youth from Campbell, Missouri, was proud to be a Marine but had a recurring worry. He had six sisters at home but no brothers. He was, in fact, the only son of an only son. "If I am killed," he said, "the family name will die, too." He mentioned a girl named Thelma who he believed would be willing to help him save the family name if he lived.

The company had at least one malcontent. Pfc. Donald J. Ruhl of Joliet, Montana, often grumbled about orders he considered unreasonable and made trouble for himself by bucking them. He chafed at the tedious repetition in the company's training schedule, and, considering his helmet a useless trapping, kept trying to put it aside in favor of a baseball cap. His attitude earned him the disapproval of some of the men who had to work with him, but he seemed to feel they had no right to judge him until they had seen him perform in combat.

Frank L. Crowe of Cambridge, Massachusetts, was the company bugler, or "music," and the captain's runner and bodyguard. His rank was "Field Music 1st Class." Although five feet eleven inches tall, Crowe weighed only 126 pounds. He was strong and healthy; there was just no way he could gain weight. Highly proficient at table tennis, Crowe used to spend his liberties in the States visiting recreation halls in search of competition, and usually held his own with the best of his challengers. "Music" also enjoyed visits to the Hollywood Canteen, and he never forgot the night he jitterbugged for a few seconds with Carole Landis, one of the most exciting beauties of the era.

Easy Company had men from nearly every state in the nation and from all walks of life. A variety of accents were heard. There were farmers and ranchers, former members of the Civilian Conservation Corps, former merchant seamen, bank personnel, store clerks, truck drivers, plumbers, electricians. Some had joined the Marines right out of high school, while others had interrupted college studies. Corporal Robert A. Leader, a sandy-haired New Englander, was preparing for a career as an artist, and had been attending the Boston Museum of Fine Arts when he decided to enlist.

Taken all together, the men of Easy Company were much like the men of the other companies of the 5th Amphibious Corps. A sketch similar to the foregoing could be drawn for each company.

In latter December, 1944, the 4th and 5th Divisions, both encamped in the Hawaiian Islands, received orders to rendezvous at Pearl Harbor. The 3rd Division, still on Guam and 3,000 miles closer to the objective, would not embark until later. This unit had been designated as the corps' floating reserve.

The men of the three divisions were not only superbly trained but also in excellent health. Their hearts were strong and their muscles well toned, their appetites and digestion were in the best possible order, they had been immunized against some of the worst diseases, their teeth had been checked and repaired where necessary. These things were epitomized by bronzed faces with gleaming grins.

An aggregation from the cream of America's young manhood, the Marines, alas, were also like well-nurtured and sleekly matured livestock ready for the slaughterhouse. And in truth, a slaughterhouse is exactly what the Japanese had prepared for them.

5

TOWARD THE OBJECTIVE

As the men of the 4th Marine Division, encamped on the Hawaiian island of Maui, began packing up to sail for Pearl Harbor, Pfc. Jack R. Helm, a replacement who had never been in combat, noticed something curious. One of the division's veterans was daubing black paint on his helmet cover, knapsack, cartridge belt, and even his dungarees. He told Helm the Marine Corps was all wrong in making the men scrub everything with soap and water until it gleamed almost white. This made the men too conspicuous. "Everything," he said, "should be dark." In this case he was more correct than he realized. Iwo Jima's beaches were composed of gray volcanic sand.

Even as the 4th Division boarded its transports at Kahului, Maui, Tokyo Rose mentioned the fact in one of her nightly broadcasts. The men of the 4th listened to her more carefully after that, figuring they might very well learn more about upcoming events from her than from their own officers.

This was a time when rumors and scuttlebutt flew about everywhere. But even the most naive Marine and sailor had learned that such information could not be trusted. According to Signalman 2nd Class Robert L. Collyer, of the attack transport *Sibley*, a piece of scuttlebutt was usually "a modified version of a revised revision with qualifications and additions."

The 5th Division troops moved down from the heights of Hawaii by truck and by rail, boarding ship at Hilo, where they had landed about four months earlier. This time there were no cheering crowds. In an effort to preserve as much secrecy as possible the port area had been declared off limits to all civilians but dock workers. The transports slipped away quietly, some of the Marines standing on deck and watching the great peaks of Mauna Loa and Mauna Kea fade over the horizon.

The transports soon reached Pearl Harbor, a busy place in mid-January, 1945. Either tied up at its docks or anchored in its expansive waters were nearly 500 vessels: aircraft carriers, battleships, cruisers, destroyers, smaller men-of-war, troop transports, cargo transports, hospital ships. Some of the vessels were formed into convoys from time to time as the Marines, Navy, Coast Guard, and a few attached Army amphibious units went out among the islands for extensive invasion rehearsals. In the harbor, gigs and landing craft left long wakes as they hurried about among the anchored vessels or performed missions from ship to shore. Oil tankers and water tenders slipped about performing their vital servicing duties. Barges laden with stores from the docks saw to it that the various cargo vessels were brought to full supply.

It had taken months of work by Army, Navy, and Marine supply units to gather all of the necessary materials for the operation. In addition to the countless tons on the vessels, additional items had been stockpiled among the Hawaiian Islands and in the Marianas, to be airlifted to Iwo Jima as needed. The supplies ranged from items of the first urgency such as ammunition, food, and water, to things such as flashlight batteries, pencils, and shoelaces. Special orders had been issued about the toilet tissue: It was to be stored under tarps to keep it dry. Naturally, the stationery for writing reports was accompanied by carbon paper for preparing them in triplicate. Nearly all of the men knew the supplies included cigarettes and liquor, but few were aware of the burial equipment and the thousands of wooden crosses.

As they had arrived off the island of Oahu and made their approach to the entrance of Pearl Harbor, many of the Marines, sailors, and soldiers had got their first look at Diamond Head, the white sands of Waikiki Beach, the pink towers of the Royal Hawaiian Hotel, and the city of Honolulu. The harbor itself had beautiful hills in its background. The troops were eager to explore, and they were granted liberty, twenty-five percent of the total force each day. With thousands at a time on shore, it was fortunate the bars were not open. The men swam at Waikiki, some even trying their luck on the surfboard. In Honolulu they found such attractions as curio shops, tattoo parlors, shooting galleries, photo booths, and hamburger stands. There were, of course, hula shows, too, but some of these were a disappointment, the dancers being a mixture of thin school-girls and stout matrons.

Seaman 3rd Class Chester B. Hack, a Coast Guardsman serving on an LST (a 315-foot landing ship with a tank deck in its bowels), enjoyed going ashore just to absorb Oahu's exotic atmosphere. Some of his shipmates shared his feelings, but many did not.

He was on duty on deck one intoxicatingly beautiful day, envying the men of the crew who were ashore, when one of them returned early. Chet asked why he had come back when his liberty had several hours to run.

"Nothing to do," the sailor said. "Bars all closed. No women available. Just nothing to do."

As he watched the sailor go below, Chet shook his head. "That man," he said to himself, "could go around the world and see nothing."

Late in January the various elements of the fleet moved slowly out of the harbor and formed for the long trip westward. As the huge convoy got underway, the men on central vessels could see gray silhouettes on all horizons. The weather remained sunny and pleasant, and the ocean's waves were gentle and blue-green.

On the second day out, the troops finally learned where they were going. Maps made from aerial photographs suddenly appeared everywhere—rolled maps, folded maps, wall maps, contour models attached to tables. They were surprising in their detail, a great many of the island's defenses being accurately depicted. Gathered in groups with the maps as centerpieces, the troops were briefed on all aspects of the invasion. Most grew sober as they began to realize what they were up against.

The days allotted to briefings soon gave way to a day on which there was a great piece of horseplay. Early in February the fleet crossed the 180th meridian, or the International Date Line, and all men making their first crossing were subject to an initiation (at the hands of those who had crossed before) into the domain of the meridian's ruler, the Golden Dragon. This applied to enlisted men and officers alike, and it was somewhat humiliating. Heads were clipped in weird patterns, mustaches were halved, saltwater hosings were administered. In the end the victim had to kneel on the deck and kiss the bare foot of a man dressed as Neptune, the god of the sea.

Why he was not dressed as the Golden Dragon was not explained. Perhaps dragon costumes were hard to come by.

No one escaped this initiation. One enlisted Marine ran below-decks and tried to hide, but several strong men went after him. As they were dragging him up the last gangway, he was heard to shout, "I demand to see my commanding officer!" As it happened, he saw this man very soon. He was on deck being initiated.

At this point in the voyage the Marines were advised they would be allowed to send notes home saying they were going into battle but giving no details. Thousands of men sat on the decks of their ships in the sun and wrote these messages, some saying no more than something like this: "Am at sea, headed for combat. In case I am not able to write again for a while, don't worry. I'll be okay. Will write as soon as I can." Many mothers, fathers, and wives who received these notes never heard from their young Marine again. The next message they received was from Marine Corps Headquarters in Washington, D.C.

Between February 5 and 7 the convoy anchored and refueled in the spacious lagoon at Eniwetok in the Marshalls, taken by the Americans a year earlier. There was little to see here except a shoreline strewn with combat debris, the stumps and splinters of palm trees, and a community of Quonset huts. Swimming call was sounded each day, and hundreds of men bobbed about in the lagoon's milky waters.

The fleet moved on to Saipan in the Marianas, coming to anchor there on February 11. Saipan had gleaming beaches, velvety green contours, and a series of jagged hills. The sight was of special interest to the Marines of the 4th Division, who had been a part of the assault on the island eight months earlier. They were surprised to see a destroyer move in and shell a rocky area where some die-hard Japanese guerrillas had been spotted. Saipan had changed dramatically. In place of the burnt cane fields strewn with enemy dead were long white airstrips. The nearby island of Tinian, also well known to the 4th, had similar strips. It was from these places that the B-29s were making their runs to Japan.

Each morning during their stay in the area, the men of the convoy were treated to the sight of the giant planes taking off, one after the other in a seemingly endless stream, as they headed for their targets. More than once the men's fascination turned to horror as a bomber failed to lift its great load and crashed into the sea, exploding for half an hour afterward, its crew lost.

Unknown to these spectators was that the morale of the B-29 crews was dragging at this point. They were developing an obsession about Iwo Jima, a perpetual threat to their missions and their lives. All were aware the island could be converted from a dark peril to a glistening asset if America took it.

The assault elements of the landing force—the first ten waves—were now placed on board an array of LSTs. These Marines had trained for the invasion by going over the rail of the larger attack transports (APAs) and descending rope nets into landing craft drawn alongside. Now they learned they would make the assault in an entirely different way. They would climb aboard amphibian tractors (LVTs) lined up in the dark holds of LSTs, and pass through opened bow doors and down a ramp into the sea. It wasn't a bad way to go, except that the little LVTs bobbed mercilessly in the water, sometimes sickening even men with strong stomachs.

A final invasion rehearsal was conducted, with Tinian the objective. The Marines were not actually landed; their craft merely made a run toward the beach and then drew away. The sea was rough, and the men in the amphibian tractors were greatly relieved when the order came for the vessels to climb back up the ramps into the holds of the LSTs.

During the last-minute preparations before the run to Iwo Jima the men were dusted with DDT powder as a defense against the island's insects. This was done with a generosity that would have dismayed later generations. In a memoir written some years after the war, Lieutenant George Stoddard of the "typical company" says: "We probably had enough DDT in our systems to kill Iwo Jima's insects by spitting at them. Those that bit us must have been surprised to discover they were committing hari-kari."

At this time Lieutenant Stoddard, along with all the rest of the officers in the landing force, had a curious problem, one related to military courtesy. In training, great emphasis had been placed upon saluting and "sirring." But in combat the officers did not want to be conspicuous, since they were high-priority targets for enemy snipers. Concealing their insignia, they tried to look like ordinary enlisted men. The troops were supposed to knock off all saluting and sirring and call them by their first or last names.

Asks Stoddard: "How do you undo what has been so ingrained in

Bird's-eye view of Marines in landing craft during invasion rehearsal off Tinian in the Marianas.

the minds of well-disciplined troops?" It wasn't easy. When a man accidentally called an officer "sir" and was chastised with "Don't call me 'sir'!" it was not unknown for him to respond with, "Sorry, sir!"

The new system gave the enlisted men a certain power over their platoon leaders. These officers had better measure up on the battlefield! A platoon leader who roused the ire of a certain type of Marine just might find that Marine running up to him, saluting, and shouting at the top of his lungs, "Here I am, lieutenant, sir!"

The campaign's various elements, each the product of an enormous amount of planning and preparation, were now nudged into a whole. Overall responsibility belonged to Admiral Raymond A. Spruance, commander of the Fifth Fleet. In direct command of the invasion was Vice Admiral Richmond Kelly Turner, probably the world's leading authority on amphibious warfare. Traveling as an observer on Turner's flagship, the USS *Eldorado*, was the Secretary of the Navy, James V. Forrestal. Also on this vessel were Marine Generals Holland Smith and Harry Schmidt.

Task Force 58, a special unit under Vice Admiral Marc A. Mitscher, was on its way to Japan to deliver a powerful diversionary and covering attack, and an amphibious support force under Rear Admiral William H. P. Blandy was headed for Iwo Jima for three days of preliminary bombardment. Holland Smith had argued with the Navy for a longer bombardment period, but was told that this would throw the campaign's timetable out of order and was probably unnnecessary anyway. Smith was disturbed by the decision. "I could not forget the sight of Marines floating in the lagoon or lying on the beaches at Tarawa, men who died assaulting defenses which should have been taken out by naval gunfire."

The American submarine service was a part of the operation, its vessels sent on special assignments. B-24s and other aircraft from the Marianas continued their work against Iwo, Chichi, and Haha. The air forces in the southwest Pacific and even Allied air commands in India were helping. Their missions were to pound bases on islands southwest of Japan and on the Asian mainland that might send air reinforcements to the home islands or to Iwo.

The assault shipping sailed from Saipan in sections. Leading off on February 15, four days before D day, were the LSTs bearing the Marines of the 4th and 5th Divisions who were to land with the first ten waves. They were accompanied by some of the smaller men-of-war. The main body of the vessels followed on the sixteenth. Aboard the troop transports, along with the rest of the men of the 4th and 5th Divisions, was a regiment of the 3rd, that division having joined the convoy from its camp on Guam. Sailing on February 17 and bringing up the rear were the transports carrying the remainder of the 3rd Division and its attached units.

A certain optimism was evident among the men of the 3rd. As the assault's floating reserve, there was a possibility they would not be landed. And even if they were, it would not be until the beachhead was established and conditions for survival had improved. They congratulated each other on their luck. But the feeling was not unanimous. One veteran sergeant was heard to say: "The trouble with luck is that it runs out."

It was about 700 miles from Saipan to Iwo. The Marines spent most of their time on deck. Those on the smaller transports, in fact, were quartered there. Firearms were cleaned and recleaned, and combat knives and bayonets were honed to a fine edge. Some of the men played cards; others read tattered paperback books taken from packs or pockets. Officers assembled groups for briefings and exercise periods, and chaplains conducted special religious services. Out on the sea, porpoises and flying fishes gave pleasing performances. At night, men hung over the rails to view the phosphorescence of the water that brushed past the dark metal hulls.

The Marines ate in the ships' galleys. Saltwater showers were available belowdecks. The regular toilet facilities, however, had been reserved for the Navy or Coast Guard crew and the Marine officers. The enlisted Marines had makeshift facilities. Erected on deck near the rail was a metal trough with two skimpy wooden seats. It was set at right angles to the rail, with an end extending out over the sea, and a continuous flow of water kept it flushed. The contraption was sanitary enough, but there was no screen around it. A man had to sit there, his bare buttocks gleaming, before the eyes of half the men on deck.

The Marines had been advised to be very careful not to fall overboard. It was explained that a convoy's sailing pattern could not be disrupted for a rescue mission. In spite of the warning, a man in one of the convoy's LST sections got careless. According to Coast Guardsman Chet Hack of LST 763:

"We got the man-overboard signal from the ship ahead of us. We turned to port to avoid hitting him and threw him a life preserver, but had orders not to stop. We could not hold up twenty-four ships for one man. Looking back, we could see him waving his arms, and it broke our hearts that we couldn't help him. We hoped that one of the destroyers or other small men-of-war that were cruising around to protect us would pick him up, but we never heard that one did."

While the various divisions of the assault fleet churned steadily toward Iwo, the island had the attention of Admiral Blandy's amphibious support force, composed of aircraft carriers, battleships, cruisers, destroyers, and other men-of-war. They approached the objective during the dawn of February 16. Meanwhile, the task force under Admiral Mitscher, lying only sixty miles off Japan, was launching its planes. After two days of damaging strikes in the Tokyo area, Mitscher's force would swing toward Iwo to back up the landing.

The Japanese on Iwo observed the approach of Blandy's force with awe. Heard everywhere were such exclamations as, "I have never seen so many ships in my life!" Most of the men decided the situation was hopeless. Said one to a comrade, "Let us die happily together." General Kuribayashi broadcast this announcement: "All shout *Banzai* for the Emperor! I have the utmost confidence that you will all do your best. I pray for a heroic fight."

On the previous evening Kuribayashi had radioed Tokyo that he had learned the Americans were on the way and that now was the time for the Imperial Navy to do what it could to help him. The navy sent back word that it would not come out now but would wait until April 1, at which time it would drive the Americans all the way back to their mainland. It was the kind of reply Kuribayashi had expected.

The workhorses of Blandy's force were its six battleships and five cruisers, assembled from diverse stations. The *Nevada, Texas, Arkansas,* and *Tuscaloosa* reached the Pacific through the Panama Canal after supporting the landings in North Africa, Normandy, and southern France. The *New York* had come through the canal after supporting the North African landings and doing convoy work in the Atlantic. The *Idaho* and *Tennessee* had come directly from West Coast shipyards after undergoing repairs for damages sustained during extensive operations in the Pacific. The *Pensacola, Chester,* and *Salt Lake City* had been shelling the Volcano-Bonin group of islands, including Iwo, intermittently since November, 1944. The *Vicksburg* had been commissioned in June, 1944, and was seeing her first combat.

Each of the heavy vessels had been assigned its own particular segment of the island, and the firing began about 7 A.M. It was not random and hasty work, but a slow, careful probing for targets. Spotter planes were catapulted from the ships for the purpose of seeking out targets and helping the gun crews gain maximum accuracy by reporting on their hits. Unfortunately, the day soon turned cloudy, and the bombardment's effectiveness was severely curtailed.

Minesweepers operated with little interference along the coasts, but the carrier planes that attacked the airfields and Mount Suribachi during breaks in the overcast found antiaircraft fire heavy. Forty-two B-24s from the Marianas, reaching the island at a time when the clouds were thick, turned back without releasing their loads.

A single Zero rose from the island. It zoomed up behind a slow-moving spotter plane, missed with its burst of fire, and roared on by. The American pilot, naval Lieutenant Douglas W. Gandy, fired his machine gun into the Zero's tail, and, to his astonishment, it went down, crashing among some cliffs—a kind of David-and-Goliath victory.

At 6 P.M. the fleet withdrew to the sea for the night. All in all, it had been a disappointing day. Among the hundreds of targets marked for destruction, only a very few had been accounted for. When informed of this, Holland Smith was appalled. Only two days of the bombardment period remained.

By the next morning the weather was clear and visibility was good. A dozen minesweepers sailed to within 750 yards of the shore, and soon several of the big support vessels, stationed about 3,000 yards out, opened up over them. The Japanese answered this fire with their shore batteries, and the *Tennessee* received a hit that wounded four men but did no other damage. The sweepers found no mines, reefs, or shoals, but they drew fire, both small-arms and 40-millimeter. The cruiser *Pensacola* moved in to provide close support. A heavy Japanese gun got her range, and within three minutes she had taken six hits. She drew off with her crew fighting fires and plugging holes near her waterline. Her casualties numbered seventeen dead and 120 wounded, her executive officer being among the dead.

The cruiser might have fared even worse had not the Japanese gun been dismounted by its recoil. Watching the vessel move away with smoke pouring from her decks, the crew chief lamented, "We could have sunk her! We could have sunk her!"

At 10:30 A.M. the ships deployed for a special event. It was time for the Navy's underwater demolition teams (UDTs), or frogmen, to go to work. Said to be "half fish and half nuts," these swimmers were required to go in and check surf and beach conditions, look for obstacles the Japanese may have emplaced, and destroy any they found—all of this in plain view.

The bombardment diminished during this deployment, and numbers of Japanese surfaced to see what was going on. They were impressed as much by the enemy's nonchalance as by his power. Many of the sailors were hanging over the rail and peering at the island as though they were on tour boats, and across the water came the unmistakable sound of popular music from record players.

To cover the UDT operation, the heavy gunfire support vessels began a slow, deliberate barrage. Inside their position, about 2,500 yards from the islands, seven destroyers formed a line that paralleled the eastern beach, which was nearly two miles long. Twelve LCI gunboats armed with rockets and 20-millimeter and 40-millimeter guns passed through them. The LCIs, fresh from stations in the tropics, were a strange sight with their zigzag orange and green camouflage. The frogmen—more than a hundred of them in small, fast boats pressing shoreward along the two-mile front—were covered with cocoa butter to cut the water's chill, and with silver camouflage grease.

Now carrier planes joined the operation, making crashing rocket runs along the beach. Additional rockets were poured in by the LCIs. It all began to seem to the Japanese, who were unaware of what was really happening, that the assault was beginning. They believed the twelve LCIs to be filled with Marines. As a matter of fact, the initials LCI stood for "Landing Craft, Infantry," but these particular vessels had been converted to gunboats. They loomed as easy targets for the artillerymen in the bunkers at the base of Mount Suribachi at the southern end of the island, and for those hidden in cliffs at the northern extremity of the beach. These were navy personnel, not directly answerable to General Kuribayashi. They knew that Kuribayashi did not want anything done until the Marines were jammed up on the beach, but the targets were too tempting, and they opened fire. Some of the army's mortar crews, machine gunners, and riflemen joined in. The LCIs fought back with their rockets and guns.

The small boats containing the swimmers, who looked like marble statues in their grease, continued their run toward the beach. As mortar shells and small-arms fire began to strike around them, some of the men managed to grin and make jokes. "What the hell," said one, "it all counts on twenty," meaning that this was just another part of the trek toward retirement. As the boats neared the beach, they suddenly swerved into courses parallel to it, and, one by one, the swimmers flopped out. As soon as a boat had dropped its last man, it began zigzagging wildly toward safety at sea. The abandoned frogmen began their investigations. When mortar shells or bullets splashed too near them, the men sought safety underwater. Glancing toward the terraces that made up the beach, they sometimes saw riflemen aiming at them.

The LCI gunboats, only about a thousand yards offshore, had run into serious trouble. According to a Japanese observer: "Our artillery laid down a fierce barrage. The continuous smoke and noise of the explosions were terrific." This man was aware that hits were being made, but he was unaware of the full extent of the damage. All twelve of the gunboats were struck; nine were so badly shattered they were put out of commission, one having to be abandoned. The conduct of the officers and men during the ordeal was superb. They remained at their stations and kept up the fight as long as was humanly possible. Forty-seven were killed and 153 wounded. One commander, Lieutenant Rufus G. Herring, wounded three times, later was given the Congressional Medal of Honor, and ten other commanders won the Navy Cross.

The destroyers behind the LCIs were involved in this action. One was hit and sustained seven men killed and thirty-three wounded. Carrier planes continued active, and the heavy support vessels kept up a steady fire, also laying a smokescreen along the beach to facilitate the recovery of the frogmen by the same craft that had taken them in. These daredevils had completed their mission, finding the water free of obstacles and of a good depth right up to the beach. Some of the men even brought back sand samples in tobacco bags. Only one swimmer had been lost, presumably the victim of mortar fire. One boatman died of a gunshot wound in the head.

Casualty being removed from LCI gunboat battered by Japanese shells.

That afternoon fresh UDT teams made the same kind of examination of the western beach, the second-choice landing area. Heavy-gunfire vessels, destroyers, and carrier planes supported the mission, keeping up a constant fire and laying down smoke. The enemy's resistance was brisk, but all of the swimmers and boatmen got through it safely. One mine was discovered and detonated. The western surf and beach were otherwise clear and would be suitable for landing if necessary.

The B-24s from the Marianas were able to complete their run that day, reporting an excellent record of hits on the target. Iwo's air forces had diminished to insignificance. Two operable Zero fighters were hidden in a concrete revetment at the second airfield, and their pilots were ordered to take them up and ram the largest warships they could reach. One pilot complained of a severe headache, and said he would not be able to perform the mission. He was told he was going to die anyway, but he still held back. A volunteer stepped forward and took his place. The camouflage was torn away, and the two planes roared down the strip and into the air, heading southward toward Suribachi. Over the volcano they were caught in artillery fire, and both tumbled into the sea.

Kuribayashi could not be too unhappy with the results of the unauthorized firing on the LCIs. He believed that a landing attempt had been repulsed, and reported the incident this way to Imperial General Headquarters in Tokyo. Admiral Ichimaru and his men were radioed a commendation. But the attack on the LCIs had been a mistake. Many Japanese gun positions hitherto invisible to the Americans were now marked on their maps. During the afternoon, some of these positions were destroyed.

But that night the atmosphere on board Admiral Blandy's flagship, the USS *Estes*, was grim. Only one more day of bombardment remained, and not even the landing area had been neutralized, let alone the other parts of the island. Lieutenant Colonel Donald M. Weller, the Marine gunfire officer who was working with the Navy, urged that the last day's bombardment be concentrated on the fortifications overlooking the beach. The admiral was quick to agree to this.

By dawn on Sunday, February 18, the weather had turned gray again, with visibility only fair. At 7:45 Blandy ordered his ships to "close beach and get going." He specified that the heavy batteries at the base of Suribachi and those overlooking the landing area from the north absolutely had to be destroyed. The vessels approached to within 2,500 yards of shore and commenced their bombardment. Carrier planes operated as the weather permitted. Again the visiting B-24s had to turn back without dropping their loads.

The work of the gunfire support vessels had its effect. When the bombardment ended at 6:30 P.M., an analysis revealed that out of 200 targets in the landing area, nearly half had been destroyed or heavily damaged. In breakdown, this amounted to eleven coast defense guns, twenty-two dual-purpose guns with five-inch bores, sixteen large blockhouses, and about forty-five pillboxes.

That evening one of the underwater demolition teams that had survived the hazardous work of the previous day came to grief in an unexpected way. The men were sitting in the mess hall of their vessel, the APD *Blessman*, some writing letters home while others played cards, when a Japanese plane winged over and dropped two heavy bombs. One landed in the water, but the other made a direct hit on the mess hall, and the ensuing sheet of fire rose so high into the night it could be seen for twenty miles. Eighteen members of the team were killed and twenty-three were wounded or burned. Similar casualties were suffered by the vessel's crew. Stronger than the smell of smoke and powder was the odor of burning flesh.

Those UDT men who escaped harm joined in the firefighting efforts that saved the ship. As they operated their bucket brigade, silhouetted against the flames, with the vessel's ammunition exploding in bursts, they maintained their devil-may-care image by singing "Anchors Aweigh." The singing stopped, however, when the time came for them to retrieve the charred bodies of their comrades from the wreckage.

The scheduled three-day bombardment was over. Admiral Blandy's next move was to send a message to Admiral Turner, whose flagship was approaching Iwo with the assault shipping: "Though weather has not permitted expenditure of entire ammunition allowance, and more installations can be found and destroyed with one more day of bombardment, I believe landing can be accomplished tomorrow as scheduled if necessary." He had permission from his superior, Admiral Spruance, who had accompanied the task force that went to Japan, to delay the landing one day if he thought an additional day's bombardment was needed, but Turner felt that the original plan should not be modified, that a sufficient amount of additional destruction would be accomplished by the two-hour bombardment scheduled to precede H hour, the time of landing.

Marine General Holland Smith, aboard Turner's ship, did not oppose the decision. He had wanted the bombardment to start earlier, not to run over its scheduled closing date. Smith's worries were now general ones: "The eve of D day at Iwo Jima found me unable to suppress a deep emotional surge. The imminence of action and the responsibility for the most appalling operation we had yet undertaken weighed heavily."

On this Sunday evening, as the flagship approached Iwo, many of its sailors and Marines were carrying a small card they had been given by the ship's chaplain, Curt Junker. On it was a prayer from the year 1645 composed by one of Oliver Cromwell's generals, Sir Thomas Astlie, before he went into battle: "Lord, I shall be verie busy this day. I may forget Thee, but do not Thou forget me."

On all of the vessels in the assault force, orders covering the arrival at the objective had been posted on the bulletin boards. Included with the special notes posted on the *Missoula*, an attack transport, was the following: "Laundry for the ship's officers will be taken Sunday night as usual. Due to the uncertainty of operational conditions, it is not known when this laundry will be returned."

That night Tokyo Rose was especially informative. She named many of the ships connected with the operation, identified the various Marine units, and disclosed where the ships had picked them up. She told the Americans that however tough they had considered their previous landings, all had been easy compared to the one they were facing.

6

THE ASSAULT BEGINS

The dawn sky was turning from leaden gray to pale blue, and the pre-H-hour bombardment had reached a crescendo as the Marines of the assault waves, standing combat-loaded on the weather decks of their LSTs, got the order to go below and board their assigned amphibian tractors. On each ship the procedure was the same, the men descending by means of a metal ladder to the dimly lit hold where the tractors stood in two lines, facing forward. When the bow doors were opened and the ramp lowered to the water, one could peer out of the hold as from a cavern. Motors started by the Navy coxswains set up an ear-numbing clatter and gave off exhaust fumes that burned the eyes and thickened the throat.

The Marines climbed in, remaining on their feet. Space was at a premium, since they were encumbered with packs, gas masks, canteens, helmets, and an assortment of weapons and ammunition. Soon the throbbing tractors began moving forward jerkily, one by one, toward the bright opening, their tracks clanking and screeching on the deck. Each nosed up momentarily as it reached the ramp, then plunged clumsily into the water, raising a splash and throwing its occupants hard against one another. A quick acceleration carried the craft away from the mother ship.

Soon nearly 500 tractors were bobbing around in a sea now glimmering with warm sunlight. In one of the craft, a Marine sang: "Happy D day to you! Happy D day to you! Happy D day, dear Marines, happy D day to you!" In one way, it *was* a happy D day. The weather, which could have made it terribly difficult for the Marines to get ashore, had chosen to cooperate—at least for the time being. The air was a fine 70 degrees and the sea was relatively calm. From Admiral Turner's flagship came the announcement: "Boating, excellent; visibility, excellent." The breeze was just brisk enough to set the fleet's hundreds of flags and pennants waving proudly, their colors bright in the sun.

The Japanese who peered from cave entrances and apertures in bunkers and pillboxes were almost incredulous at the size of the fleet after its augmentation, during the night, by the arrival of the assault shipping from Saipan and of several men-of-war—including the battleships *Washington* and *North Carolina*—that had supported the attack on Japan. The horizons, east and west, looked as though mountain ranges had risen upon them. A radio operator informed Imperial Headquarters in Tokyo, "We are doomed. The enemy is firing on us from both seas." Even as the island shook under the bombardment, some of the Japanese could not help but admire the fleet's majesty and the symmetry of the landing preparations. Pfc. Kiyomi Hirakawa, watching from a cave on Suribachi, found himself thinking, "How systematic and beautiful!"

The small craft loaded with Marine rifle companies had formed into slowly circling groups and were awaiting the signal to head for the Line of Departure, where they would form abreast for the dash to shore. Other landing vessels of various sizes were also standing by. They contained high-priority support units such as tank and artillery battalions, rocket sections, communications men, engineers, Seabees, and medical teams. Some of the craft were filled with ammunition, rations, water containers, signal equipment, and other supplies.

H hour had been set for nine o'clock, and the gunfire support vessels, some lying only a thousand yards offshore (much closer to the island than the circling assault craft), were not losing a moment. They were, in fact, laying down the heaviest pre-H-hour bombardment in history, the explosions coming with the rapidity of drumbeats. Smoke and dust hung over Iwo in great white, yellow, and gray clouds, blotting out its sunlight. The island doubtless had not been rocked like this since the ancient day when Mount Suribachi had last erupted.

Numerous Marines in the landing craft wondered whether the bombardment would leave any of the Japanese alive. Later they would wonder whether any had been killed. One Marine who hung over the gunwale of his craft to take a close look at the island was reminded of something he had heard from an observer aboard ship. The island *did* look like a floating mummy case, with Suribachi the head. The image was a chilling one.

Each man had his own thoughts, many later confessing to having uttered silent prayers. There were those who believed that God would keep them safe, however high the casualties. On the other hand, some had premonitions of death, going so far as to give away such possessions as money, watches, and rings. The young recruits were not sure what to make of the situation. Many had joined the Marines "to see action," but now a dawning had come that action was likely to be a terrible thing. A very few, among both recruits and veterans, felt truly aggressive, eager to land and begin fighting, believing themselves to be alert enough and clever enough to survive. Bravado was commonplace. One man tilted back his head, cast his eye across the sunny sky, and announced, "What a perfect day to die!" The main concern of at least a few was seasickness. An acute sufferer said later that, danger or no danger, all he wanted was to get his feet on dry land.

There were men whose anxiety was etched on their faces, but few gave the feeling a voice. It is not true, as commonly believed, that a group of people sharing a perilous experience grow stronger if they make a free confession of their fears. This is more likely to edge them toward panic. The strength of such a group depends upon how adept each person is at keeping up a courageous front.

At 8:05 the naval gunfire was temporarily lifted, and seventy-two carrier-based bombers and fighter planes thundered to the attack. Suddenly the operation's motif was blue—blue sky, blue water, blue planes. Rockets, bombs, and machine gun bullets were showered on Suribachi, the beach, and the rugged high ground that overlooked its northern extremity. Then forty-eight additional fighters, including twenty-four Marine Corsairs, flashed in and hit the same areas with napalm and more rockets and machine gun bullets. As soon as the last planes droned away, the gunfire support ships, having maneuvered into their final positions, opened up with renewed fury.

"Everything is coming off like clockwork!" thought Gunner's Mate 2nd Class Louis Berard of the crew of the attack transport *Missoula*. And the same satisfaction was felt by countless others who were backing up the Marines and had been working for many months toward this critical moment.

Now fifteen B-24s from the Marianas appeared over the island and added nineteen tons of bombs to the Navy's deluge of shells and rockets. Another thirty planes had been assigned to this strike but had been delayed by bad weather between the Marianas and Iwo.

At 8:30 a number of rocket ships armed also with 40-millimeter

American carrier plane strike on defenses overlooking northernmost landing beaches.

guns began moving abreast toward the island. After loosing a storm of missiles against the beach defenses, they veered off to the right and left to make way for the first wave of the assault. Nearly seventy armored amphibian tractors were now heading shoreward along a two-mile front. They carried no troops but were mounted with 75-millimeter pack howitzers and machine guns, their mission to take up positions on the beach and provide cover for the landing of the waves of troop-carrying craft that were beginning to follow at 250-yard intervals.

Some of the troop-filled tractors passed close by battleships and cruisers firing at point-blank range. Viewed from the tiny craft, hardly more than corks on the water, these vessels looked amazingly huge. Their gray plating rose cliff-like toward the decks that held the big guns. Sailors stood along the rails looking down, some waving coffee cups and others making victory signs. One Marine thought he heard a sailor shout, "Go get 'em, you damned glory hounds!"

Corporal Bill B. Faulkner, a Kansan riding with the first assault wave, would never forget his encounter with one of the battleships: "It was in our path, so we made a half-circle around it, and just as we lined up again it fired—and us right under those big guns. The fire rings came out over us, and we could see the projectiles starting off. And that concussion! For a moment we thought our little tractor would be driven under."

At 8:57, a few minutes before the armored tractors were scheduled to reach the island, the naval gunners lifted their landing-zone fire and began to train their weapons on inland targets. It was part of the general plan that they support the landing with a rolling barrage. During this interval the Marine Corsairs returned to strafe the beach. They roared in from the south past Suribachi, dropped close to shore as they fired, then peeled off over the sea. Additional runs were made 500 yards inland.

As the naval gunners commenced firing at their new targets, they caught some of the Japanese in the open, among them the 309th Independent Infantry Battalion, assigned to protect the northern half of the first airfield. In about sixty seconds, one forty-man unit was reduced to ten. Among the stunned survivors was Pfc. Nosaro Fuji, who fled northward to the second airfield, where he took refuge in a cave.

For American purposes, the two-mile stretch of beach had been divided into seven segments. Starting at the base of Suribachi on the left, they were Green Beach, Red Beach 1, Red Beach 2, Yellow Beach 1, Yellow Beach 2, Blue Beach 1, and Blue Beach 2. The initial landing was being made by the 23rd and 25th Regiments of the 4th Division on the right, and the 27th and 28th Regiments of the 5th Division on the left.

The armored tractors climbed out of the water at 9:02. They had been firing rapidly on the way in, but now they were hindered by a

Photo by Lou Lowery

Scene on board landing craft as Marines head for beach.

sandy terrace that ran parallel to the water's edge and ranged up to fifteen feet in height. Some were able to churn their way up the terrace front, but others found it necessary to back off into the surf to resume an effective fire.

Up to this time the Japanese had sent only a few shells and some scattered small-arms fire toward the assault waves, most of the defenders abiding by General Kuribayashi's wishes to allow the Marines to establish a crowded beachhead before hitting them. But one troop-filled tractor was sunk: the men went under and some did not reappear, victims of either shrapnel or the weight of their packs, weapons, and helmets. Survivors who had shed their gear were pulled from the water by Marines of a luckier vessel.

Supply Sergeant Raymond A. Dooley, heading shoreward near Suribachi in a tractor of the sixth wave, heard the crack of bullets going over just above his helmet. This was the first time during the war that Dooley had been shot at, and he found himself thinking: "They say a miss is as good as a mile. I'll take the mile."

Japanese antiaircraft crews were busy against the dive-bombers, fighters, and two-man observation planes. Major Raymond W. Dollins, the 5th Division's chief air observer, was over the island, and the men of the fleet who were tuned to his radio frequency heard him sing, "Oh, what a beautiful morning; oh, what a beautiful day. I've got a terrible feeling everything's coming my way!" It was a colorful touch, and listeners laughed in appreciation. A few moments later the major's plane, trailing flames, plunged into the sea near Suribachi. Both Dollins and his pilot were killed.

At 9:05 the first wave of troop-carrying tractors churned to a stop at the edge of the surf. The ramps at the rear of the vehicles rattled down, some splashing into the water, and within moments nearly 1,400 Marines, scores with soggy feet, were spread along the two-mile front. The smell of cordite from the last friendly fire on the beach was still heavy, but making a deeper impression on many was that the freshly washed sand sloping from the waterline held no footprints, a forceful reminder they were the first Americans ashore.

The men wasted no time crossing this wet ribbon and flinging themselves against the face of the first terrace. There were three of these, one above the other, created by a violent storm two years earlier. They led up to a plateau that held the first airfield. The sand—or volcanic ash—was light and loose. Those men whose first thought was to dig a foxhole found the sand flowing back in almost as fast as they could scoop it out. It occurred to at least one Marine with a farm background that the job was like trying to dig a hole in a bin of wheat.

The Marines having started to land, island is still obscured by smoke and dust of pre-H-hour bombardment. Mount Suribachi dimly visible at left.

Japanese resistance, in accord with General Kuribayashi's plan, was still light. The gunners on the American vessels believed their rolling barrage, hitting the island in an arc around the landing zone, was responsible for this. Sporadic small-arms fire snapped and whined about, and an occasional mortar shell *whoomped* along the beach. Light or not, the fire took a toll. On the extreme left, the Marines of the first wave noticed an armored tractor standing quietly in the surf, two men hanging grotesquely over the sides of its gun turret. Their arms dangled, and they were very still.

But the first wave did not linger near the surf. Other waves were coming in behind and it was necessary to start the inland movement at once. Defenses were light on the terraces, since the Japanese had anticipated the hammering this area would get by naval gunfire. But the sand itself was a formidable enemy. The Marines had been trained to make movements like this with the greatest possible speed, but now they could only plod, sinking ankle-deep at every step and leaving elephantine footprints.

The weight of their gear made matters worse, and items were dropped. Among the first things to go was the gas mask, carried in a clumsy pouch at the waist, its strap over the opposite shoulder. This was considered an unnecessary trapping, though the pouch was of some small use for carrying—against regulations—apples and oranges and other things that did not fit readily into the pockets. Numerous men soon decided to lay aside their packs, too, intending to return for them later. Right now, weapons and ammunition were all that seemed to matter.

Except for the twisted and bloody remains of a few Japanese who had been caught in the bombardment, the enemy was not in evidence. The island looked uninhabited. But the Marines, recalling their shipboard briefings, knew they had been thrust into the worst possible situation. On their left loomed Mount Suribachi, ostensibly an extinct volcano but in reality a fortress. Up ahead, on that long, sandy plateau with the many contours, was a maze of half-buried bunkers and pillboxes. On their right was the rugged ridge and cliff area that looked down on the beach in the same manner as Suribachi. Every move they made could be watched. They were like ducks in a shooting gallery.

One Marine, after sizing up the situation, did a curious thing. He took his combat knife and cut a slit in the seat of his trousers and in his underwear. To the comrades who looked askance he explained that

With Mount Suribachi looming over them, 5th Division Marines start
moving inland.

now he was not only completely ready for emergency bowel movements but could have them without exposing the white of his buttocks
to enemy snipers.

Among the thousands of Japanese observers was Seaman 1st
Class T. Koizumi, an antiaircraft gunner in the high ground north of
the beach. He could see the long line of Marines plodding inland, and
noted that when the leading groups were about 200 yards from the
water, "any and all Japanese weapons commenced firing." This
included artillery, mortars, rockets, machine guns, and rifles, a new
and busy combination of noises added to the rumbling fire from the
American naval vessels. As scores of shells raised sand spouts among
the Marines and they were temporarily stopped, Koizumi cast his eye
to the beach and out over the water, the nearer reaches of which were
filled with a variety of small craft, heading in. Shells had begun to
land among them, too, and some were taking hits. But the general

picture, Koizumi noted, did not change: "The enemy continued the landing. To my regret, there were no Japanese naval vessels, nor aircraft."

One of the Marines under fire on the first terrace was Corporal Leonce "Frenchy" Olivier, of Eunice, Louisiana, a Pacific veteran. He said to the men near him, "This is going to be worse than Tarawa." Olivier had won the Silver Star for his part in that bloody assault, so the prediction was respected, if not exactly welcomed.

By this time the sounds of combat included a new and shriller note. Heard everywhere was the cry: "Corpsman! Corpsman!" Two of these men accompanied each rifle platoon. They were actually naval personnel, but had lived and trained with the Marines from the start, and had developed the same *esprit de corps*. Also a part of the landing were naval medical teams led by doctors, whose job was to set up aid stations and field hospitals, and to evacuate the wounded to the hospital ships offshore.

Never did a battle's medical personnel have a tougher or more dangerous job. The corpsmen in the front lines had to move among the wounded in plain view of the enemy, without so much as a shrub to conceal their movements, and the doctors and corpsmen in the rear had to set up their hospitals on the beach against the first terrace, an area that was taking as many shells as the front. Not only did medical personnel in both places become casualties, but the doctors on the beach saw some of their patients from the front re-wounded or killed.

In the 5th Division zone, Navy Lieutenant Paul Bradley, a regimental chaplain, moved among the wounded men, stopping at each to utter a few words of comfort. He knelt beside one Marine just as a bullet entered the man's side. Father Bradley did not flinch, but the words of comfort he had begun were supplanted by the administration of last rites.

Soon the beach held gatherings of corpses shrouded in the ponchos the men had carried for protection against the rain. Since the Japanese had a large number of heavy-caliber weapons, casualties were often badly mangled. Entrails were torn out and strewn across the sand. Heads, arms, and legs were carried yards from torsos. One shell burrowed directly beneath a Marine lying on his stomach, the explosion lifting him as though he were as light as a rag doll. His lifeless body rose about fifty feet in the air before plummeting back to the sand.

A large American flag was flying from one of the gunwales of an LCVP—a landing craft that held perhaps twice as many men as an

An aid station on the beach.

amphibian tractor and had its ramp at its forward end—as it approached the beach. This was a bold gesture on the part of the occupants, since they must have known the flag was a special invitation to enemy fire. The Marines were carrying their display of defiance to the limit, shouting lustily as their vessel cut through the surf and thrust its prow against the shore. Then as the ramp dropped to the sand and the men bolted out they took a direct artillery hit, and their spirited shouts were instantly replaced by cries of anguish and confusion.

Another of the early casualties was a man at the front who was blinded. Led to the beach by a comrade, he had a hand clasped to a bandage over his eyes, and there was blood on his cheeks. He stumbled every few steps because of irregularities in the sand. Still another front-line Marine had his jaw shattered, the fragments hanging by shreds of skin and flesh, and blood saturating his breast. Given emergency aid in preparation for fuller treatment aboard a hospital ship, the man at first refused to leave the island. Unable to talk well enough to be understood, he dropped to one knee and began tracing a message in the sand. But the letters simply kept filling in. At last he rose, gave the sand a scuffing kick, shrugged, and allowed himself to be led to the waterline for evacuation.

Perhaps a hundred yards from the beach in the 5th Division

zone, Corpsman Gregory Emery came upon a Marine lying on his back against his pack, a large, bloodstained battle dressing on his bared midriff. An "M" drawn in red on his forehead told Emery he had been given morphine. Groggy and near death, the Marine asked Emery to reach into his pack and take out a photograph for him. The corpsman found it to be an 8 by 10, flecked with shrapnel holes, of the man's wife and newborn child. Emery gave him the photo, and, unable to do anything more for him, crawled from the spot. Soon stopping to look back, he saw the Marine give his dying gasps, holding the picture before his eyes to the last moment. The corpsman turned away. There was work to be done among the living.

The island was now emitting a sustained medley of combat sounds. Shells were whining and crashing, machine guns and rifles were rattling, and men were shouting. Overhead, the noise of the carrier planes waxed and waned as they performed their covering missions. A steadier drone was added by the spotter planes that continued to help with the bombardment from the vessels offshore.

A great part of the battle's ferocity must be ascribed to its concentration. When all of the troops of the assault were ashore, the island would be one of the most heavily populated seven and a half square miles on earth. There would be no room for tactical maneuvering that might save lives, the Marines having no choice but to go directly against the fortifications. At no time were they safely out of range. Units in reserve were obliged to dig in just a few yards behind front-line troops, and often took as much fire—sometimes even more. Conversely, when a unit was relieved of forward duty it was likely to find its retirement area very much like the front.

As one man put it: "Front lines? There aren't any goddam front lines. This whole island is a front line."

Even during lulls in the enemy's fire there was no feeling of safety, for the men knew they were within easy range of a host of weapons, and that they were being closely observed. The sensation of being watched over gunsights by hundreds of hostile eyes was nearly as trying as being under fire. The nervous strain from this situation was of such an intensity and so prolonged as to be unique in the history of warfare.

Initially, the hottest beaches were those of the 4th Division on the right, with the 3rd Battalion, 25th Marines, in the most unenviable position. It was the unit closest to the ridge, broken by cliffs, that overlooked the beach from the north. Before the landing, General Clifton Cates, commander of the 4th Division, had said, "If I knew the name of the man on the extreme right of the right-hand squad of the right-hand company of 3/25, I'd recommend him for a medal before we go in." The hero's identity was to go unrecorded.

This outfit had been in tough spots before, and the men called themselves "the ghouls of the 3rd Battalion." They had written a kind of humorous dirge, sung to the tune of Chopin's *Funeral March*, dealing with the cheapness of their lives and the comfort of having government life insurance. Each time one of them died, the song proclaimed, the bright side was that "ten thousand dollars went home to the folks."

Commander of the 3rd was Lieutenant Colonel Justice M. Chambers, recently turned thirty-seven years old, six feet two in height, and seemingly fearless on the battlefield. He had been wounded at Tulagi in the Solomons, then had to fight the Japanese from the hospital, which they raided. He was credited with driving them off almost singlehandedly. At Saipan he survived being blown off a hill by a shellblast. The colonel's vigorous way of striding around had earned him the nickname "Jumpin' Joe." He was popular with his men, and they had given him a birthday party aboard ship on the way to Iwo. Their improvised card teased him about having turned too old for combat. Actually, he *was* almost too old. Had he been an enlisted man instead of a battalion commander, he probably would have been called "pappy." This was the common designation for Marines in their late thirties.

Now, during the early moments of D day on Iwo Jima, Jumpin' Joe Chambers and his 3rd Battalion ghouls faced northeastward and, with the 1st Battalion of the 25th Marines on their left, began a dogged advance toward the formidable ridge and cliff area. This move would not culminate until late in the day.

Just to the south of these two battalions of the 25th, the 1st and 2nd Battalions of the 23rd, also of the 4th Division, were trying to reach the first airfield but had been slowed by a storm of shells and bullets from bunkers, pillboxes, ditches, and trenches that stood in the way. Even some of the defenses badly damaged by the Navy were participating. Among the first men killed was a company commander, Captain John J. Kalen, hit by small-arms fire. Kalen had a brother on board the heavy cruiser *Chester*, lying off Iwo. He was Lieutenant Commander Robert L. Kalen, a gunnery officer engaged in trying to clear a path for the Marines by directing fire over their heads. The commander would not learn of the captain's death until the campaign ended.

A sunny-faced sergeant in the 1st Battalion, 23rd, Darrell S. Cole of Esther, Missouri, led a machine gun squad against a set of sand-covered pillboxes blocking his platoon's progress. From their dark apertures came both small-arms fire and hand grenades. When Cole cut loose at the slits, the missiles quit coming. Then the machine gun jammed, and the Japanese resumed their work, their bullets and grenades pinning down not only the squad but the whole platoon. Chagrined at his failure, Cole dropped back and circled around to the rear of the pillboxes with some grenades of his own, tossing them through the low entrances. Each muffled explosion, accompanied by escaping debris, told of occupants destroyed. Cole went back to his lines for more grenades and repeated his performance. As he was completing still another attack, convinced that most of the Japanese were dead, a survivor flipped out a grenade that exploded at his feet. He died instantly, unaware that his work had earned him the Medal of Honor.

Cole's battalion was the last, or southernmost, unit in the 4th Division zone, its left flank touching the right flank of the 1st Battalion, 27th Marines, 5th Division. Fighting with this battalion was a famed Marine hero, Gunnery Sergeant John "Manila John" Basilone, the first enlisted man in the Corps to win the Medal of Honor in World War II. On Guadalcanal, during a rainy night in October, 1942, Basilone, the leader of a machine gun section, had used his weapons in a desperate but skillful way to help stop a heavy Japanese attack. After that, Manila John could have had a commission and the choicest duty in the Corps, but he wanted only to remain an enlisted man in a combat unit. Having landed on Iwo Jima with one of the earliest waves, Basilone was leading his machine gun platoon toward the southern tip of the first airfield when he was killed by a mortar shell.

On the left of Basilone's battalion, fighting the same kind of battle, was the 2nd Battalion, 27th Marines. Two battalions of the 28th Marines, 5th Division (the 1st and 2nd), completed the line. Their left flank was only about 400 yards from the base of Mount Suribachi. The men of the 1st Battalion had been assigned the most dramatic mission of the day. The island was only 700 yards wide in this area, and it was their job to isolate Suribachi by pushing across with all possible speed. The mission accomplished, the entire regiment was to place itself on line across the island and bring the volcano under attack. It was of the utmost importance that the 550-foot eminence be taken quickly, for it was a key position, commanding not only the beach but about two-thirds of the island, and functioning as both a fortress and an observation post. As long as the enemy held it, the movements of the bulk of the landing force could be clearly observed and the information could be relayed to the gun crews of widely scattered emplacements.

General Kuribayashi had foreseen the attention that would be paid to Suribachi, and he had made it a semi-independent defense sector. It was held by about 2,000 men under Colonel Kanehiko Atsuchi. At fifty-seven, Atsuchi was considered by some too old for this strenuous command, but he had an amiable disposition and was well liked. Kuribayashi had ordered the colonel and his men simply to stand fast and to kill as many Marines as they could before they themselves were annihilated. They were told, in direct terms, to make Suribachi their tomb.

With its brushy approaches, ashen dome, and fissures and shadows, the volcano was a forbidding sight. The bombardment was causing it to smoke in spots, but in other places it was twinkling in retaliation. Although it was honeycombed with caves and tunnels right up to its summit, its chief defenses were in a belt about its base. The bombardment had given these special attention, and some had been turned to rubble, but many were still strong.

The Marines of the 1st Battalion, 28th, in their rapid push across the island, bypassed Suribachi's belt, their left flank remaining about 400 yards from it. Their main concern was the defenses in front of them. All the while, however, Suribachi looked down on them and peppered them with the fire of both light and heavy weapons. They also took fire from their right flank, where no friendly forces were yet operating. The defenses they were attacking began about halfway across the island and remained thick to the opposite shore. If this was not a suicide mission, it was something awfully close to it.

The battalion made its attack with the usual two-company front, C Company on the right and B Company on the left, the platoons moving abreast. But this field-manual formation was quickly disrupted. Shellbursts ripped up and down the lines, and small-arms fire zigzagged everywhere. Men died and men were wounded. Whole squads were pinned down, while others found weak spots and slogged on through. Some of the bunkers and pillboxes were assaulted; others were bypassed.

Soon the companies were strung out in two battered columns extending toward the rear. The dead remained where they fell. The wounded were dragged into holes, tended by corpsmen, and then left. The helpless had an extra worry. The Japanese, though mostly unseen, were everywhere—in the bunkers and pillboxes and in trench systems and antitank ditches. Woe to the wounded Marine who fell into their hands!

Even areas in which all of the enemy had been killed could not be considered permanently cleared. According to an account written by Sergeant Al C. Eutsey of C Company: "When we secured a pillbox we would put up a white flag to signify it had been taken care of. I looked into several of these and saw no sign of life. A little later these same pillboxes opened fire again. The Japs could maneuver everywhere by means of underground passageways."

Eutsey soon learned something that all of the rest of Iwo's Marines, to their dismay, were learning about the same time. It was unsafe to remain in the open, but it could be equally unsafe to take cover. Eutsey explains: "The Japs had their mortars zeroed in on some of the trenches they had dug, and on some of the shell craters. When these trenches and craters were filled with Marines, they would open fire, killing and wounding many."

So unorthodox was the 1st Battalion's charge across the island that the company commanders, who were supposed to be directing operations from command posts behind the lines, were involved in some of the heaviest fighting. Captain Phil E. Roach of C Company took a bullet in the knee, and his executive officer, Captain Harold E. Rice, received a disabling crease in the back of the neck. Captain Dwayne E. Mears, commander of B Company, helped reduce several pillboxes with his .45 pistol and made it almost all the way across the island before he fell with a fatal wound in the throat.

The first troops to reach the cliff overlooking the western beach were six men of B Company under Lieutenant Frank J. Wright. The time was 10:30 A.M., only ninety minutes after the landing. These men were quickly joined by a fragment of C Company under Lieutenant Wesley C. Bates. A few more men of B Company arrived next. Everyone had had close calls. One of Bates's men had a heel shot off a shoe, and there were bullet holes in his dungarees and pack, but his skin hadn't been touched. The crossing had been completed so fast that an American destroyer firing at the western cliffs, unaware the Marines were there, loosed two rounds that struck the cliff directly beneath the spot where three men were digging in. Lieutenant Bates had gotten across the island unscratched, but now, as he went back to urge other units of his company forward, he was shot through the forearm. Although the bone was broken, Bates continued in action.

The action maintained its fury. Gunnery Sergeant Harry L. "Hap" Mowrey, who had trained C Company's demolitions men, now saw his work pay off. He had been uncertain about one man, Sergeant Martin J. Queeney, who was different from the other trainees. Queeney did not drink, smoke, or swear, and was unathletic. He had never even learned to swim. In the minds of many in the company, he did not qualify as a true Marine. But now, when the advance was delayed by a bunker emitting heavy fire and Mowrey called upon Queeney, the sergeant coolly took a satchel charge, made a flanking approach to the mound, and shoved the charge into its back entrance. In a moment there was an explosion and a cloud of smoke and dust. Jumping to the top of a nearby knoll, Queeney clasped his hands over his head and gave the "all's well" signal, and the advance was resumed. The sergeant went on to assault other defenses in the same way. He would not survive the battle but died a much-respected Marine and a winner of the Navy Cross.

C Company's Corporal Bill Faulkner learned early that a helmet was a valuable thing. He was leading his fire team out of a crater on the way forward when a shell exploded just in front. He and a man beside him were thrown back into the crater, but neither took more damage than a huge gash in his helmet.

A little later, Bill Faulkner was crossing a small, level area when something akin to a manhole cover hinged up a few yards ahead. It was resting on a Japanese helmet, and two very surprised eyes were staring at him from this "spider trap." The lid dropped at once, and so did Bill, his rifle at the ready. When the Japanese did not reappear, Bill crawled to a nearby sand mound, where he discovered the entrance to a tunnel cutting down into the earth, possibly connected with the spider trap, and, in any case, requiring attention.

The tunnel was already under the observation of Corporal Conrad F. Shaker, another C Company man, and Bill said to him, "Let's give it a grenade."

Shaker rejected this idea, and drew his combat knife. He had used this same primitive approach at other fortifications that morning, each time successfully. It was no different this time. He slipped down into the darkness of the tunnel, was gone for a few minutes, then emerged with his knife bloody and carrying several souvenirs of the enemy's underground life, including two pens. But Shaker's luck had run out. As he climbed the sand mound to shout to some Marines farther back, he was shot through the head and fell dead across the summit.

A youth who belonged to Shaker's squad, unaware of what had happened, approached Bill Faulkner and asked, "Where's Shaker?"

Bill pointed and said, "There. He's done."

The youth could not accept the sight. He began crying and said, "I gotta find Shaker!"

Bill slapped him across the face and grabbed him by the shoulders, saying, "Shaker is gone!"

A corpsman approached then, and took over. When Bill left, the youth was still crying.

Faulkner soon came upon Sergeant Thorborn M. Thostenson, who was down on one knee, engaging in a rifle duel with a Japanese inside the entrance of another tunnel. The sergeant would duck as a bullet sang by his ear, then return the fire, all the while grumbling and swearing. At last he tossed in a grenade, and the tunnel was quiet. Thostenson explained to Bill that he had had a particular grudge against that Japanese, for the first bullet from the tunnel had hit his pack and broken a bottle of Four Roses he was carrying.

By this time A Company, which had landed in reserve but was right behind companies B and C, had been committed to the attack. Even before the company got off the beach, a key man, its radio operator, went down with a shattered foot. He set up the radio where he fell and used it to good advantage until he passed out.

A platoon leader who pushed up on the first terrace ahead of his men turned around and shouted, "You'd better get the hell up here if you want to win this war." A moment later he was lying dead.

One man quickly set about winning himself the Medal of Honor. Corporal Tony Stein, formerly a toolmaker in North Dayton, Ohio, was armed with a "stinger," an air-cooled machine gun he had taken from a wrecked Navy fighter plane in the Hawaiian Islands and made into a hand weapon. Exposing himself fearlessly to seek out enemy positions, Stein covered his platoon's advance with torrents of fire.

Machine gunner operating near Mount Suribachi.

Each time his ammunition ran out, he stripped off his encumbering gear (including his helmet and shoes), found a wounded comrade and helped him back to the beach, grabbed more ammunition, and returned on the run to the front. His singlehanded attacks accounted for at least twenty of the enemy.

More and more Marines filtered through to the west coast and took up the fight there. Pfc. Eual D. McRoberts, who served with a C Company machine gun crew, remembered using up a large amount of ammunition: "We had to shovel the empty shells away so we could turn the gun from right to left."

By noon the operation to isolate Mount Suribachi was assured of success. But the fighting and mopping up would continue for the rest of the day.

7
A VIOLENT AFTERNOON

The unit that landed just behind the 1st Battalion of the 28th as it began its charge across the neck of the island was the regiment's 2nd Battalion, under Chandler Johnson, its mission to support the 1st and prepare for the main event, the regiment's attack on Mount Suribachi. Making up the 2nd Battalion were companies D, E, and F.

At this point, Captain Dave Severance and his men in E Company had no visions of glory. They hadn't made the landing in a position of honor, but in reserve. The peppery battalion commander, Johnson, had given the forward positions to companies D and F because he considered them to be best qualified for the work. Easy Company's first assignment was to do nothing more than make its way to a preselected assembly area to the right of its landing place and about a hundred yards in from the beach.

The men had landed on the extreme left of the ninth wave, only a few hundred yards from Suribachi, its gray hulk looming over them. Although trembling and smoking under the impact of shells from the sea and rockets from aircraft, the volcano remained stubbornly active, adding its own noises to the din. Colonel Atsuchi's men were firing both at the Marines crossing the island and those crowding the beach.

Lieutenant Keith Wells and his 3rd Platoon were the closest to Suribachi and had the farthest to travel in their move northward along the beach (away from the volcano) toward the company's assembly area. Two men were quickly wounded—Pfc. Bert M. Freedman in the foot by small-arms fire, and Pfc. John J. Fredotovich in the side and in the thigh by a mortar burst. Shortly afterward, Private John G. Scheperle had his BAR shot from his hands. The weapon was ruined but Scheperle's wound was light. He remained in action.

During a brief halt in the move, several men took cover against the first terrace-front at a spot where it was about six feet high and sharply inclined. With the group was Corporal Robert Leader, the art student from Massachusetts. Leader suddenly found himself completely buried, an artillery shell having exploded in the sand above his head, causing it to give way and come down on top of him. Two of his friends leaped to his aid. Somewhat confused about what had happened, Leader felt himself being uncovered, pulled free, and dusted off roughly, and heard one of his rescuers ask, "Are you all right?" He was relieved to be able to reply that he was.

Meanwhile, Pfc. Leo Rozek discovered that even the act of digging a foxhole on Iwo's beaches could be perilous. He was busily scooping away the sand with his hands when he felt his fingers strike a smooth object, and discovered to his horror that he was clawing at the side of a land mine. Moving quickly to another spot, he started to dig again, and, incredibly enough, uncovered a second mine. He was more fortunate with his third try, but had barely taken cover when Lieutenant Wells ordered another advance.

During the next stop along the beach, Corporal Charles W. "Chuck" Lindberg had his helmet nicked by a mortar fragment. Lindberg was a former Marine Raider who led the platoon's assault squad and was also one of its flamethrower men. Square-set and muscular, he had a jovial rough-and-ready manner that made him popular. Half a finger was missing from his left hand, and the men had often reminded him, during field problems, that he was well equipped for range-indicating. (When a man estimated the distance to a target and wanted to relay the information to fellow Marines without breaking silence, he held up one finger for each hundred yards of the estimate, and the men enjoyed telling Lindberg, who took his impairment lightly, that he was the only one in the platoon who could indicate ranges in fifty-yard units.)

The platoon's new stopping place soon became very warm. Two large landing vessels (LSMs) pushed their prows up on the beach to unload supplies through their bow doors, and promptly drew artillery fire. Crashing shells began to raise waterspouts in the surf about them. Most of the shrapnel that came in the platoon's direction was high, but a few fragments thudded into the terrace-front. Keith Wells was on his feet when the shelling began, and turned to watch it without ducking. Corporal Harold Keller, veteran of several campaigns with the Raiders, rose and yanked him down, and the unceremonious act saved the lieutenant from injury or death, for a huge fragment sped over him as he hit the sand.

The artillery fire soon subsided, and Wells led the platoon up the terraces and inland about a hundred yards to Easy Company's assembly area, a high expanse of open sand that the enemy's gunners were presently neglecting. The spot was found without much difficulty by all units except Second Lieutenant Edward S. Pennell's 2nd Platoon, which had been set ashore in the wrong spot and was having trouble getting oriented.

Lieutenant George Stoddard and the 1st Platoon congratulated themselves on completing the trip without having taken any casualties. Small-arms fire had given them some close calls. One man had a bullet pass between his back and a pack of explosives he was carrying. He found a slit in his dungaree jacket and a matching slit in the pack. Another man who thought he had picked up a stone in his shoe discovered a bullet just beneath his insole. Still another had two holes in his helmet that seemed to indicate he had been shot through the head. The bullet had followed the helmet's inner contour, not even scratching the liner.

Easy Company's assembly area was near the 28th Marines' command post, and the regiment's commander, Colonel Harry B. "Harry the Horse" Liversedge, soon called for Dave Severance to report to him at once. The colonel explained that he was expecting the sector's Japanese to launch a counterattack. Was Dave ready to move out? Dave was obliged to respond that the 2nd Platoon was still absent.

"Be ready to go in five minutes," snapped the colonel, "or I'll give you a general court-martial!"

Dave returned to his command post and looked up and down the crowded beach. The 2nd Platoon was not in sight. Dave did not hesitate. He went back to the colonel and announced in his usual calm manner that he was ready to move. Happily, no counterattack developed, and the 2nd Platoon soon arrived.

The approach of noon found the men of Easy Company still in reserve and still drawing only light fire in spite of their lofty and very visible position. Many occupied themselves by studying Suribachi, perhaps half a mile away. They were seeing it for the first time from the angle at which it would have to be assaulted. Its flanks dropped to meet the sea, but the near side was semicircled by brush-covered approaches that held a 1,300-yard belt of blockhouses, bunkers, pillboxes, mortar pits, caves, tunnels, trenches, and other defenses. Because of the brush and the enemy's camouflage, the Marines could see nothing of this elaborate defense setup except the dark shadows of a few cave entrances and the jagged concrete walls of several blockhouses that had been blasted by the Navy. The shellfire and the attacks from the air continued, raising great puffs of smoke, volcanic ash, pulverized rock, splintered brush, and other debris.

From their unique vantage point, Easy Company's Marines could watch another great show, the one on the beach. Resistance to the landing activities had grown since the company had come ashore. The beach was receiving steady artillery and mortar fire, and a chain of destruction was being forged at the water's edge. Useless landing vessels, trucks, jeeps, and other pieces of equipment were settling haphazardly into the surf-soaked sand. The scene included lifeless bodies, many badly torn, reddening the water that lapped about them.

Hostile fire wasn't the only cause of the rapidly mounting congestion. As jeeps and trucks emerged from their landing craft they often bogged down in the sand before they cleared the ramp. Unless a Caterpillar was on hand to tow a stranded vehicle free at once, the craft, its bow pinned to the beach, usually broached and swamped. To worsen matters, the sea was gradually rising again.

Litter begins to accumulate at shoreline.

Jeep sticks in sand as shore party uses crane to unload supplies.

One of the enemy's most decisive blows was struck against a 5th Division rocket section. As the four truck-mounted launchers rolled from their vessels they were subjected to artillery fire, and three were quickly blasted out of commission. The one that remained, however, was able to go into action, and a ripple that it fired into the slopes of Suribachi caused a tremendous explosion. The Marines on the beach, assuming that an enemy ammunition dump had been demolished, raised a loud cheer.

The invasion's artillery support was only now preparing to land, but the tanks had been coming in since mid-morning. In spite of the stability provided by their tracks, some had trouble clearing their landing craft ramps. Once ashore, they were plagued by congestion, land mines, the soft sand of the terraces, and antitank fire.

A man on the beach in the 4th Division zone who watched one of the tanks start inland later related: "It was trying to edge over the first terrace when it was hit by a mortar that blew off its right tread. Marines began trying to get out of the turret. Another mortar lit right on the turret. The tank spread apart a little. All the Marines were killed."

A number of tanks were lost, but some were waddling into action. Their appearance at the front was viewed with mixed emo-

Sherman tank wrecked by land mine and artillery fire. Crew escaped unhurt.

tions. Although their power was welcomed, they drew so much enemy fire that it was unsafe to be near them.

Conditions on the beach were seriously impeding the landing of supplies. Only the highest-priority items—such things as ammunition, communications equipment, medical supplies, rations, and water—were being brought in. Amphibian tractors, amphibian trucks (some of which were Army vehicles with Army crews), and "weasels"—small boat-like tracked vehicles without ramps—proved invaluable during this stage of the battle. Instead of unloading on the beach, many took their precious cargoes directly to the front lines. Sometimes they came up against active defenses, and their operators suddenly found themselves involved in the fighting. The vehicles were prime targets for shellfire. Those that survived to make the return trip often transported casualties, men who were relieved to be going but who were apprehensive about taking a shell in their midst, a distinct possibility.

At intervals along the landing zone were naval beach parties led by beachmasters equipped with bullhorns that could be heard, above the crash of shells and pounding of the surf, for 500 yards. These officers were also in radio contact with the fleet. It was their job to supervise the landing and unloading of both troop and cargo vessels, create supply dumps, keep critical items moving inland, and evacuate casualties. They were aided not only by their own parties of Navy men but also by shore parties composed of Marines and Seabees.

The Seabees were assigned a variety of tasks. Carpenter's Mate 3rd Class Delmer Rodabaugh had landed as a "checker," carrying five fat notebooks of forms listing the various supplies that were scheduled to come in over his section of the beach. He was supposed to check the items off as they arrived. The confusion that developed turned this job into a joke, and Rodabaugh soon laid aside his notebooks, picked up a box of ammunition, and started inland. Topping the first terrace, he came face to face with a Japanese soldier sitting in a shallow hole and staring at him. The man was dead, and Rodabaugh circled around the body and continued his trek.

Many other Seabees assisted in moving ammunition off the beach, loading themselves with as much as they could carry. They were obliged to go "over the top" three times while negotiating the three terraces. Shipfitter 3rd Class John C. Butts, Jr., a strapping man of twenty-four who had a wife and child at home in Salt Lake City, Utah, made four such runs, carrying his loads all the way to the front lines. On his fifth trip, as he was going over the top of the third terrace, he was killed by a Japanese sniper. Two of his buddies divided his load and finished the run.

On the beach, specially trained teams of Seabees probed for mines and destroyed those they found. Others used demolitions to blow up some of the worst tangles of debris at the water's edge. Under the steady shellfire, Seabee casualties mounted. A seven-man crew manhandling a 37-millimeter gun off the ramp of an LCVP was grunting and swearing under the strain when a mortar shell exploded in its midst, wounding or killing all seven.

Among the most important men helping to fight the battle of supply were the Seabee Caterpillar operators, whose work included towing bogged vehicles free, digging revetments for supply dumps, and fashioning roads along the beach and through the terraces toward the front lines. While preparing to land one of the heavy Cats from the hold of an LSM, Machinist's Mate 1st Class Alphenix J. Benard, a brawny construction worker from Escanaba, Michigan, encountered an unexpected problem. The ship was in the proper position, its prow on the beach, its doors open, and its ramp down. But as Benard was about to jockey the heavy Cat out of the hold, he noted that the sand in front of the ramp was covered with dead Americans. "I was so horrified," he said later, "that I almost fell off my seat." But he hesitated for only a moment. His Cat was needed ashore, and the dead were beyond feeling. Gritting his teeth, he drove down the ramp and churned over them.

Early afternoon found the attack progressing only a yard or two at a time. The island's neck had been crossed, but this had done nothing to weaken the strength of the torso extending northward. The first airfield, about 700 yards in from the beach, was still in enemy hands, and the 25th Marines had not taken the ridge and cliff that overlooked the landing zone from the right. The invasion was not moving as fast as the high brass had anticipated. Of course, these same men had predicted that the entire battle would be over within a few days, ten at the most.

At this stage of the operation, an American aerial observer reported, Iwo Jima looked like "a fat pork chop, sizzling in the skillet."

Japanese shellfire remained the chief deterrent to the advance. This is not to say that bullets were not thick and punishing, but bullets were not so terrible to face. A man need only drop into a shallow depression to avoid them, and the Japanese from whose weapons they came could be spotted and destroyed. It was different with artillery and mortar shells, and shrieking rockets. Their origins were usually a mystery, some coming from far off. And however deep a man dug, he knew a shell could seek him out. Under a barrage, with the earth shaking and the air filled with heavy explosions and the whir of shrapnel and sand, he felt terrified and helpless. There was nothing he could do but cringe in his hole and pray he would be missed. If he was hit but was lucky enough to keep his life, he had a new worry. It was quite possible for him to be hit again.

Perhaps no Marine who landed on Iwo Jima survived wounds from a greater number of shells than Second Lieutenant Benjamin F. Roselle, Jr., who, about 1 P.M., went ashore on the extreme right of the 4th Division zone as the leader of a six-man naval gunfire liaison team. Weighed down with radio gear, Roselle and his party plodded inland over the sand for about 200 yards, at which point one of the men was felled by an artillery shell. Roselle took up the man's gear, and the team started forward again. Shortly a mortar blast knocked Roselle and two others off their feet. The two were able to rise, but Roselle could not. His left foot and ankle were hanging by shreds of muscle and flesh, the bone was in splinters, and his blood was pouring into the sand. Not a man to panic, the lieutenant managed to joke about the misfortune while the unwounded men applied a tourniquet to his leg. He ordered the wounded to return to the beach for evacuation.

Then another shell found the range. Two men were killed, and several fragments penetrated Roselle's good leg. He was now left with only one man who had not been hit, and they hugged the sand as the shellfire continued. It was being delivered by pattern, and it was possible for Roselle to make a good guess as to where each new blast would take place. Suddenly he cried, "Hold tight!" and a shell exploded almost on top of them. The lieutenant was hit for the third time, in the shoulder. The other man's right leg was torn off. He crawled away, awkwardly trailing the bleeding stump, and Roselle was left alone with the dead.

Then a fourth shell literally bounced him off the sand, and shrapnel ripped into both his thighs. He was still fully conscious as he settled down, and for some reason he began to wonder what time it was. As he lifted his left arm to look at his wristwatch, a fifth shell exploded right beside him. The watch was torn from his wrist, and a jagged red hole was left in its place. The bone had been fractured.

By this time Roselle was in terrific pain, but he was also seething with rage. He said later, "I think this is what kept me alive." He took no further hits, and was soon found by a team of medical men working their way in from the beach. His arm was splinted and he was evacuated to a hospital ship, where his treatment included the amputation of his dangling foot.

General Kuribayashi followed the progress of the battle from the headquarters blockhouse above his living quarters at Iwo's northern end. He was in contact with all of the units on the island, and also with Imperial Headquarters in Tokyo. One of his first messages to headquarters announced that the Iwo Jima garrison was donating 125,000 yen to the national treasury. As soon as the invasion had become a fact and the men had no more use for their currency, they had burned it. Kuribayashi also reported to Tokyo on the garrison's bravery, citing individuals for special acts and recommending them for posthumous promotion. The general would continue this policy throughout the battle.

For a time during the afternoon the Americans on the beach

were granted a respite from the shellfire as the Japanese raised their guns and trained them on the sea. The regimental reserves, which had been circling in their small boats (LCVPs) for hours, were forming abreast along the Line of Departure and were starting in. As the shells began to hit the water, raising tall silver spouts as they exploded, a Marine in a hole near the first terrace-front stood up and took a long look. He might have been speaking for every man on the beach when he said, "Thank God! They're firing at somebody else!"

The reserve battalions were given a hotter reception than the assault battalions. As they neared shore the shellfire increased. Some of the boats took hits that mangled Marines in groups and left the unhurt spattered with blood. Other boats were menaced by small-arms fire, bullets thudding against their square fronts or creasing their sleek sides. Men flinched involuntarily at the whine of ricochets. A number of Japanese in high positions managed to drop their bullets directly within. The cry, "I'm hit!" was frequently heard, and here and there a man slumped amid his comrades without a sound.

Led by Captain LaVerne Wagner of Dubuque, Iowa, K Company, 3rd Battalion, 23rd Marines, 4th Division, headed for Yellow Beach 1. The companies of the 23rd that had made the original assault were now several hundred yards inland, near the first airfield. It was the mission of Wagner and his men to proceed to the front and relieve one of these companies. Ordinarily, a reserve company like Wagner's

Fourth Division Marines pouring from beached landing craft.

would have had little trouble landing and marching inland. By this time the beach and the area stretching toward the front should have been reasonably quiet. But in this battle very few of the usual conditions prevailed.

As the boat in which Captain Wagner was traveling rammed its bow against the beach, machine gun fire was crackling overhead. The men wanted to get out fast, but the ramp would not lower. Wagner ordered a jump over the side. One man who rose up was hit in the face and shoulder. The rest made it, dropping into waist-deep water, pushing to the beach, and running for shell holes. The beach was crowded with men, many of them wounded and awaiting evacuation. One Marine had been blown in half, his entrails scattered.

Shells continued to seek their targets, and within a few minutes a fragment smashed the walkie-talkie carried by Wagner's radioman. All of his platoons having landed, the captain began his move toward the front. The machine gun, in some unknown position off to the right, had found the range again, adding its crackle to the shellbursts. Men began to fall. Inland about fifty yards, Second Lieutenant James P. Mariedas jumped into a hole and came face to face with a live Japanese, one bypassed by the assault troops. A tussle ensued, and Mariedas managed to stab the man to death with his own bayonet.

The company's front was studded with bunkers and pillboxes, some retaining the sand that had been heaped over them, others showing sides of bare concrete. Most had been assaulted with flamethrowers, hand grenades, and demolitions, and their crews were dead. One or two of the structures were smoldering inside, and emitting smoke and firecracker-like pops and snaps as their ammunition exploded. But one large bunker opened up with machine gun fire. Captain Wagner called for a tank, and one of the huge dark-green machines came lumbering forward, its engine throbbing and its tracks creaking and clanking. Its fire, however, had little effect on the concrete walls, and none of the missiles entered an aperture. Some troops on the left of K Company circled behind the fortification and threw several grenades into its entrance. This had a curious effect: A dozen grenades came flying out the front. Finally a few men of K Company circled to the rear and kept throwing grenades through the entrance until the occupants were silenced. Entering gingerly, a Marine discovered three dead men and seventy-five grenades lined up on a shelf, all ready for throwing.

As Wagner's platoons at last moved up behind the assault troops who were dug in facing the airport, they drew artillery fire and took cover. Soon they discovered that one of the enemy installations that was delaying the advance of the assault troops was an antiaircraft gun that had been depressed to parallel the sand. A squad of K Company men worked its way around the flank of this position, and a rifleman shot the lone gunner through the head. Closing in, the Marines were astonished to find the man not only alive but able to walk and talk, even though his brains were oozing through a hole in his temple. He became the first prisoner taken in the Yellow Beach area.

By this time K Company had suffered thirty casualties. Captain Wagner said later: "Theoretically, we hadn't even been committed to the battle. We were still in reserve."

Watching the invasion from the sea were nearly a hundred correspondents—American, British, and Australian—representing wire services, radio networks, and magazines. Some of these people had covered other invasions, both in the Pacific and in the war's European theater, but they had seen nothing like this. The battle was unique not only in its fury but also in its setting. All areas of the field could be taken in with one sweeping glance. It was almost as though the whole thing had been arranged with spectators in mind. They were able to watch a major invasion—the first penetration of Japanese territory—as they might have watched a football game.

The newspeople, however, were located within the battle's arena; they were with the fleet that was supporting the landing force with ponderous shellfire. Between the viewers and the shoreline, innumerable landing craft were active, some heading in with troops and supplies, others coming out with cargoes of wounded. Aircraft darted about over the island, conspicuously active against Mount Suribachi and the northern cliffs toward which elements of the 25th Marines were still fighting. The wreckage on the beach was outlined against the first terrace. One observer compared the scene to a long line of frame houses that had been hit by a tornado. The shore parties and other men on the beach could be seen, as well as the artillery crews who were struggling to get their weapons into position for firing. Tanks looking like beetles moved about behind the front lines. Numerous other tanks were still, having been knocked out by mines or antitank fire. Some were burning. The men in the front lines were harder to see, but could be picked out by observers with good glasses.

Robert Sherrod, covering the battle for *Time-Life*, was disturbed by the volume of the enemy's shellfire. He saw one burst after another raise debris on the beach and on the slopes leading to the first airfield. Having accompanied the landings on Tarawa and Saipan, Sherrod was well aware of the capacity of such bursts to sunder human flesh.

The correspondent soon had a disquieting experience close at hand. An LCVP flying a Red Cross casualty flag came alongside his vessel as he stood at the rail. The boat was delivering three psychiatric cases for treatment on board, and one of the men was twisting and turning on his stretcher, all the while screaming at the top of his lungs. Thought Sherrod: "There is war at its worst."

About 5 P.M. Sherrod prepared to go ashore. A few correspondents had preceded him, among them Keith Wheeler of the *Chicago Times*. Wheeler was returning to the fleet to write his D day story at the same time Sherrod was starting in, and they met. "I wouldn't go in there if I were you," said Wheeler. "There's more hell in there than I've seen in the rest of this war put together." But Sherrod went in, and was soon crouching in a foxhole in the 4th Division zone.

In the 5th Division zone near Suribachi, Captain Dave Severance and Easy Company had left their reserve position and were now in action. They had been ordered to follow the men of the 1st Battalion, 28th Marines, who had crossed the neck of the island. The Company's job was to help mop up and to become part of the defense line the 1st was setting up on the opposite coast.

The first few sand mounds with dark apertures were silent as the company approached, but then one cut loose with machine gun fire. There was a general lunge for cover, some of the men finding craters or depressions, while others dropped behind a foot-high terrace that happened to be handy. Lieutenant Keith Wells made a flying leap into a shell hole and came into contact with a dead Japanese. The corpse was lying on its back with its abdominal organs exposed and buzzing with flies. Wells landed right on top of the man, and his knees sank into the exposed organs. "After that," recalled the lieutenant, "my pants legs smelled so bad that at one time I almost cut them off."

Easy Company was spared the necessity of dealing with this pillbox when two tanks came forward and knocked it out. Congratulating themselves on their good fortune, the men rose and continued the advance. About halfway across the neck, the open sand gave way to patches of scrubwood. Pillboxes and bunkers, connected by trenches, were thicker here, but most had been knocked out and stood quiet beneath their covering sand, some having a conical appearance and others resembling igloos. A number had patches of grass and other low vegetation growing on them.

The area also held networks of antitank ditches, and Easy Company filed through a chain that led in the direction of the west coast. Lining the sandy sides of some of these deep recesses were groups of 1st Battalion wounded, awaiting evacuation that was being delayed because of their distance from the landing zone. Teams of stretcher bearers had not been able to reach them. Swathed in bandages showing patches of blood, some were lying with white faces and closed eyes, while others sat and watched the company pass. There was little exchange of conversation. One of the company's men admitted later: "I found myself disliking to pay the wounded too much attention. Thinking about them increased my awareness that I might at any moment be sharing their plight."

The day was waning when Easy Company reached the defense perimeter the 1st Battalion had set up along the brushy high ground overlooking the western beach, and the company became part of the line, digging in near a large bypassed mound. Since this particular mound had been quiet all day, the 1st Battalion had assumed it was nothing more than a supply house, but Easy Company eyed it with suspicion, for it was big enough to hold an artillery piece. Keith Wells wanted to blow it, but a 1st Battalion officer who outranked him insisted he would only be wasting the charge.

As soon as the lieutenant had his platoon's line set up, he went to investigate some patches of brush in the mound's vicinity. He took with him Pfc. Donald Ruhl, the company malcontent, who seemed impatient for action. Wells was armed with a Thompson submachine gun and Ruhl had his Garand rifle, or M-1, to which he had attached his bayonet. Ruhl had much earlier discarded the helmet he hated and was wearing only a fatigue cap.

While the two men were kicking about in the brush, the bypassed mound suddenly came to life. A heavy door rolled open, and a three-inch fieldpiece, its muzzle flashing orange, began to boom shells along the perimeter. Wells was about to alert his platoon for an attack on the bunker when he saw that a 1st Battalion squad was already moving against it. Led by a tall, husky second lieutenant, the men closed in swiftly, their maneuver partly screened by a scattering of bushes. Then the bunker began to spit machine gun bullets, and the advance came to a halt as one of the leading Marines crumpled and died.

The next move came from another direction. A Marine rushed the bunker with a shaped-charge, an explosive designed to concentrate its force in one direction. He scrambled to the top of the mound, scratched away an area of sand, planted the charge, then bounded for safety. A loud blast followed, and a hole was driven down through the concrete and into the bunker. The measure wasn't strong enough to finish the occupants, but it made them hasten to close the doorway they had been firing through. Another Marine then climbed the mound and dropped a thermite grenade through the shaped-charge hole.

Meanwhile, Wells and Ruhl had been working their way closer to the bunker, and as the thermite grenade started to generate intense heat and smoke within, they became an important part of the assault. A door that faced them was rolled open, and a cloud of white smoke billowed out. A cluster of green sneakers appeared at its base, and the two men opened fire. Wells let go an entire forty-round Thompson clip, and Ruhl emptied his eight-shot Garand. Three Japanese stumbled out of the smoke and fell to the ground. One made a feeble effort to rise, and Ruhl hurried forward to finish the job with his bayonet.

A moment later Wells saw a hand grenade arc toward Ruhl from a nearby thicket. At the lieutenant's cry, "Look out—grenade!" Ruhl dropped flat, and the fragments lashed out harmlessly. Wells slammed a fresh clip into his Thompson and ran toward the thicket. He was staking his life on the probability that the Japanese, since he had done no shooting, was without a firearm. The lieutenant crouched low as he entered the brush. Dusk was setting in, and he knew his best chance of locating his quarry lay in spotting a silhouette against the sky. But a complete search convinced him the grenadier had escaped, probably into a hole somewhere.

Returning to the bunker, Wells found Ruhl engaged in a struggle with one of the 1st Battalion Marines who had made the initial assault. The man was temporarily deranged and was trying to wrest Ruhl's rifle from him, apparently wanting to use its bayonet to mutilate the fallen Japanese. "Give it to me!" he shouted, his eyes glistening with tears. "Those son of a bitches killed my buddy!"

"Take it easy! Take is easy!" Ruhl pleaded, straining to break the man's grip on his weapon. Ruhl had already used his bayonet, and all three of the Japanese were dead. In a moment two of the crazed Marine's friends reached the scuffling pair and pulled the offender away. He calmed down as they led him back to their unit's section of the perimeter.

Easy Company had had its first real test in combat, and had measured up. Keith Wells had been right about the bunker and had conducted himself commendably in the action against it. He had demonstrated that his demeanor on the training field, when he had quoted from Jenghiz Khan and talked dramatically of his battlefield intentions, had not been idle bravado. He was actually the resolute fighting man he imagined himself to be. Donald Ruhl, too, had proved himself to be aggressive and capable. Criticized in training for his discontent and rebelliousness, he had let the men know that he intended to "show them" when he got into combat. And he had made a good start. After the bunker encounter, Ruhl asked to become the lieutenant's permanent runner, a job that would involve repeated exposure under fire, and Wells was glad to have him.

At the other end of the landing zone, the 25th Marines, 4th Division, had now mounted the ridge they had been pressing toward all day under unremitting fire. Colonel Jumpin' Joe Chambers and his 3rd Battalion "ghouls" seized control of the clifftops, where they found several concrete bunkers smashed by the Navy, and also many pillboxes, trenches, caves, and other defenses still furiously active. The battalion had been 900 strong when it landed. Now it numbered 150 combat effectives. A large part of this loss had been caused by disorganization and was only temporary, but many a ghoul had been killed or wounded. The indomitable Chambers was still on his feet, an inspiring figure in his dusty fatigues, but nineteen of the battalion's officers had been felled.

As they fought to hold the heights, their weapons flashing in the gathering dusk, the ghouls continued to suffer, but soon relief troops began to come up behind. The ghouls were permitted to withdraw a hundred yards to the rear, where perhaps they would be slightly safer than at the front. It would be hours before the exchange was completed. As the ghouls trudged rearward by platoons—their mouths parched and gritty, their nerves frayed and their muscles complaining, a number with bandaged wounds—they began to realize the extent of their losses, and to miss their vanished comrades.

As a result of this day's fighting, they knew all too well, many a ten-thousand-dollar insurance check would "go home to the folks."

The fleet had landed additional 4th and 5th Division reserves— the 24th and 26th Regiments—late in the day, and about 40,000 men were now ashore. Although the beachhead was relatively secure, it was less than half as deep as the landing plan called for. Casualties for the day were about 2,500 killed, wounded, or missing, plus another hundred psychiatric, or "combat fatigue," victims.

8
THE FIRST NIGHT

Iwo's night came on suddenly, the sun seemingly extinguished by its plunge into the western sea. To the Americans ashore, the blanketing darkness seemed almost to have a physical weight. Its effect on their vision increased the threat to their lives. The ground they occupied was completely unfamiliar to them, while the Japanese knew it intimately and had been trained to deal with an occupying force. It was obvious that a bad day was to be followed by a worse night. Many a man who had spent the daylight hours hoping and praying he would survive the battle was now concerned only with getting through the hours of darkness.

The temperature soon dropped to about 60 degrees and seemed lower to the Marines after their months of duty in warmer climes. As the chill penetrated their thin dungarees, those men who had laid aside their packs and blanket rolls began to wish they had not. The rations in the packs, however, were not missed. Few men had eaten much, if anything, all day, and there was little hunger now. Most stomachs were heavy with apprehension.

Even some of the reassurance provided by the fleet had been lost, many of the vessels having withdrawn to night stations. The carriers had reclaimed their planes. Remaining behind were a scattering of hospital, supply, and gunfire support ships. Mortar-armed gunboats concentrated their fire on the high ground dominating the 4th Division beaches, while destroyers, using searchlights, looked for targets on Suribachi and along the coasts. The missiles from some of their guns included tracers that left vivid streaks of light that often terminated in sparks when rocks were struck.

The destroyers also fired star shells that burst high in the air and descended slowly under silk parachutes, giving off a dazzling yellow illumination. The island became an eerie mass of highlights and shadows, all in motion. To the Marines at the front, most of whom were dug in for the night, the star shells were both an aid and the cause of repeated false alarms. Visibility was enhanced, but many of the restless shadows of shrubs, rocks, and mounds of sand were mistaken for skulking Japanese.

The enemy's shellfire continued, with pyrotechnics added, each burst accompanied by a red and yellow arc with jagged extremities. The most fearsome missiles were 675-pound spigot mortars that shrieked weirdly as they wobbled through the air and burst so heavily that they shook the earth over a wide area. Hardly less jarring were 550-pound rockets launched in the north from crude wooden troughs. Neither of these giant projectiles was very accurate. Moreover, the enemy's supply of both was limited. Most of the smaller missiles—rockets, mortars, and artillery shells—were amply stocked and were used at night almost as effectively as in the day.

Second Lieutenant Cyril P. "Pete" Zurlinden, a public relations man with the Fleet Marine Force, was lying in a shell hole about 200 yards in from the beach when a dazzling burst raised him bodily amid flying sand and an ear-pounding concussion. He landed on his back, his momentary confusion giving way to an awareness that something terrible had happened to him, though he was uncertain what it was. In the shadowy light of a star shell, Pete looked down at his body. He did not know what to make of it. There was a leg and foot jutting sharply sidewise from the vicinity of his left thigh. His next move was to take a long draft from a canteen of whiskey he was carrying. Then, in the dim light, he looked at the leg and foot again. He decided they were not his; the angle was too absurd. He called to a man dug in near him, "I've got a leg in here. I'm going to throw it out."

As Pete seized the leg and tried to move it, great pain swept over him. The leg not only belonged to him but was still strongly attached, the shattered bone notwithstanding. Pete called for a corpsman, but none was near enough to hear. Something had to be done. Probably the best thing to do, he thought, was to straighten the leg. Taking swigs of whiskey to help counteract the stabs of pain, Pete spent an hour at this job. Then he lay back and drew his right foot up behind his left knee, which not only supported the mutilated limb but helped stem the flow of blood. He was fairly comfortable now, except that his right leg kept going to sleep. Help did not reach Pete until morning, but a surgical team on a ship offshore saved his leg. Some months later, back in the States, Pete escorted his bride-to-be to a dance.

Many others were wounded or killed as they lay in holes that night. Sometimes they were first tormented by a number of near misses flashing and roaring about them and showering them with sand and dust. Then as they lay shuddering and praying the barrage would end or at least move somewhere else, the big one dropped in with them, the power of its burst increased by the confinement of the hole. One of the direct hits was scored on the command post of the 1st Battalion, 23rd Marines. Instantly killed were the battalion commander, Lieutenant Colonel Ralph Haas, and his operations officer, Captain Fred C. Eberhardt.

There were hundreds of narrow escapes. One Marine literally had his hair parted by a mortar shell, a large fragment slicing through his helmet from front to rear and almost halving it. Correspondent Robert Sherrod found himself in the center of one of the barrages. "The heavy shells burst around my foxhole every few seconds in a furious tattoo. In the midst of this thunder and lightning there was a thud in the bank of my foxhole, next to my left arm. I reached over and dug out a piece of hot steel that must have weighed a half pound."

The Japanese did not neglect the shoreline, where the landing of supplies continued amid the wreckage. Fire became so heavy on the Yellow and Blue beaches that they were closed at eleven o'clock. Farther south, a limited number of landing craft still operated, and bulldozers went on with their work of freeing bogged equipment, digging revetments, and making roads. The landing craft exchanged their supplies for wounded men lying on stretchers at the foot of the first terrace, blankets over them and their faces white in the light of the star shells.

Among the landing craft were amphibian trucks (DUKWs, or "ducks"), some of which belonged to the Army and had black crews. One of these tracked vehicles churned up on the beach just north of Mount Suribachi and encountered Marine Supply Sergeant Ray Dooley. The driver suggested the load of supplies be taken inland: "You lead us, Sarge!" Dooley climbed aboard, and the duck clattered up the terraces and made a sweep behind the front lines, where Dooley and the crew tossed out rations, water, and ammunition as they went, leaving the items in a long trail across the sand. Back on the beach, Dooley helped the crew load the duck with wounded, and it headed out for a hospital ship.

Among the other small landing craft, none was harder to handle in the rising surf, and in the current that swept past the island from north to south, than the LCVP, that flat-bottomed rectangular plywood shell, completely open to the sky, whose forward section dropped to form its ramp. The night sea was filled with such boats, their mother ships having withdrawn and left them behind. Equipped with radios, they cruised about in assigned areas, answering calls as they were needed. Gunner's Mate 2nd Class Louis Berard, who served on one of the craft of the attack transport *Missoula,* said later that "the big ships fired over our heads at targets on the island all night long, and the star shells lit up the water around us." According to Signalman 2nd Class Bob Collyer, of the attack transport *Sibley,* the LCVPs bobbed like corks: "When it comes to amphibs, there are only two kinds of stomachs—damned tough, or none at all." Collyer had a good stomach. His chief problem that night was to avoid being distracted from his duties by the fireworks on Iwo, which he found a constant fascination.

The supply dumps on the beach were imperiled by more than shellfire. General Kuribayashi had organized "wolfpacks" of three or four men each. Their job was to slip through the Marine lines with demolitions and hand grenades and blow up dumps that held ammunition and fuel. Whether or not the men got back to their own lines was inconsequential. One of these teams reached a 4th Division depot that held two boatloads of ammunition, gasoline, and flame-thrower fuel. It went up with a tremendous roar and a sheet of fire that could be seen all over the island, and the concussion collapsed foxholes for yards around. A Navy doctor and a Marine major sharing a hole were buried and nearly suffocated before winning the struggle to free themselves. Gasping for breath, they crawled away amid the red glare of flames and the din and debris of secondary explosions.

Howlin' Mad Smith, at this time still on board Admiral Turner's flagship, notified his subordinates on the island to be prepared for a large-scale counterattack the first night. "We will welcome a counterattack. That is generally when we break their backs." But a counterattack never developed. Kuribayashi had no intention of wasting his forces by flinging them against an entrenched enemy. Instead he had schooled them in infiltration tactics such as those used by the men who blew up the supply depot.

It was well known to the Marines that Japanese soldiers were skilled night fighters. This had been learned in confrontations on other Pacific islands. The enemy's daring frequently went beyond

Western understanding. There were Marines who swore that a night-creeping Japanese would sometimes feel about in a foxhole very carefully until he touched a body, his purpose being to make sure it was warm lest he waste a hand grenade on a corpse.

On Iwo, infiltrators had a special advantage. They could make use of the network of caves, tunnels, and trenches and arrive among the Marines in totally unexpected places. Some of the Marines believed they heard movements through the earth directly beneath their foxholes, and they very probably did. Actual attacks were scattered, but no one in the lines was exempt from the threat, and few men slept. Most kept a firm grip on their weapons and peered with wide eyes through the star-shell light at the shadowy sand, rocks, and brush about them, and were sometimes startled by even the peregrinations of sand crabs. The acute tension and the night's chill forced many men to clench their teeth to keep them from chattering.

The strongest attempt at infiltration was made in the zone occupied by the 27th Marines, at the southern end of the first airfield. A hundred or more Japanese started down the runway and were met by a hail of rifle and machine gun bullets, plus a barrage from the 13th Marines, an artillery regiment. They were soon stopped. Those not killed or disabled slipped back into the holes that had produced them.

Infiltrators came by sea as well as by land. A Seabee near the surf was looking out over the water when a log came floating down from the north, borne past by the current. It seemed harmless enough, but suddenly it made a sharp turn. The Seabee opened fire, and a dead Japanese rolled off, later washing up on the beach.

In another section of the surf lay a derelict Japanese vessel from which an enemy radioman directed artillery and mortar fire. Not a true infiltrator, he had been lurking there all day with Americans all around him. On hearing a clicking noise made by the radio, a Marine alerted two or three comrades, and the group crept up to the derelict. Scanning the dark interior until they found the right shadow, they shot the man dead.

The Marines belonging to the 1st Battalion, 28th Regiment, who were in foxholes along the cliff overlooking the western beach near Suribachi, were astonished to see a barge full of Japanese soldiers push out from the base of the volcano and come northward along the coast. The vessel nudged up on the beach just below the Marines, who let go a fusillade of rifle fire. Several of the enemy dropped dead on the barge, others tumbled into the surf, and still others, some of them wounded, broke for the brush a few yards from the water, doubtless intent only on escaping.

In their foxholes scattered about just inland from this cliff area, Dave Severance and Easy Company, the flag-raisers-to-be, had their own share of experiences with night-prowling Japanese. BAR man Art Stanton spotted three men trying to reoccupy a neutralized bunker, which looked like nothing more than a huge mound of sand. One man was standing at the base, while the other two crept up the slope toward an opening at the top. Stanton fired first at the man at the base, dropping him lifeless, then swung his fire up the slope. "By the time I had downed the second Jap I was unable to see even the bunker because of my muzzle blast. I could see nothing but balls of fire for a long time afterward." The third man escaped.

One of Easy Company's squads had taken cover at a spot where two thigh-deep enemy trenches crossed each other at right angles. When a shadowy figure came up the segment in which Pfc. Edward S. Kurelik was lying with his BAR, Kurelik did not fire but called out a challenge, thinking the figure might be a Marine. There was an exclamation in Japanese, and a hand grenade exploded with an orange flash at Kurelik's side, wounding him in the thigh and foot. Others in the squad let loose with rifle fire and hand grenades as the Japanese darted away, but the result was uncertain. Pharmacist's Mate 2nd Class John H. Bradley was dug in some yards from the squad, and after yelling for the men to hold their fire he crawled over and tended to Kurelik's wounds.

In another Easy Company area, a Marine was crouched in a shell crater he had taken as his foxhole for the night when an infiltrator slipped in beside him. The Marine leaped from the hole screaming, "Jap! Jap!" Since orders had been issued for everyone to stay low until dawn, the Marine was mistaken for the infiltrator, and a friend in a nearby hole shot him down, the scream turning to gurgled breathing, then silence. The Japanese got away. The Marine who did the fatal shooting was devastated by remorse. His platoon leader, George Stoddard, tried to console him with the assurance that his reaction had been a natural one.

Not all of the infiltrators were bent on slaughter. There were those like Seaman 1st Class T. Koizumi, whose job was reconnaissance. He had spent a long day at his antiaircraft gun north of the landing beaches, and had retired to his night shelter only to be ordered to "take three men and reconnoiter the enemy around the southern coast."

Exchanging solemn goodbyes with comrades, the patrol picked its way among rocks, sand ridges, and patches of brush, trying to avoid the light of the star shells and the searchlights of the destroyers. The men were amazed at how the terrain had been changed by American naval shells since they had last seen it. With a few bullets cracking over their heads and an occasional shell from their own forces falling near them, they managed to pass through the Marine lines to a spot on one of the terraces overlooking the southern beach, where landing activities had continued. Inching closer, they neared a hole in which a black sentry, a Seabee, was standing. He was armed with a BAR, whose trigger he fingered nervously as he studied the shadows about him, his ebony features highlighted by the star-shell light. He did not see them.

"We were armed with hand grenades," says Koizumi, "but it was our duty to return to our own lines without challenging the enemy."

They slipped away, making it safely to the edge of their lines. Here an American shell exploded near them, and one man was badly hurt. The others carried him to a shelter that held a doctor, then went to their own shelter, where they reported on the landing activities and received the congratulations of their comrades for making it back alive.

For the Americans, the night dragged wretchedly. The hours at last edged toward dawn, a continuation of patchy illuminations and moving shadows; of medleys of small-arms fire intermingled with hand grenade bursts; of the shrieking, crashing, rumbling, and flashing of shellfire; of slaughter and mutilation, with their ugly patterns of blood; and of anguished cries for help.

"The first night on Iwo Jima," reported newsman Robert Sherrod, "can only be described as a nightmare in hell."

9

CARNAGE ON TWO FRONTS

February 20 dawned cloudy, but the Americans found it a beautiful sight. True, the daylight reemphasized the multiplicity of the island's defenses, but it also ended the infiltration threat. Along with this boon, there was a lull in the enemy's shellfire. As the Americans began stirring and flexing muscles that had stiffened, voices that had been held to a whisper rose again, some of the men reverting to their usual unrestrained profanity as they discussed the night's events.

New events were not lacking. One occurred at the artillery bunker that Lieutenant Keith Wells and Pfc. Don Ruhl had helped to reduce the previous evening. The men who had made the first rush on the bunker approached it at dawn out of curiosity and to look for souvenirs, and they flushed an unarmed Japanese from its dark interior. As the man began to run for his life, the Marine who had gone berserk after the death of his friend whipped out his combat knife and bounded into pursuit, urged on by the others: "Get him! Get the bastard!" Winning the race, the Marine seized his quarry by the shoulder and drove the knife home savagely again and again. The Japanese crumpled, bleeding profusely from the neck and side. A dozen observers cheered as he died.

The Marines in positions overlooking the eastern beaches were encouraged to see, in the early light, the fleet reassembling in full strength in the waters offshore, and the renewed movements of the smaller vessels indicated that the landing activities were being pressed in spite of enemy fire and a high surf. But the scene at the water's edge was now almost indescribable. All along the two-mile landing zone the debris had thickened to such an extent that incoming vessels had serious trouble finding places to beach. Lying every few yards was a wrecked or bogged LCVP, amphibian tractor, tank,

Tank and amphibian tractors blasted by Japanese artillery.

halftrack, or jeep. Some had been flipped over by mines or heavy shells. Bulldozers and Caterpillars sat crippled on roadways they had been building, and cranes brought in to unload cargo lay on their sides or reached up at impossible angles. Also scattered about were water cans, ammunition boxes, rifles, gas masks, packs, blankets, ponchos, toilet articles, and letters and photos from home, and many of these things were torn by shrapnel or riddled by bullets. Commonly, they were splotched with bloodstains turned brown. Some of the surf-washed dead were now almost wholly covered by sand. Here and there, all that showed of a corpse was a foot or an upstretched hand.

Dawn saw special efforts being made to evacuate casualties it had not been possible to take out during the night. In spite of the many problems, a system was being established. Several LSTs doubling as hospital ships lay about 2,000 yards offshore to receive emergency cases and serve as control centers. The regular hospital ships were farther out. Auxiliary facilities were provided by some of the troop and cargo vessels. The attack transport *Sibley*, for example, was equipped to handle 325 ambulatory and 150 stretcher cases. The

Sibley took on her first casualties that morning. According to the ship's historian:

"Bunks were available in the regular sick bay and troop officers' quarters for the seriously wounded, and troop compartments A and B for the ambulatory cases. The wardroom was turned into a sorting station.

"The wounded men were brought alongside in a 'P' boat [LCVP]. If possible the boat was raised to the rail of the main deck and unloaded. When the boat could not be davit hoisted, slings were attached to stretchers, and the wounded lifted out singly. Willing mess stewards and corpsmen carried the patients from the main deck into the wardroom. The more seriously wounded were brought to the operating room as soon as possible.

"Gradually the wardroom filled up with wounded Marines. The ambulatory cases sat in chairs, their heads, legs or arms covered with filthy, bloody bandages. Some still tense from the agony of battle sat bolt upright, staring stonily ahead and shaking spasmodically. The majority, however, reclined patiently in the chairs. There was little or no conversation. Doctors and corpsmen moved silently up and down the room, giving an encouraging word or stopping by a particular patient for further examination."

It seemed strange to some of the Marines to hear phonograph music playing softly in the background. Frank Sinatra was singing "Nancy with the Laughing Face."

On the morning of the second day the battle for Iwo Jima developed into two distinct operations. In the extreme south, the three battalions of the 28th Marines, 5th Division, occupied a line across the neck of the island facing southward toward Suribachi. Just to their north, or behind them, the 26th and 27th Regiments of the 5th were arced across the southern tip of the first airport in preparation for a drive northward. On the right, or northern, flank of these regiments, the three regiments of the 4th Division—the 23rd, 24th, and 25th Marines—were also set for a northerly swing, their left having reached the airport and their right anchored in the cliff area near the eastern beach.

The 3rd Division, made up of the 3rd, 9th, and 21st Regiments, was still in floating reserve. Only the 21st was actually close to the island, having traveled from Saipan with the second contingent of the 4th and 5th Divisions. The vessels holding the 3rd and 9th Regiments

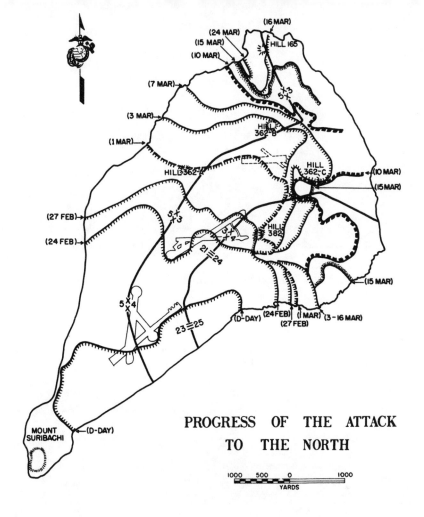

(16 MAR)
(24 MAR)
(15 MAR)
(10 MAR)
HILL 165
(7 MAR)
5·3
(3 MAR)
(1 MAR)
HILL 362-B
HILL 362-C
(10 MAR)
HILL 362-A
(15 MAR)
(27 FEB)
5·3
(24 FEB)
HILL 382
3·1
21≡24
(15 MAR)
5·4
(D-DAY) (24 FEB) (1 MAR) (3-16 MAR)
(27 FEB)
23≡25

PROGRESS OF THE ATTACK
TO THE NORTH

MOUNT SURIBACHI ·(D-DAY)

1000   500   0   1000
YARDS

had sailed a day later and were fifty or more miles to the southeast in their prescribed reserve area, which they had reached during the night. Admiral Turner and General Smith were hoping the 3rd Division would not be needed on Iwo; that it could be saved for the Okinawa operation, scheduled to follow.

Artillery, naval gunfire, and air preparation for the attack on Suribachi and the drive northward began soon after daybreak. The front lines were marked with panels of white cloth so the airmen would not bomb and strafe the Marines, an idea that worked well except in those areas where the enemy sneaked out and stole the panels.

The attacks north and south were begun simultaneously at 8:30 as the Marines moved from their holes with weapons at the ready, the riflemen with fixed bayonets. Company assault squads moved along bearing demolitions and flamethrowers, the filled tanks of the latter

Communications team advancing inland on February 20, D plus 1.

An Iwo Jima phone booth. With Japanese mortar barrage in progress, this front-line communications man is calling to the rear for artillery support.

weighing about seventy pounds. Wherever possible, cover for the advance was provided by machine guns and mortars.

The Japanese responded with a deluge of artillery, mortar, and small-arms fire, and the attacks were instantly slowed. A particular problem at first was the inability of the tanks to operate because their maintenance sections were not yet ashore. According to the special action report of C Company, 5th Tank Battalion, attached to the troops attacking southward: "We had eight tanks to place in action, but no fuel or ammunition was available. Salvaging from knocked out tanks and redistribution was started. A heavy mortar barrage was placed upon us and we were forced to move to another position. Work had no sooner started in the new position and the barrage was upon us again. This occurred three times, as there was no place which we could move where we would not be under direct observation by the enemy on Mount Suribachi."

The left half of the line facing the volcano was in open sand, while the right half threaded through patches of scraggy vegetation. The terrain leading to the base was a wasteland of sand, broken rocks, and extensions of the stunted brush. Although the heaviest defenses were in the fringe of green at the base, the cave and tunnel entrances scattered up the barren slopes held some light artillery pieces, mortars, and machine guns. The entrances were also perfect observation posts. The attackers could be observed even when they jumped into shell holes.

Tactically, the problem of Suribachi was a simple one. Lieutenant Colonel Robert Williams, executive officer of the 28th, expressed it this way: "A frontal attack, surround the base, locate a route up, then climb it!" The hard part was the frontal attack. It was true that the Marines, with all their supporting units, had Colonel Atsuchi's remaining troops considerably outnumbered, but this was not so much an advantage as a necessity. Sound military practice calls for troops attacking a fortified position to outnumber the enemy three to one. Not that the Marines actually at the Suribachi front had this kind of edge. Their numbers were probably about equal to the numbers they faced.

The 28th attacked with the 2nd Battalion on the left and the 3rd Battalion on the right. The 1st Battalion, which had made the dash across the neck of the island the day before, was in reserve, its mission to mop up positions behind the lines.

The situation at the front made good leadership essential, and it was nowhere better provided than in the 2nd Battalion zone, where Chandler Johnson commanded. In training, the colonel's mercurial temperament had kept the battalion somewhat jittery, and his temperament did not change on the battlefield. He still fumed and swore when he was angry, and still found things to laugh about. What began to impress the men was that he not only knew how to handle a battalion under fire but seemed altogether fearless. He strode about unflinchingly, wearing nothing on his head but a fatigue cap and carrying no gear except a .45-caliber pistol thrust into his right hip pocket. When he stopped to consult with one of his subordinates he often stood erect, gesturing and pointing authoritatively and making no effort to keep the enemy from learning he was a senior officer. Johnson, of course, was breaking the rules. It is the job of a colonel in charge of a battalion to commit his companies from a command post behind the lines, paying visits to the front only when he is unable to size up a situation through regular channels of communication. But Johnson's frequent appearances in highly dangerous spots were an inspiration to the men. And in this battle, inspiration needed all the sustenance it could get.

Even as the colonel was leading a seemingly charmed life at the front that morning, the regimental command post in the rear was targeted for mortar fire. A few minutes before it started, Staff Sergeant William T. Vessey, a combat correspondent, stood up to watch an aircraft attack on Suribachi. "This will be one to tell the kid about!" he said. The shellfire killed him. There were two direct hits on the command post, and several other men were killed or wounded.

At the front, the tanks joined the fight at about 11 A.M. In firing positions not far behind them were the 37-millimeter guns and the 75-millimeter halftracks of the regimental weapons company. From the rear, artillery missions were fired in close succession by the 3rd Battalion, 13th Marines. Ships on both flanks lobbed in shells, and the carrier planes continued their runs. Suribachi rumbled, quaked, smoked, and spewed debris. But the Japanese managed to keep firing back, and by noon the attack had gained no more than 75 yards. Only about 125 yards would be added during the afternoon.

Better progress was made by the 5th Division units attacking toward the north, their left flank on the west coast and their right about 1,000 yards inland. Much of this terrain was relatively open. Although it led to the main cross-island defenses, it was not amenable to heavy fortification. Scattered bunkers and pillboxes, however, took their toll, and so did artillery and mortar barrages. Land mines were also a constant hazard. These Marines shed their share of blood, but gained 800 yards by day's end.

Fifth Division Marines pause for briefing during earliest phase of drive up west coast.

A commander of one of the tanks, Second Lieutenant William O. Jarvis, had a singular encounter with a Japanese soldier. After planting a mine in the tank's path, the man secreted himself in a nearby clump of bushes, his rifle ready. The blast tore a track from the tank, and the heavy machine swung around and stopped. Jarvis threw open the turret hatch and thrust up his head and shoulders to assess the situation, his .45 pistol in his hand. He caught sight of the Japanese raising his rifle, and shot him through the head before he could fire. As Jarvis and his crew emerged from the crippled tank, they were attacked by several more Japanese, whom they managed to kill.

A rifleman with the 26th Marines, Pfc. Jacklyn H. Lucas, won the Medal of Honor that day. While crouched behind a row of his comrades lying prone, Lucas saw two enemy grenades land just in front of them. Making a flying leap over the men, he landed on one grenade and reached out and pulled the second one under him, absorbing both bursts. The action doubtless saved his comrades from death or injury. Military history records no shortage of men who have thrown themselves on a single grenade, but men who have smothered two are hard to find. And still rarer, if not unknown, are men who have fallen on two grenades and remained alive. Although Lucas suffered myraid painful wounds, he was left with a disability no more serious than a partly crippled arm. Five months after the battle, healed and firmly on his feet, he paid a visit to the White House to receive his award.

Attacking on the 5th Division's right up the center of the island, the 4th Division's left wing kept abreast, its objective to sweep to the north end of the first airport. Some of the Japanese fell back through tunnels under the strips and resumed the fight from defenses on the other side. Others sniped, until they were killed, from inside wrecked planes. The airport was taken by noon, but the Marines left wounded and dead almost every yard of the way. This wing of the attack now faced toward the southern tip of the second airport and the first line of General Kuribayashi's cross-island defenses.

The 4th Division's right wing, since it had come ashore on the

Fourth Division Marines fighting at hand grenade distance.

beaches farthest north, was already facing the first of the cross-island defenses when the attack was launched at 8:30. On the eastern shore, these began on the cliffs Jumpin' Joe Chambers and his ghouls had taken the previous evening. The nature of this coastal ground was viewed with astonishment by Captain Frederic A. Stott of the 1st Battalion, 24th Marines, the unit that had bolstered the battered ghouls during the night: "At the water's edge were giant rocks which, after a short space of level terrain, rose in a cliff line to the table land on top. This lower shore area was sufficiently rugged with a plentiful supply of caves, small canyons, and fixed fortifications. But atop the cliff the terrain almost defied passage. Trees and vines twisted in confused fashion over an area in which erosion and excavation had created cuts, dips, rises, and pinnacles which made direct-line progress impossible. Rock piles and dirt mounds jutted everywhere, and no man could be certain that the ground ten feet to his front was devoid of Japs." This wing of the attack made few gains.

Behind all fronts, units in reserve were subjected to shellfire and even small-arms fire, the latter coming chiefly from bypassed fortifications. In the Suribachi area, the men of the 1st Battalion, 28th, assigned to mopping up the ground they had taken the day before, killed about seventy-five of the enemy. According to Sergeant Al Eutsey of C Company: "Flamethrowers blazed at pillboxes and bunkers, and satchel charges were used to blow them up. Gunnery Sergeant Hap Mowrey was one of the busiest men in our company. He was in the thick of everything, doing an excellent job of getting things done."

Says Mowrey himself: "Sometime in mid-afternoon word came that a patrol was needed to meet a halftrack that was bringing in ammunition and food but would not travel without protection. We were getting some fire from Suribachi and from spots in the north. Sergeant Benjamin J. Rybiski and I were the point men of this patrol. We found the supply vehicle and started back, meeting other Marines along the way, some of whom were casualties, apparently having been hit from Suribachi. We received some small-arms fire. As we got closer to our company we saw a Jap scurry through the brush and disappear. Rybiski jumped up into the halftrack, manned the turret-type machine gun, and sprayed the area. Then we approached a bunker.

"Almost in a detached way I saw a yellow arm flick out and vanish. In an instant I felt the impact of the grenade. I was thrown off my feet, my helmet spun away, and my rifle and bayonet flew out of my hands. I got the feeling I had been cut in two. I lay for what seemed an eternity but what was surely only a few seconds, and then learned I could wiggle my toes. I knew I was alive. Apparently the grenade had exploded in midair, about waist high. I got to my knees, and Rybiski came and helped me to my feet. We were able to get back to the company. I had multiple wounds, chest and abdomen. I believe the chest cavity was rapidly filling with blood, because breathing became extremely difficult and I could no longer walk. Four men from the company volunteered to take me to an aid station. There were no stretchers, so a poncho was used."

Mowrey eventually reached an evacuation station on the beach. "Consciousness was fleeting. For me the war had ended." His work during those first two days earned Mowrey the Silver Star.

Lieutenant Wesley Bates, of the same company, was still in action in spite of the broken arm he suffered during the fight to isolate Suribachi. An assault he led during the mopping up is described by Corporal Bill Faulkner: "We moved north to knock out a gun emplacement. Had three engineers with us to probe for mines. They found some and blew themselves all over us. Bates, with his arm getting worse, told us to follow in his footsteps, and we made it across the minefield. Neared the bunker. Its gun was a big one, and its approaches were protected by machine gun nests. We got rid of them and moved to the bunker's rear. Used satchel charges on the ventilator three or four times. Must have really shaken them up.

"In a bit, a whole shower of hand grenades came flying over the top, thrown from the other side. Everyone was jumping every which way. Luckily, very few exploded. Then some wounded Japs came charging around the bunker. We tried to fire but our weapons were jammed with sand. I finally got off a round. The Japs turned and ran right into a machine gun we had set up to cover the attack. We moved around to the front of the bunker and found several Japs, all wounded but jabbering and trying to pull the pins of grenades. Bates tried his Japanese on them, asking them to surrender, but no luck. Five or six guys tried to shoot them, but all rifles were jammed. Finally a rifle began to work, and the job was done. We blew the barrel of the big gun with a C-2 charge, then headed back to the company area."

Unknown to most Americans ashore, efforts were being made to reinforce them with the 21st Marines of the 3rd Division. The high brass had decided that this regiment, at least, was needed in the present fight and could not be saved for Okinawa. During their climb down the cargo nets into LCVPs in a high sea, some of the men missed their footing and had to be fished from the water. A wind rose during the afternoon, and this, coupled with the nearly impossible conditions on the beach, caused the landing to be canceled. The Marines returned to their transports, many of them suffering from seasickness.

Not canceled was the landing of additional artillery units; their support was urgently requested by officers in the front lines. The 105-millimeter howitzers of the 3rd and 4th Battalions of the 14th Marines, an arm of the 4th Division, had come to Iwo in DUKWs sitting in the holds of LSTs. All of the 3rd Battalion ducks made it off the ramp and into the rough water safely, but the 4th Battalion was less fortunate. Eight of its ducks swamped and sank, and a dozen men were lost with the guns. During the landing the ducks were menaced by enemy fire and beach congestion, and the unlucky 4th lost two by broaching. Of its original twelve guns, only two remained to go into action.

LST 779 took four heavier guns—155-millimeter howitzers— directly ashore, ramming its bow through the wreckage of Red Beach 1. The vessel's huge doors creaked open, its ramp rattled down, and tractors with cables not only pulled the two-and-a-half-ton weapons out on the beach but also managed to work them up the terraces and across the island to the 5th Division zone near the west coast.

A 155-millimeter howitzer opens fire.

It was not the fire of land-based artillery that bothered Japanese antiaircraft gunner T. Koizumi in his emplacement among the cross-island defenses on the heights north of the landing beaches. Koizumi disliked the sea and air strikes, finding them "more intensive than on D day." The entrance to Koizumi's shelter, which he shared with the gunners of nine other 20-millimeter weapons like his own, was partly buried by a shellburst. All of the gunners, however, continued shooting at the carrier planes, believing they were making occasional hits. "Around four o'clock, a big warship was firing, and we saw many crew members walking on the deck. Finally we volleyed this warship. In turn, it volleyed us. The fire was so heavy our commander ordered us to retreat to our shelter. When we came out in the evening, we were surprised to find that all ten guns had been destroyed." The vessel involved was the battleship *Washington*.

Correspondent Robert Sherrod had spent the day on the island and at dusk went to the beach, intending to catch a boat back to his ship to write his story. He found the shore-party people still struggling to evacuate the wounded, the congestion and the rough surf permitting few boats to make it in and out. "There were too many wounded waiting for what boat space could be provided. I turned back to spend another night on Iwo Jima."

The day's gains, which gave the Americans control of about a

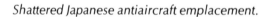

Shattered Japanese antiaircraft emplacement.

fourth of the island, had cost them nearly another thousand men killed and wounded. A further detriment to morale was that no one knew how many of the enemy had been killed, since only about 630 bodies were visible for counting.

The second night on Iwo was a repetition of the first. Star shells from destroyers kept the darkness at bay with their ghostly, wavering light. Artillery, mortar, and rocket barrages, both American and Japanese, screeched and roared and rumbled, the island sometimes seeming to shake on its foundations. Sand trickled into foxholes, and Japanese shells found targets with sickening regularity. Medical corpsmen risked their lives moving about in answer to cries for their help, and aid station personnel piled sandbags higher around the revetments that held rows of the wounded on stretchers. Bone-tired doctors rose from their night berths to minister to new cases as they were brought in.

The isolated popping of hand grenades was almost lost amid the heavier explosions, but the bursts of machine gun fire and the volleys of rifle fire were distinctive and clearly heard. Either by a Japanese shell or by infiltration, a large ammunition dump on the beach was ignited, setting off a spectacular fireworks display. The red flashes and explosions continued for perhaps an hour, sometimes diminishing briefly and then bursting forth again. During this time the island took on a flickering red glow, and seemed more than ever to resemble the popular conception of hell.

Japanese infiltrations amounting to minor counterattacks were repulsed in both the 4th and 5th Division zones. When a number of Suribachi's defenders began to mass on a plateau at the volcano's eastern base, the *Henry A. Wiley*, a destroyer covering this area, closed in to about 200 yards, switched on a searchlight, and cut loose with all of its bearing guns. The Marines in foxholes facing Suribachi watched with fascination as the plateau was raked by shellbursts and 20-millimeter tracers. The Japanese were decimated. So suddenly had the *Wiley* attacked that one enemy soldier was caught with his trousers down in the act of moving his bowels. He tipped over and died with a section of excrement half in and half out.

Individual infiltrators, often illuminated by the star shells, were busy everywhere. A 4th Division Marine was appalled to see a spectral figure rushing toward his foxhole, a rifle with fixed bayonet thrust forward. The Marine did not have his own rifle ready, but he had a hand grenade. There was no time to pull the pin. He merely threw the heavy missile with all his might. It caught the charging soldier squarely on the chest, and he drew up with a loud grunt. Throwing his rifle toward the Marine, he wheeled and fled. Even more unnerving was the experience of another Marine in the same area. A Japanese slipped into his hole and was so near he had to react with his bare hands. Getting a grip on the man's throat, he started to shut off his air. The result was a scream that so startled the Marine he let go, and the Japanese bolted away. Some of the infiltrators were not as bent on killing Marines as they were on finding an honorable way to die quickly. At the last moment, however, these men were apt to be seized by the instinct to live, and would escape if they could.

As during the first night, American landing activities continued in a limited way. The beachmaster on Yellow 1, 4th Division zone, was Lieutenant Commander Gordon A. Hebert, a veteran of World War I. He had served with the 1st U.S. Cavalry then, but had chosen the Navy when World War II broke out. "My job," he says, "was to handle all boats loaded with cargo and troops, to supervise all unloading and the evacuation of casualties. About 9 P.M. I received word that high-priority cargo was coming in, and to direct the landing. About the same time we received word to be on the alert for Jap swimmers coming in with demolition charges to be secured to hulls of boats and ships to blow them to pieces. Immediately I set a guard on the shoreline. The only shelter available was under a jeep that had been sent ashore on D day and had become mired in the sand. Enemy mortar fire continued through the night, and when the blasts came near I practically dove under the jeep and curled up like a snail. During the day I had been informed that a dead Jap lay buried under the front bumper, but inasmuch as he had not started to decompose his inert presence did not bother me. Well, no Jap swimmers came in that night, and neither did the cargo."

In the waters extending a mile or two out from shore, the plywood LCVPs patrolled and circled, awaiting calls for their services, keeping an eye out for suicide swimmers, and assisting one another when engines failed. The current past the island was strong, and occasionally a stalled boat that lost its communications and received no aid drifted past Suribachi and into the night, not to be heard from again.

These open boats, in which many crews were now spending twenty-four hours a day, had no conveniences, not even toilet facilities. Explains Louis Berard, whose craft came from the *Missoula:* "We had a couple of buckets on ropes, and each time we used them we tossed them over the side and flushed them out."

"We rotated on wheel watch," says Bob Collyer of the *Sibley.* "One of my watches brought a thud against the side. It was during a star-shell illumination, and I looked over and saw we had hit a corpse. The face reflected grotesquely, but whether American or Japanese I could not tell. A sense of absolute helplessness caused me to leave the thing far in my wake."

Two of the LCVPs cruising about that night held gruesome cargoes—dead Marines the crews had loaded from the beach during the day, stacking them like cordwood and covering them with large American flags. As it happened, no orders were available for the disposal of cargoes like this. Whenever the crews asked what to do they were told to keep circling until something was decided. Incredibly, this was to go on for two more days, and the corpses began to bloat and emit a powerful stench. At last the suffering crews secured orders to take the loads far out to sea and throw them overboard. One of the crewmen later said: "After we got through handling those bodies I could have drunk a gallon of whiskey and never felt it."

10
TO THE BASE OF SURIBACHI

The dawn of February 21, D plus 2, found the Marines on both fronts preparing to renew the attack. Their artillery opened up in the rear, and the missiles went over the front with a sizzling sound. The blasts in the enemy's lines were joined by those of missiles dispatched by cruisers, destroyers, gunboats, and diving aircraft. The push northward was falling into a pattern, a simple but painful one. The Marines were required to maintain a dogged frontal advance against heavy resistance, with no indication that conditions would soon change. In the south, however, a climax was fast approaching, the American lines now only about 200 yards from Suribachi's main defenses. At this distance the volcano loomed up ponderously. Some of the debris from the bombardment winged toward the clusters of foxholes, and the men crouched lower.

The attack would be made with Chandler Johnson's 2nd Battalion on the left, Lieutenant Colonel Charles E. Shepard's 3rd Battalion in the center, and Lieutenant Colonel Jackson B. Butterfield's 1st Battalion—the unit that had led the charge across the island the first day and had spent the second day mopping up—on the right. The 1st Battalion would be occupying only a one-company front on the western beach, which meant that Shepard's companies had more than just the center to cover. Shepard had told his men they had a twofold mission: "One, to secure this lousy piece of real estate so we can get the hell off it; and two, to help as many Nips as possible fulfill their oath to die for the emperor."

Dave Severance and Easy Company were on the 2nd Battalion's right, which placed them just left of the center of the island, where the terrain leading into the defenses was entirely open. They occupied a front of about 200 yards, with another company between them and the eastern shore. So far, Easy Company's casualties had been relatively light: two killed and thirty wounded, with seven of the latter having remained on the field, their wounds minor. Among the wounded who had been evacuated was George Stoddard, leader of the 1st Platoon, who had been shot through the left hip. His place had been taken by Platoon Sergeant Paul P. Paljavcsick.

The pre-attack bombardment ended with a forty-plane strike against Suribachi's base. Rockets slammed into the defenses and into the rocks and brush with such a terrific noise and concussion that the Marines in their holes were temporarily deafened. The volcano was hidden by clouds of smoke, dust, rocks, banyan branches, and shreds of enemy equipment. Then the planes darted away across the water and a relative silence fell. Some of the Marines stood up and began looking anxiously toward the rear for the attack's tank support, but no tanks were in sight. Once again these important machines had been delayed by refueling and rearming difficulties.

It was 8:25, time to jump off. All along the 700-yard front the Marines began to stir. Those on the beaches, east and west, simply rose and started walking toward Suribachi's flanks. On the brushy western half of the island the men threaded forward cautiously, while on the open eastern half they trotted from shell hole to shell hole. Behind the lines, the covering artillery continued firing.

Attacking through the brush.

For a few moments the hulking fortress remained still. Then it began to react. First came the crack of rifles and the chatter of machine guns. This quickly grew to a heavy rattle, and bullets snapped and whined. Then the mortars started coming, some of them visible as they made their high arc, and shortly much of the front was being blanketed by roaring funnels of steel and sand. It was as though the volcano's ancient bowels had come to life.

Although staggered in many places, the line kept edging forward. One of the men said later: "This was the kind of performance the Marines were famous for, but there was nothing glorious or inspiring about it. Most of us felt only reluctance and enervating anxiety. There seemed nothing ahead but death. If we managed to survive the first part of the attack we would only become close-range targets for Suribachi's concealed guns. I myself was seized by hopelessness. I could feel the fear dragging at my jowls.

"It is in situations like this that Marine Corps training proves its value. There probably wasn't a man among us who didn't wish to God he was moving in the opposite direction. But we had been ordered to attack, so we would attack. And our obedience involved more than just a resignation to discipline. Our training had imbued us with a fierce pride in our outfit, and this pride helped now to keep us from faltering. Few of us would have admitted we were bound by the old-fashioned principle of death before dishonor, but it was probably this, above all else, that kept us pressing forward."

The resistance on the western beach proved the most manageable, and the 1st Battalion, with its one-company front, soon picked up momentum on its way to the volcano's right flank. Its intention was to swing around the base at the water's edge. All along the rest of the front the enemy's resistance remained dogged. Dave Severance and Easy Company were caught up in some of the heaviest fighting. Keith Wells and the 3rd Platoon, on the company's right flank, had moved out first, and Ed Pennell and the 2nd Platoon, on the left, had started very soon afterward. The company's machine gun platoon provided covering fire for both units.

As they dodged from hole to hole across the open sand, the men under Wells began suffering casualties at once. Pfc. Robert L. Blevins of Galesburg, Illinois, fell with a bullet wound in the leg, and Pfc. Raymond A. Strahm, also from Illinois, took a piece of shrapnel through his helmet just above the right ear. The helmet slowed the fragment and saved his life.

A mortar that burst in a large shell hole hit two men, a small fragment breaking the jaw of one (the author), and another piece giving the second man a minor back wound. Pharmacist's Mate 3rd Class Clifford R. Langley jumped into the hole and administered first aid, making skillful use of compresses to stem the profuse bleeding of my jaw wound, the other man needing no more than a small patch on his back. As Langley finished and prepared to move on with the attack, a second shell exploded in the hole's confines. I suffered a severe calf wound. The major muscle was sliced in two, and the flesh was generally lacerated and hanging in shreds. The man whose first wound had been minor was hit fatally. Still fully conscious and outwardly calm, he lay on his stomach with both legs stripped of skin and missing patches of flesh; the right resembled a long pile of raw hamburger. Although Corpsman Langley had taken a peppering of fragments, he turned at once to his patients, binding up my calf wound and—to make the other man feel that something was being done for him—placing a tourniquet around the skinless right thigh, the white cord contrasting signally with the red flesh it was compressing. As the corpsman finished his work the second time, still another shell entered the crater. But this one was a dud. It did not explode; it merely buried itself. Langley and I watched, fearfully fascinated, as sand funneled in over the top of it. Then, with blood seeping through his clothes in several spots, the corpsman moved on with the attack.

Up ahead, some of the company's hole-hopping groups were nearing the belt of defenses in the brush fringe, and they found a degree of hope in the sight of the destruction that had been wrought by the Navy's guns and planes. From farther back, only the jagged walls of the blasted blockhouses had been visible. Now it was seen that many of the bunkers and pillboxes whose covering sand and rocks had been blown away were also damaged, that the trench system was filled with craters, and that much of the brush had been splintered and denuded and blackened by napalm flames.

But as the men began to rush the first defenses they discovered there were still plenty of live Japanese among them. Sergeant Henry O. Hansen and Don Ruhl, who had been charging in the lead with Keith Wells, ran to the top of a silent, sand-covered pillbox and promptly clashed with several of the enemy in a network of trenches behind it. While the two Marines were emptying their rifles at these men, a demolitions charge came flying through the air and landed on the sand in front of them. Ruhl shouted, "Look out, Hank!" and dived on the charge, absorbing its full blast. Hansen, recoiling off the mound, was spattered with blood and bits of flesh. With the mound between him and the enemy, he reached up and grabbed Ruhl by the foot. Keith Wells, who was crouching nearby, quickly ordered, "Leave him alone. He's dead." The lieutenant had seen Ruhl's arm fly back and reveal a gory cavity where his chest had been.

Don Ruhl, Easy Company's rebel and often the target of its criticism, had sacrificed himself to save a comrade. The deed earned Ruhl the Medal of Honor.

Sergeant Howard Snyder and his 1st Squad, 3rd Platoon, were moving up on the left flank of the pillbox now, and they took up the fight. The Japanese had begun to scurry back and forth through the trenches, talking excitedly. One seemed to be issuing commands as though trying to organize a *banzai* attack. Although such attacks had been forbidden by General Kuribayashi, the order was not always obeyed. The tradition was too strong. Snyder and Corporal Harold Keller quickly began to lob grenades into the trenches, while James "Chick" Robeson and Louie Adrian, the Spokane Tribe Indian, took turns firing with their BARs. One man would stand up and shoot until he had emptied his weapon; then the other would jump up and the first would duck to reload. After Snyder and Keller had thrown all the grenades the squad had, Wells tossed them his own and ordered more passed up to them. The two men threw so many of the heavy missiles they wore their fingers sore. The combination of grenades and bullets took their toll, and no *banzai* developed.

But then Louie Adrian, while standing erect and firing into the trenches, received a bullet in the chest. His BAR kept chugging as he crumpled to the sand. Snyder stooped over him, took a look at the wound, and said with a frown, "He's gone." The bullet had pierced the Indian's stout young heart. His death came as a severe shock to Chick Robeson, who said afterward: "We had met when we enlisted in Spokane, and we had been together constantly for fourteen months. Seeing him die so suddenly is something I'll never forget. He wasn't only my friend; he was my link with home."

By this time the 3rd Platoon's 2nd and 3rd Squads, led by Corporal Robert M. Lane and Sergeant Kenneth "Katie" Midkiff, were moving in among the leading attackers, and one of Midkiff's BAR men, big Leo Rozek, hurried forward and took up the firing. Then a Marine carrying a light machine gun moved into the platoon's zone, and Keith Wells placed him on the line. He began to make it hot for the entrenched Japanese, but was soon shot dead. Several other men tried to operate the gun but were all shot away from it. The gun itself took multiple hits and was knocked out.

During these moments a bunker that lay just ahead of the platoon began to emit a profusion of hand grenades. Many of the men were pinned down by the blasts, and not much could be done about them. Rifle fire proved ineffective, the platoon was out of grenades of its own, and Corporal Charles Lindberg's assault squad, with its flame-throwers and demolitions, had not yet made its final break through the fire being laid on the open sand. Corporal Wayne C. Hathaway, a quiet-spoken ex-Raider from El Dorado, Kansas, volunteered to go back for grenades, and Wells consented to the mission. Hathaway took with him Private Edward Krisik, an eighteen-year-old Milwaukee youth who was seeing his first action. The pair had not gone far before they were shot down, both wounded fatally. Hathaway was hit by a dumdum bullet that tore up his abdominal cavity.

Several members of the assault squad had got through with demolitions now, and Hank Hansen told Wells he thought he could get to the bunker with a charge. "I told him to try it," says the lieutenant, "because we weren't getting anywhere trying to dodge those damned grenades. He took a large demolitions satchel and put in a time fuse. Then he ran at the bunker. But instead of placing the charge at an aperture he threw it—and missed. We all had to duck, because when that C-2 went off it rocked the whole area. The dirt had hardly settled before grenades were flying like mad."

To worsen matters, Suribachi's mortarmen had begun to pull in some of their fire, and shells were starting to burst alarmingly close. A direct hit was soon scored on an amphibian tractor rattling forward with supplies. Next the barrage closed in on Easy Company's 2nd Platoon, engaged in its own heavy fighting on the 3rd Platoon's left. Says BAR man Art Stanton: "I was lying on my stomach on the sand when a shell exploded close to my feet. The powder flash went up the legs of my pants, burning large patches of skin off my hips, and the concussion threw me about ten feet in the air." Stanton gathered his senses, ignored the pain of his burns, and stayed in action. He was about to run forward to join two of his comrades, who were lying side by side on the sand, facing the front, when he saw a shell explode between their heads, killing them instantly. The same barrage wounded Lieutenant Ed Pennell, making it necessary for Platoon Sergeant Joseph McGarvey to take over. For his vigorous leadership during this first part of the attack, Pennell was awarded the Navy Cross.

For the moment, the 3rd Platoon escaped harm from the shellfire. One of the company's communications men came running up to Keith Wells with a telephone whose wire trailed across the sand toward the rear. The lieutenant, lying in a depression with several of his men, made a report of the platoon's situation to Dave Severance. Wells looked rearward while he was phoning. Back near the company command post, standing on a knoll, was battalion commander Chandler Johnson, watching the action through binoculars. The colonel was fast concluding he had underestimated Easy Company. No unit could have plunged itself into this desperate struggle with more spirit.

Chuck Lindberg had brought up the rest of the 3rd Platoon's assault squad by this time, and Wells prepared to direct the two flamethrower men against the bunker and the other busy defenses. But the effort was impeded by mortar fire, which now had the platoon's range. One of the shells soon scored a bull's-eye, bursting among Wells and four others, wounding all five. Wells, who had been lying on his stomach facing forward, was hit along the back of both legs: "I had no feeling below the waist and a burning sensation in my neck. When I reached down and felt my legs I found them all wet. I thought it was all blood, but a piece of shrapnel had exploded one of my canteens. My clothes were nearly all blown off me from the waist down, and I was full of shrapnel."

But the lieutenant did not relinquish his command. By the time Corpsman John Bradley had given him first aid and injected him with morphine, the feeling had returned to his legs. Learning that he could still move, Wells disregarded his wounds and turned his attention once more to the platoon's problems. The unit had lost a third of its men in about forty-five minutes, a casualty rate high enough to raise the threat of disorganization and panic. The men were being taxed to the limit of their endurance and had only a precarious hold on the section of line they had hit.

But then matters began to improve. Braving the mortar shells, hand grenades, and small-arms fire, Chuck Lindberg and Private Robert D. Goode, a muscular Californian, started to move against the bunker and the other defenses with their flamethrowers. The platoon's riflemen covered them by firing at the menacing apertures. The results the two men achieved were both dramatic and terrible.

Squirting streams of fire at every opening they could find, they began to destroy dozens of the enemy. The bunkers and pillboxes were turned into furnaces. Their ammunition was exploded, and shell casings, hand grenade fragments, and other pieces of debris came flying out through the smoking apertures. As the Japanese died, the platoon could smell their roasting flesh, and some of the men said later the circumstances made this seem the sweetest odor they had ever smelled.

Chuck Lindberg earned the Silver Star at this point. Although he knew he was a conspicuous target with the bulky flamethrower tank on his back, he moved among the defenses as though they were training-field dummies. "It was a remarkable example of cool-headed fighting," recalled Robert Leader, one of the riflemen who helped to cover Chuck.

Covered by two riflemen, flamethrower operator sends a blast through pillbox entrance.

Dave Severance, meanwhile, had received word at his command post that the delayed tanks were now ready to come forward from their station several hundred yards in the rear and that men from the front were needed to guide them up. The captain gave the job to the 1st Platoon, part of which was still in reserve. Three men were required, and those who went back were Corporal Bob Sinclair, Pfc. Arthur J. Kintzele, and Pfc. George C. Stolieckas. Each came forward in front of a tank, using arm and hand signals to direct it around craters, exposed mines, unexploded shells, and the scattered dead and wounded. The machines drew concentrated fire, both shells and bullets, and Kintzele was killed and Stolieckas wounded. Bob Sinclair made it all the way to the front, using his tank's external phone to direct its fire until the instrument was shot from his hand. He was not wounded, though during one of its maneuvers the tank backed over his left foot and nipped off his large toenail. All three of the guides were awarded the Silver Star.

Frank "Music" Crowe, of company headquarters, crouching in a hole with Corporal Edward O. Blankenberger, was watching as one of the tanks that had lost its escort arrived at the front: "All hatches were battened down tightly, with the operator and tank commander looking out through their prism periscopes. Enemy knee mortar shells were bouncing off the turret like Ping-Pong balls. Machine gun and rifle bullets were ricocheting off the front and the sides. The tank stopped. Blankenberger and I crouched lower. Then we looked up to see Pfc. Daniel Friday, one of the company's Indians, scramble out of his hole, exposing himself to enemy fire by standing in front of the tank, and use arm and hand signals to direct its fire at enemy positions. Several were knocked out, with Friday escaping unhurt."

Tanks were now working along much of the regimental front. Also moving up were the regiment's 37-millimeter guns and 75-millimeter halftracks. Rocket trucks farther back were sending their missiles overhead, the mild whooshing ending in the sharpest detonations on the battlefield. Supplies were coming forward in amphibian tractors, each crew unloading in a hurry, picking up a group of wounded, and heading for the rear at top speed.

Teams of stretcher bearers roamed the field, looking for casualties in obscure holes and taking great risks to get them to safety. One of the paradoxes of warfare is that it brings out not only the worst in men but also the best. Along with a brutal desire to destroy the enemy is the warmest spirit of mutual sustenance. When a comrade is hit, a man will stand up under heavy fire to call for a corpsman, and a corpsman will come running with shells and bullets striking about him. A man will give the last swallow of water in his canteen to slake a wounded comrade's thirst, uncertain where he will get his own next swallow. Or he will give up his blanket to keep a casualty from shivering, oblivious of the fact that he himself will be cold that night. On the other hand, it is common for a wounded man to feel a deep anguish not because of his wounds but because he must leave comrades who need him. Brotherhood and altruism are nowhere stronger than they are among a body of men in battle.

As tank crews, infantrymen, and demolitions experts of the 5th Engineer Battalion, working together, began to drive wedges into the belt of mutually supporting bunkers and pillboxes, the system was disrupted and its resistance began to diminish. The survivors of the trench fighting were forced to fall back to positions closer to the foot of the volcano.

The attack, of course, included many moments of confusion. One involved Easy Company's mortar section, which was operating just behind the front, sending its high-trajectory missiles over the heads of the rifle platoons and crashing about a hundred yards ahead of them. Frank Crowe and Ed Blankenberger, still in the same hole, were involved in the incident. In Crowe's words: "We were surprised to see a lieutenant from another company come rushing across an open area toward us, arms waving frantically and screaming at the top of his lungs, something about Easy Company's mortar section dropping shells on his men at the edge of the banyan trees. All we could do was direct him to the broad hole about twenty-five yards farther back where Second Lieutenant Leonard Sokol and his men were firing as rapidly as they could load their weapons. I saw Sokol lunge up from the hole, grab the accusing lieutenant by the field jacket, pull him down, and let him see for himself by looking into the sights of the mortars. Obviously convinced that Easy Company's shells were going where they were supposed to, the man scrambled away through the noise and smoke, still hollering about his men being killed by friendly fire from somewhere."

During this phase of the action Keith Wells, wearing little in the way of trousers except bloody bandages, was still hobbling around directing the 3rd Platoon's attack. In a lunge for cover when a Japanese machine gun fired at him, he got his wounds full of sand and they began to grow very painful. Corpsman Bradley gave him a second shot of morphine and made an attempt to clean and re-dress the wounds, telling him sternly that he ought to head for the rear at once and have himself properly treated. But Wells remained at the front for another half hour. Then, at last deciding he was no longer fit to command, he turned his unit over to Platoon Sergeant Ernest "Boots" Thomas and crawled to the rear on his hands and knees. Like

Ed Pennell, Wells had earned the Navy Cross. This decoration is one of those ranking just below the Medal of Honor.

It was early afternoon when the men of the 2nd Platoon led Easy Company in an important gain. Word came from Dave Severance that a naval observation plane had spotted numerous Japanese moving about among some trenches and open gun positions in the company's front. For the second time it appeared that a *banzai* attack was developing. As the company hurried to place its machine guns and BARs in strategic positions, several carrier planes hit the threatening area, and some of the explosions came alarmingly close to the company's lines. For a while after the strike the Marines waited tensely. Then the 2nd Platoon's Sergeant Mike Strank, the boisterous Czech from Pennsylvania, jumped up and shouted, "Easy Company, charge! Let's show those bastards what a real *banzai* is like." He sprinted forward, followed by others, and the surviving Japanese were overrun, some being killed and some escaping toward the volcano's base, now very close.

First to reach the base, soon after three o'clock, was Boots Thomas and a few men of the 3rd Platoon, who had been working with one of the tanks. During his days in training, Thomas had been known to blanch when required to take an injection. On the battlefield, at every moment risking a real perforation, he seemed dauntless. He climbed to the top of a silent bunker and waved his helmet in triumph, his blond hair gleaming, the sight a heartening one for a host of Marines whom the past few hours had brought nothing but feelings of terror and impending doom. Chandler Johnson was watching through his binoculars, and his tanned face cracked into a smile.

But there was still a large and active bunker in Easy Company's zone. Dug into Suribachi's slope, it had concrete walls four feet thick and held a piece of heavy artillery and a machine gun. Says the 1st Platoon's Private I. J. Fuertsch: "The tank didn't do much damage to the bunker. We fired our bazooka at it and knocked out bigger chunks of concrete than the tank's 75-millimeter. To get out of the range of the machine gun fire we worked our way around to the flank. I could hear the Japs talking inside. We got some grenades through the slits, and after that it was quiet." For good measure, the bunker was hosed with a flamethrower and its interior set afire. This brought the total number of bunkers, pillboxes, and other defenses destroyed by Easy Company to well over fifty.

When Chandler Johnson came up, chewing on an unlit cigar, he

Japanese soldiers shot down while running for cover.

was jubilant. Suribachi's bristling lines had been breached, and one of his companies had done it! To Boots Thomas he said, "Son, you've won yourself the Navy Cross. Hang on to command of that platoon." This was the 3rd Platoon's second Navy Cross, added to its Medal of Honor, Silver Star, and the twenty Purple Hearts it had earned since D day. The platoon had set a Marine Corps record—with another Navy Cross (Corpsman John Bradley) and many a Purple Heart yet to come.

The attack was now succeeding in all zones of the regimental front. The companies advancing along the east and west beaches were moving around the volcano's flanks. Although the companies of Charles Shepard's 3rd Battalion, operating on the right of Johnson's 2nd, had not yet reached Suribachi, they were not far out.

Dave Severance and Easy Company were allowed no rest after knocking out the big bunker. Johnson ordered them to move around the base of the volcano to the left. They encountered and neutralized additional defenses, including several caves. A new practice was initiated, that of attacking caves with hand grenades, hosing them with flamethrowers, and sealing them with demolitions.

On the company's left, cliffs fell to the beach. Relates Pfc. Jim Buchanan: "I looked over one cliff and saw a machine gun muzzle firing toward some troops near the water. The gun was about twelve feet below me. I was thinking about lowering a grenade on the end of a rope when a destroyer escort opened up and almost caught me with its 40-millimeters. I saved myself by dropping behind some rocks." The machine gun was silenced.

In the evening, when the time came to "button up," Easy

Company was well around the eastern side of the volcano, in a narrow, rocky area between its steep slopes and the sea. Since the 2nd Battalion troops that had advanced along the beach were now being pulled back, Severance was obliged to set up his defense line without flank support. Easy Company, in fact, found itself cut off from all friendly troops; some of the quiet defenses it had bypassed had come to life.

The company was in a difficult spot. It had several critical casualties that could not be evacuated. It was low on ammunition. Many men who had eaten little for the past three days were getting hungry but were short of rations. "All we had," says Art Stanton, speaking of the squad to which he belonged, "were a few D bars the boys had in their packs." These were chocolate bars, nutritious but hard and somewhat bitter.

The terrain, some of it solid lava, was poor for foxhole digging. In any case, foxholes would not give the men much comfort. It was believed that if trouble developed it would come in the form of grenades and bullets from above. To mitigate this danger, two destroyers moved in and began to hit the slopes with 40-millimeter shells. This brought pieces of rock tumbling down and raised the threat of a major slide. The captain had set up his command post against the volcano, and now he moved it out nearer the water. When the star shells began illuminating the island at dusk they revealed the men of Easy Company crouched among the rocks with faces upturned, eyes scanning the flickering slopes. Many a Japanese soldier was seen where none existed. Along with everything else, the weather was turning bad. The wind became brisk, raising the surf and producing small, eerie whistles in the fuselage of a wrecked Japanese plane, and a cold rain began falling.

The attack northward that day had seen the best gains made by the 5th Division Marines moving up the west coast. The going had been rough enough, but only now were these men approaching the heavy cross-island defenses the right wing of the 4th Division had been struggling against since it landed. The day's gains on all fronts increased American holdings to a strong one-third of the island. Again about a thousand casualties had been sustained, bringing the total for the three days to about 4,500.

As a result of General Kuribayashi's radio reports to Imperial Headquarters in Tokyo, the Japanese people knew the American

Destroyer standing off eastern coast of Mount Suribachi.

beachhead had been well established. The Tokyo newspaper *Mainichi* reported: "We must now realize that it is not impossible for the enemy to attempt a landing on the homeland. The homeland has indeed become a fighting front." But the evening "Home and Empire" broadcast took a more defiant stand. Admiral Turner, who had destroyed so many Japanese in his advance across the Pacific, must not be allowed to return to the United States alive. He must be killed "to put to rest the many souls who have paid the supreme sacrifice."

Even as the broadcast was being made, twenty-five *kamikaze* aircraft from Japan were hitting Turner's invasion fleet off Iwo. Upon their arrival in the area the ships closest to shore threw an umbrella of antiaircraft fire over the beachhead, thousands of tracers rising through the dusk and piercing the rain clouds. "Condition Red" had been set on the island, and the Marines waited tensely for the bombs to fall. But the suicide pilots were interested only in the fleet. They managed to bomb or ram five vessels, inflicting varying degrees of damage. The worst casualties were two of the aircraft carriers. The *Saratoga* suffered more than 300 killed and wounded, and was so badly damaged she had to head for Pearl Harbor. The *Bismarck Sea*, swept by fires that could not be contained, exploded and sank, and over 200 of her crew were lost in the dark, rain-swept waters. All of the Japanese planes were either shot down or destroyed in ramming. Not one pilot survived.

At this stage of the war, Japan's *kamikaze* corps was becoming a

Crew of Saratoga *fighting flames after* kamikaze *attack.*

formidable weapon. It was in a class by itself. Usually, when a nation develops a new weapon it is quickly copied by other nations. But Japan's new weapon remained unique. As one American naval officer put it: "Nobody else is going to get the *kamikaze* boys, because nobody else is built that way."

Kelly Turner had remained safe on board his flagship, the *Eldorado*. When the alert ended, he and Holland Smith went to the wardroom to see a motion picture, one of the many that Hollywood provided for the men overseas. Keith Wells of Easy Company's 3rd Platoon was there, too, for even the flagship was handling casualties. The lieutenant's legs were stiff and painful, but he could walk. It was a strange contrast: Wells watching a movie aboard a ship glowing with warmth and comfort while his men huddled, wet and fearful, at the base of Suribachi. Even stranger was the fact that Wells would much rather have been with his men than on the *Eldorado*, and was pondering a plan to escape from the ship and return to the island.

11
THE FLAG RAISING

It was still raining when dawn came on February 22, D plus 3. Atop Suribachi hung a restless fog, portions of which rolled down over the crater's rim and gathered in the higher fissures. Inside the volcano, and in the defenses at the base not yet overrun, were some 800 or 900 Japanese, many bearing flamethrower burns and other wounds, all aware the end was near. Some squatted near candles and made final entries in diaries, or wrote letters they hoped might in some way reach their families.

Colonel Atsuchi sent a radio report of conditions to General Kuribayashi, requesting permission to take the survivors out in a grand *banzai* charge. In his curt reply, the dedicated general ignored the request: "I had imagined the first airfield would be overrun quickly, but what has happened to cause Mount Suribachi to fall in only three days?"

In the Suribachi sector, as in the north, Kuribayashi wanted organized resistance maintained to the last moment. He had begun to believe that an occasional well-conceived counterattack might be useful, but he remained opposed to the traditional *banzai* attack. That its use led to nothing but disorganization and early defeat had been proven on other Japanese-held islands the Americans invaded. It was largely because the majority of Kuribayashi's troops obeyed his orders to make maximum use of their defenses, supporting each other in an organized manner as long as possible, that Iwo Jima was so difficult to conquer.

That morning the three battalions of the 28th Marines prepared to tighten their grip on Suribachi's base. Easy Company, in its isolated spot on the southeastern side, had gotten through the night with no serious trouble, for the infiltrators had concentrated their efforts on the volcano's northern and western zones. One of the first things Dave Severance noted at daylight was that the spot against the slope where he had first established his command post had been covered by a rockslide caused by the destroyers. Easy Company's wounded were taken off the rocky beach by a life raft from the fleet, and some ammunition and rations were floated in. The company's contact with the units in front of Suribachi was soon reestablished, the interposed Japanese having vanished.

It turned out to be a relatively free day for Easy Company. Chandler Johnson ordered Severance to consolidate his position and resupply. The chief peril came in the form of a bomb that a friendly plane dropped on the company by accident. No casualties resulted, though the concussion lifted Chick Robeson from a hole in which he was dozing and knocked the breath out of him.

At Colonel Harry Liversedge's regimental command post in front of the volcano, the day began inauspiciously when a Japanese artillery shell from the north made a direct hit, killing the regimental surgeon, Lieutenant Commander Daniel J. McCarthy. But the work against the volcano went forward on schedule. The day's heaviest fighting was done by the men of the 3rd Battalion, who had not reached the base the day before. The rain continued, and the low-hanging clouds helped to amplify the now-familiar sounds: the detonations of shells, demolitions and hand grenades; the rattle of machine guns and rifles (though some of these weapons fell silent as they became clogged with wet sand); and the shouts and curses of excited men, together with shrill cries for aid from the wounded and dying. Among the American weapons, only the flamethrowers performed in anything like a quiet manner, going into action with a metallic click, a whoosh, and a

Japanese victim of flamethrower assault.

Photo by Lou Lowery

low-keyed roar. These were doubtless the most terrifying sounds the enemy heard.

Interpreter questioning wounded Japanese prisoner.

There were instances of hand-to-hand fighting with knives, bayonets, and swords when Japanese soldiers suddenly darted from cover to lunge at their attackers or to make a break for the caves at Suribachi's base. One Marine, charged by a saber-swinging officer, caught the blade with his bare hands, wrung it free, and hacked the officer to death with it. This Marine left the island with two heavily bandaged hands, and with the sword clutched firmly to his breast.

During the bloody activities a Marine officer who could speak Japanese took a loudspeaker into the front lines and called upon the surviving defenders to surrender, but the appeal was ignored. The only prisoner taken was a wounded man found lying on his back almost completely buried in the sand at the bottom of a shell crater. He was pretending to be dead, a grenade a few inches from his right hand. When he saw that he had been found out, he did not reach for the grenade but raised the hand and used the first two fingers to signal for a cigarette. Given one, he submitted to capture and interrogation.

On the far right, where the 1st Battalion was operating, one of the craters held a Japanese on his back and feigning death in a similar way, eyes half closed, a pistol lightly covered with sand in his right hand and sword buried near his left. As Corporals Bill Faulkner and Robert Wells skirted the crater on their way forward, Wells kept his eye on the man. They were nearly past when Wells suddenly wheeled and fired. Faulkner asked why he had done so. The answer: "His eyes followed us around the crater." The Japanese was now truly dead.

One of the caves the Marines approached during the day held a surprise. A Marine yelled, "Come out, you damn Japs!" and was answered in perfect English, "Go to hell, you damn Yankees!" This Japanese and his comrades came to a hellish end when the cave was assaulted with a flamethrower and demolitions.

By the end of the day the fight for the volcano was largely won. The network of caves in the dome still held a few hundred live defenders, but the front and flanks of the base had been occupied in strength, while patrols from the flanks had met at the water's edge in the rear. "Tomorrow we start climbing," said Harry Liversedge.

It had been an especially bad day for the regiments attacking northward, all of which were now either enmeshed in or approaching the fringe of the main cross-island defenses. By mid-morning the settling clouds made it impossible for the carrier planes to operate, and rain and patches of fog also caused visibility problems for the tanks. Mines had been planted in many places, and several tanks had tracks blown off or were otherwise crippled. As the infantry started forward, Japanese bullets streaked from sodden mounds and misty hillside crevices, and artillery and mortar shells accompanied the rain from the clouds. The smoke from the bursts remained at ground level, and the smell of cordite was pungent. Along most of the line, casualties were far out of proportion to gains, the loss among officers being particularly high.

The 21st Regiment of the 3rd Division, having landed the previous day (after failing in its attempt to land on D plus 1), had been placed on line in the center, between the two original divisions. The men were on a heavily fortified slope leading to the southern end of the second airfield. Having spent the night in the rain, these fresh troops were as disheveled and sand-smudged as the veterans, the only difference being that their whiskers were shorter. Their best efforts in their uphill fight advanced their irregular front from 50 to

250 yards and cost them dearly. F Company of the 2nd Battalion was so badly battered it had to be relieved.

As it happened, the 21st was facing the best Japanese troops on the island, the 145th Regiment under Colonel Masuo Ikeda. The unit's hundreds of defenses included artillery bunkers whose guns were sighted to fire straight down the runways the Marines were trying to take.

The only heartening development of the day occurred in the zone occupied by the 25th Marines near the east coast. Jumpin' Joe Chambers and his 3rd Battalion ghouls, still fighting in spite of their terrible D day battering, requested rocket support against a hill in their front, and two rocket trucks came forward. They launched shattering ripples, and about 200 of the enemy were driven in confusion from their hillside defenses. The ghouls had several machine guns trained on the area, and, with exultant shouts, the crews opened up. Many of the enemy fell dead at once. Others were killed as they tried to crawl away after first hits. Still others dodged and jumped and ran as the bullets cut up the hillside about them. Of those who got away to new cover, several left trails of blood. This was probably the hardest blow struck against a group of Japanese in the open since the battle began.

Marine rocket unit launching a barrage.

The ghouls enjoyed a surge in morale, but it was only temporary. That afternoon their beloved Jumpin' Joe took a machine gun bullet through the collarbone. The corpsman who reached him almost as soon as he fell stuffed the wound with gauze, for the lung had been punctured and the hole was wheezing. The regimental surgeon soon arrived and took over. Then Captain James C. Headley, who had campaigned with the colonel before Iwo, approached and urged him to get up, adding, "You were hurt worse on Tulagi." But Chambers could not get up, and needed help even to get on his stretcher. Four of his men carried him to the beach, and Headley took over the battalion. Chambers would survive, and his leadership on Iwo earned him the Medal of Honor.

Surf conditions during the day made it extremely hazardous for the smaller landing craft to operate, and the evacuation of casualties was impeded. Many of the unfortunate men were obliged to spend long hours lying on their stretchers in the rain, ponchos tucked about them and helmets tipped over their faces.

In spite of the high surf, the landing of supplies from the larger craft, which rammed their bows up on the beach and were unloaded through their big doors, was accomplished at a good pace. Functioning especially well was the station on Yellow 1, near the center of the landing zone, where Gordon Hebert was beachmaster. That morning the fleet beachmaster had come by on a tour of inspection, congratulated Hebert on his work, and told him he would be recommended for a decoration. Says Hebert: "By this time we were pretty well organized. Though there was still plenty of confusion on the beach, with thousands of men milling around, enemy fire in our area subsided to a minimum during the day, and we were able to unload many ships. But we encountered a terrific rainstorm in the afternoon, and we got soaked to the skin in spite of all our foul weather gear."

Farther to the south, on Green Beach, Corporal Wilbur A. Young had charge of a group of Marines unloading the big craft as they came in. A college graduate who had taught school in civilian life, Young had turned down a chance to become a Marine Corps officer, becoming instead a drill instructor at the recruit depot in San Diego. He had helped to train twelve platoons, and found this deeply satisfying. Young's present responsibility was something very much different, but he was up to it. He relates: "We were unloading an LST. It was raining, and we were under mortar fire. The men were tired and miserably wet. I went to the galley and asked the man in charge if he had any coffee that we could give the workers. He replied there was plenty but that he would have to check with the skipper, who was 'very particular.' He returned with the news that the skipper said he wasn't going to give coffee to everyone coming aboard. I immediately ordered the men to leave the ship and start unloading an adjacent one. The skipper saw us starting to leave and began yelling that we couldn't quit and leave him exposed to fire. I told him that I was in charge and could unload any ship that I wished. My men were soon drinking coffee."

Unloading operations as seen from bow of an LCI rammed up on beach.

The unloading continued after dark. The vessels holding critical cargoes remained on the beach all night, and some had to keep their engines running. Explains Coast Guardsman Chet Hack: "This created a terrible vibration, but it was the only way to keep the ship from broaching—going sideways—one way or the other. Sometimes a dead Marine would float by a ship and go right through the props, an awful thing that no one could do anything about." One vessel, LST

807, spent the night on the beach as a volunteer hospital ship. The crew became temporary corpsmen, and doctors operated in the wardroom. More than 200 cases were handled, and only two men died.

The number of heavy support vessels lying off Iwo Jima diminished that night. Task Force 58 left for another strike against Japan, to be followed by one against Okinawa. This meant a reduction in close air support for the Marines. Also reduced at the same time was the number of shells fired at the island by the vessels that remained. Lavish expenditures had put a great dent in supplies, making economy measures necessary. This diminution was expected to be offset by the Marines' own artillery, now well established on the island, with ammunition coming ashore in a steady flow.

February 23, D plus 4, dawned clear. The Americans in their holes and the Japanese peering from caves and slits saw the sun come out of the sea and make silver silhouettes of the vessels comprising the fleet's eastern wing. The sunshine would not last, but the encroaching overcast would at least be thin. The rain was over for a while.

Beach scene on February 23, invasion's fifth day.

This was the morning Harry Liversedge wanted the 28th Marines to "start climbing." There was a problem, however. Although Suribachi was only 550 feet high, its slopes were so steep that a coordinated move could not be made. There appeared to be only one practical route up. It lay on the northeast slopes, which the 2nd Battalion was facing, and so it was Chandler Johnson who got the order to "secure and occupy the summit."

The colonel decided to send up an assault patrol provided by Dave Severance, whose men were still in their position around the volcano's east side. The job went to the company's 3rd Platoon, led originally by Keith Wells and now by Boots Thomas. This unit had more than proved its combat efficiency. It almost seemed as though the high-spirited Wells had been granted the fifty men he had wished for in training, the fifty who weren't afraid to die and could take any position. But the twenty-five men still on their feet no longer looked or felt like crack combat troops, being very dirty and very tired. They were not seeking new challenges; they would have much preferred to rest on their laurels. But it is a military aphorism that men who perform well in battle are rewarded with further assignments.

About 8 A.M. Lieutenant Hal Schrier, Easy Company's executive officer, assembled the platoon, its thin ranks bolstered to forty men by a machine gun section. Schrier led the column, now officially a patrol, back around the volcano to 2nd Battalion headquarters near the northeast base. Chandler Johnson was found standing outside an improvised pup tent. In accord with the colonel's contempt for Japanese shells, the tent was not in a sheltering hole but at ground level. Johnson was sipping from a cup of steaming coffee, wearing his fatigue cap with its visor bent upward, and smiling. He was apparently pleased with the way things were going. While Johnson and Schrier consulted, the men were issued an abundant replenishment of cartridges, hand grenades, demolitions, and flamethrower fuel. They were also provided large water cans from which they filled their canteens. During these preparations they were joined by a radioman, two teams of stretcher bearers, and a photographer, Staff Sergeant Louis R. Lowery of *Leatherneck* magazine.

As the patrol prepared to move out, the colonel handed Schrier a folded American flag that had been brought ashore by the battalion adjutant, First Lieutenant George G. Wells, who had been carrying it in his map case since obtaining it from the *Missoula,* the attack transport that had borne the battalion to Saipan, its staging area.

Johnson's orders were simple. The patrol was to climb to the summit, secure the crater, and raise the flag. The men hoped fervently that their mission would prove as matter-of-fact as the colonel made it sound, but most had serious misgivings. Harold Keller said later: "When I looked at the two stretchers that were being sent along, I thought to myself, 'We'll probably need a hell of a lot more than that.'" But Johnson had already sent small patrols probing up the slopes, and they had returned safely. Now the colonel telephoned regimental headquarters and requested that the fleet be notified what was happening and told to withhold all fire in the Suribachi area.

Falling into an irregular column, the patrol headed directly for the volcano's base. The men moved briskly at first, soon passing a Marine howitzer that had taken a direct hit from an enemy gun in the north. Two of its crew lay dead beside it. A little farther on they passed several enemy corpses, one of which was badly mutilated. All were buzzing with green flies. When the route turned steep and the going became difficult, Lieutenant Schrier sent out flankers to guard the vulnerable column against surprise attack. Heavily laden with weapons and ammunition, the men climbed slowly and were forced to stop from time to time to catch their breath. Some areas were so steep they had to be negotiated on hands and knees. Although several cave entrances were sighted and watched uneasily, no resistance developed.

Starting its climb up Suribachi, patrol passes Japanese corpse.

Photo by Lou Lowery

Far below, the Marines semicircling the volcano's northeast base watched the patrol's laborious ascent. Said one: "Those guys ought to be getting flight pay!" Also watching, many with binoculars, were hundreds of men of the fleet.

The patrol reached the outside of the crater's rim sometime before ten o'clock. Hal Schrier called a halt here while he took stock of the situation. He could see two or three battered gun emplacements and some cave entrances, but there were no Japanese in evidence, so he signaled the men to start filing over. Howard Snyder was first, Harold Keller second, and Chick Robeson third. Then came Schrier, followed by his radioman, and Leo Rozek. Robert Leader, the Massachusetts art student, was seventh. Fully expecting to be fired at, he hoped that number seven was really the lucky number it was supposed to be. As the men entered the crater they fanned out and took up positions just inside the rim. They were tensed for action, but the rim caves and the yawning reaches below them remained silent. At last one of the men stood up and urinated down the crater's slope, but even this insulting gesture did not bring the Japanese to life.

While half the patrol stayed at the rim, the other half began to press into the crater to probe for resistance and look for something that could be used as a flagpole. Harold Keller, moving in the lead, made the first contact with the enemy: "The Jap started to climb out of a deep hole, his back toward me. I fired three times from the hip, and he dropped out of sight." Several caves then began to disgorge hand grenades. The Marines in the hot spots replied with grenades of their own, some of which came flying back out of the dark entrances before exploding.

Even while this action continued, Robert Leader and Leo Rozek discovered a long piece of pipe, apparently the remnant of a rain-catching system, and passed it to the summit. Waiting with the flag were Hal Schrier, Boots Thomas, Hank Hansen, and Chuck Lindberg. Thomas fired a shot through the pole near the top, and the others laced the flag on tightly. At 10:20 A.M. the pole was planted and the Stars and Stripes, seized by the wind, began to whip proudly over the volcano. The date February 23, 1945, had suddenly become historically significant. Mount Suribachi was the first piece of land under the direct administration of Tokyo to be captured by American forces during World War II. The cost to the 28th Marines: about 900 men killed or wounded.

Lou Lowery's photo of first flag raising, taken for Leatherneck magazine. Identified are: Sergeant Henry O. Hansen (without helmet), Platoon Sergeant Ernest I. Thomas (seated by flagpole), First Lieutenant Harold G. Schrier (at Thomas's right shoulder), Pfc. James R. Michels (on guard with carbine), and Corporal Charles W. Lindberg (standing behind Michels).

As Leatherneck photographer Lou Lowery put the great moment on film, the tired, unshaven observers below pointed and shouted, "The flag's up! The flag's up!" Some wept, while others cheered and clapped one another on the back. The electrifying news began spreading at once to the units all around the base and to those fighting the main battle to the north. Men sprang from their foxholes under fire to pass the word along.

On the beach near the center of the two-mile landing zone, Gordon Hebert's signalman ran up to him and said, "They've just raised the flag on Suribachi!" The beachmaster verified the statement with a quick use of his binoculars, then turned his public address system to its highest volume and announced the event up and down the beach and to the nearer vessels of the fleet, some of whose crews had been too engrossed in their work of unloading supplies to watch the patrol's ascent.

Cheers were already arising on the decks of the vessels close to the volcano and also on those farther out. Marine Lieutenant Robert West of the cruiser *Salt Lake City*, which had been involved in the Iwo operation since the earliest softening-up activities, found the moment "tremendously thrilling." More and more voices joined the cheering, the whole chorus accompanied by a frenzied medley of fog horns, whistles, and bells. To Gordon Hebert, standing on the beach, it sounded "like the applause after a touchdown at a football game." Says Coast Guardsman Chet Hack: "Talk about patriotism! The uproar almost shook the sky."

On the volcano's summit, which commanded a view of most of the Americans on the island and most of the encircling ships, a few Marines waved in response to the tribute. But the patrol's gratification was qualified. All of the men were concerned about the effect the sight of the colors would have on the enemy. There was the possibility of a response not only from the Japanese close at hand but also from artillerists in the north. The men had raised the flag but were by no means sure they would be able to defend it.

No shells came just then, but the flag was soon challenged by the enemy on the summit. First a rifleman stepped out of a cave and fired at the photographer and Chick Robeson, who were crouching in a hole together. The Japanese missed. Robeson whipped up his BAR, fired a long burst, and the man went down.

"You got him!" said Hal Schrier.

The body was quickly seized by the feet and dragged back into the cave. Then a Japanese officer stepped out. Grimacing bitterly, he lunged toward the flag-raising group brandishing a sword with only half a blade. Howard Snyder advanced to meet this attack with a .45 pistol, taking deliberate aim as the man bore down. But when the trigger was pressed, there was nothing but a metallic snap as the weapon misfired. Snyder had to scramble out of the way, but a dozen others were now alerted to the cave threat, and a volley of rifle fire turned the one-man charge into a headlong tumble.

Marine at far left examines body of enemy officer shot while charging from cave. Other two Marines are alert for further trouble. Shortly after taking this picture, Lou Lowery, obliged to dodge a Japanese hand grenade, tumbled fifty feet down outside slope of volcano.

The Marines who moved against the resisting area were met by a flurry of hand grenades, the cave being a large one with several entrances. It actually held about 150 of the enemy, but no more chose to come out, perhaps because they felt bound by Kuribayashi's order prohibiting *banzai* attacks. It is possible that some were casualties of the fighting below who had sought the cave as a refuge. Flanking the openings, the Marines again responded with grenades of their own, the flamethrower men operating where they could.

Photographer Lowery, covering the action at considerable risk, soon had another close shave. He was near one of the entrances. "Someone inside," he said later, "rapped a grenade against his helmet to start the fuse, then lobbed it at me." Lowery was forced to leap down the outside of the volcano. Tumbling for fifty feet before he caught hold of a bush, he broke his camera. Inside, the film was safe.

Groups of Marines from below began joining the patrol at the summit to help with the mopping up. The entrances of the big cave were blown shut with demolitions, and scores of the enemy were sealed in alive. Work of a similar nature was still going on at the volcano's base and had been started on its outer slopes.

Chandler Johnson, at his headquarters near the northeast base, craned his neck for another look at the snapping banner on the summit. Then he turned to his adjutant: "Some son of a bitch is going to want that flag for a souvenir, but he's not going to get it. That's our flag. We'd better get another one up there." Johnson had a second reason—a wholly practical one—for replacing the first flag. It was small, measuring only fifty-four by twenty-eight inches, and this restricted its morale value.

At Johnson's order, Second Lieutenant A. Theodore Tuttle went to the beach looking for a big flag, and boarded LST 779. The ship's communications officer, Ensign Alan S. Wood, happened to have in his stores a flag that was eight feet long and four feet eight inches wide. He had found it at a naval salvage depot in Pearl Harbor. Later, it occurred to Wood that this was a fitting place for Suribachi's banner to have come from, since it was a symbol, at least in part, of America's avengement of the Pearl Harbor attack.

While Wood went for the flag, Ted Tuttle made a visit to the ship's galley, and when he went ashore with his mission accomplished his jacket, tight at the waist, was bulging with sandwiches and apples he planned to share with comrades. Johnson was about to send Tuttle up the volcano with the flag when he decided to give it instead to Pfc. Rene A. Gagnon, who was starting up with some batteries for Hal Schrier's walkie-talkies. During the climb, Gagnon met several men of Easy Company's 2nd Platoon, including Sergeant Mike Strank, who were also ascending, and when the group reached the summit Strank took the flag, approached Schrier, and announced: "Colonel Johnson wants this big flag run up high so every son of a bitch on this whole cruddy island can see it."

At this time Pfc. Wayne Bellamy and several other members of A Company, 1st Battalion, were poking around partway down the outside of the volcano on the north side. They heard someone shouting from above that a pole was needed for the new flag. Says Bellamy: "There was a large tangle of steel and debris just in front of us. It looked like an emplacement that had been blown apart. We found a length of pipe but had to move a lot of other steel to get it. I helped to take the pipe within a hundred feet of the summit, then sat down and rested."

Photo by Bob Campbell

First flag comes down as the second goes up.

When the new flag was secured to the pipe, Schrier ordered that it be raised at the same moment the small flag was lowered. The new raisers were Mike Strank, Rene Gagnon, Navy Corpsman John Bradley, Ira "Chief" Hayes, Corporal Harlon H. Block, and Pfc. Franklin R. Sousley—all of Easy Company, though Gagnon had been detached to Battalion Headquarters. Three new photographers were on the scene: Joe Rosenthal of the Associated Press and two Marine photographers, Sergeant Bill Genaust and Private Bob Campbell. Genaust had a motion picture camera. As the flags were exchanged, the time about noon, Rosenthal and Genaust concentrated on the large one, while Campbell got a shot of both.

Joe Rosenthal's picture, which soon became famous, was later criticized by some as having been "posed," or "staged," or as depicting a "reenactment." Existing as proof of the falsity of the charges, though not widely known, is Bob Campbell's photo, made a moment after Rosenthal snapped his. The small flag is nearly down, and the large one is just beginning to float free as its raisers struggle to secure the pole in the rocks. The whole scene is obviously spontaneous. Rosenthal photographed the authorized replacement of a small flag with a large one, and under combat conditions.

He later described his great piece of military art as the product of a set of accidental circumstances: "The sky was overcast, but just enough sunlight fell from almost directly overhead, because it happened to be about noon, to give the figures a sculptural depth. Then the 20-foot pipe was heavy, which meant the men had to strain to get it up, imparting that feeling of action. The wind just whipped the flag over the heads of the group, and at their feet the disrupted terrain and the broken stalks of the shrubbery exemplified the turbulence of war."

From the flagship *Eldorado* a landing boat approached the beach as the big banner went up. In it were Holland Smith and Secretary of the Navy James Forrestal, who had insisted on making a visit to the island in spite of the general's protest that it would not be safe. The sight of the colors flashing vividly on the gray peak filled both men with the deepest pride, and Forrestal said, "Holland, the raising of that flag means a Marine Corps for the next five hundred years."

Smith and Forrestal remained on the beach for about an hour, and Marines came flocking to shake the secretary's hand. Shells were landing within a hundred yards, and Smith was worried that the concentration of men around Forrestal would invite a barrage. Forrestal seemed indifferent to the danger. Smith was greatly relieved when the two of them were back on the landing craft and making their return to the flagship.

Meanwhile, a runner from the beach appeared on the rim of the crater and shouted congratulations to the flag raisers from Smith

Second flag raising, photographed by Joe Rosenthal of the Associated Press. Left to right are: Pfc. Ira H. Hayes, Pfc. Franklin R. Sousley, Sergeant Michael Strank, Pharmacist's Mate 2nd Class John H. Bradley, Pfc. Rene A. Gagnon, and Corporal Harlon H. Block.

and Admiral Turner. A Catholic chaplain, Father Charles F. Suver, was preparing to say Mass at the summit, and several Marines were helping him build an altar of rocks. Nearby, Easy Company's Robert Leader found himself talking with a correspondent from the *London Times*. Down in the crater a BAR chattered.

There was still considerable mopping up to do, but the Suribachi saga was ending. The 28th Regiment, holding its present position, was about to become the corps reserve.

12

PRESSING THE MAIN ATTACK

February 23, which brought complete and spectacular success to the Marines in the south, was another bitterly punishing day for those in the north. This front, stretching across the island from east to west, was now about two miles from Suribachi, with the land between in American hands, though it still held numbers of live Japanese. Between the front and the northern sea was another two miles, the broad part of the island containing General Kuribayashi's main defenses. The terrain itself, described by an American newsman as looking "like hell with the fire out," was made up of barren plateaus, craggy hills, cliffs, twisting ravines and gullies, crumbling boulders, and struggling brushwood. The defenses numbered in the thousands, many of them mutually supporting. There were blockhouses, bunkers, pillboxes, caves, tunnels, trenches, mortar pits, rocket pits, machine gun nests, spider traps, dual-purpose antiaircraft positions, stationary tanks, antitank ditches, minefields, and booby traps.

No sector of the first line of defenses was tougher than the center, at the second airport, where Japanese Colonel Ikeda commanded and where the 21st Regiment, 3rd Marine Division, was trying to break through. Practically no gains were made on February 23, determined fighting notwithstanding. The regimental chaplain, First Lieutenant John P. Lee, a Northern Baptist from Glendale, California, marveled at the men's spirit: "They would get up on the airfield, then they would get knocked off. Then they would make it again."

One platoon's attempt was inspired by the raising of the big flag in the south. In charge of the unit was Sergeant Eric "Mom" Sandstrom, who had decided that Iwo Jima was "no place for Swedes." He had graduated quickly from squad leader to platoon leader, all men of higher rank having been felled. Sandstrom relates:

"As we lay in holes that were never too deep, someone yelled, 'Mom, look behind you!' I rolled over on my back and saw the most beautiful thing I have ever seen, Old Glory flying from the top of that pile of rock and sand, Suribachi. After we had been pinned down for so long, no one said a word. I got up, and, to a man, we walked forward across the airstrip." But Japanese fire increased, Sandstrom's men began falling, and this gallant advance, like the rest, resulted in a withdrawal.

The day closed with both the center and the left of the American front in about the same position as when the attack began in the morning. On the right the 4th Division made gains of 100 to 300 yards. Nothing about the day's fighting was very encouraging. Although everyone knew the island would be taken—the sight of the flag on Suribachi was all the confirmation of this that anyone needed—the time element was becoming uncertain.

It was all a deeply sobering business: trying to advance against an ingeniously concealed enemy, receiving fire not only from the front but from bypassed defenses on the flanks and even in the rear, suffering casualties and more casualties. If you remained unhurt you nevertheless knew you might take a savage blow at any second. You hoped fervently the wound would not be fatal. Huddling in a hole during a barrage, you tried to protect those parts you worried about most, holding an elbow across your face or positioning your rifle stock as a shield for your genitals. You began to realize that you would be willing to give up an arm or a leg for the privilege of staying alive. Throughout the ordeal, you were obliged to watch the mutilation and destruction of others, often at a range so close that you were splashed with blood. While attacking at your side, your best friend might be disemboweled by a shell fragment, clutch at the cascading viscera as he fell, then lie there with his fingers entangled in the mass and looking up at you with a plea for aid you could not give, his eyes soon glazing over and closing forever. Fortunately for one's sanity, such horrors were partly assuaged by shock. The scenes seemed not quite real.

It was just as well that the Marines were unaware of the tenor of Japanese communications on the twenty-third. One battalion commander at the front reported that his headquarters bunker and its caves were now within the American lines and were under attack by hand grenades and flamethrowers, and that he had lost contact with his various units. "Nevertheless," the message concluded, "the fighting spirit of all men and officers is high. We shall continue to inflict as much damage as possible upon the enemy until we are all annihilated. We pray for final victory and the safety of our country." Admiral Ichimaru, his headquarters in the extreme north near Kuribayashi's, radioed his superiors in Tokyo that the real struggle for Iwo was yet to come. "Every man of my command fully realizes the importance of this battle for the future of the nation and is determined to defend this island at any cost, fulfilling his honorable duty."

During the night, numbers of Japanese fulfilled their honorable duty by carrying on with the usual infiltration tactics. By this time many of the Marines were sleeping from sheer exhaustion, the peril unheeded, and some of the sleepers lost their lives. Generally, however, there was a response to the threat with small arms, hand grenades, and mortar shells. Again, hand-to-hand encounters occurred, the enemy usually getting the worst of them since the Marines were bigger and stronger. Sometimes one Marine would grab the infiltrator while another killed him with a carefully placed rifle shot, or with a bayonet or knife.

The Japanese shelling also continued, directed not only at the front but at rear areas, the beach, and the summit of Suribachi. Harold Keller and Chick Robeson were dug in right under the flag. The sound of its flapping might have brought them a certain comfort, had it not been for Japanese antiaircraft fire and buzz bombs (large rockets) that came out of the north and seemed to be trying for the pole. Fortunately, the buzz bombs were sighted too high and passed overhead and plunged into the sea. But the two men decided that when morning came they would move to a less sensitive spot. From the earth beneath them, all through the night, came the sound of muffled explosions. The Japanese sealed in the caves were killing themselves by holding grenades against their stomachs.

Remarkably, a few Japanese survivors of the five-day fight managed to slip through the American forces crowding the southern third of the island and make it to their own lines in the north. Among them was a young naval lieutenant and three or four of his men. Their uniforms torn and bloodstained, they arrived at the headquarters of naval Captain Samaji Inouye, and the lieutenant explained he had come to report that Suribachi had fallen. He was greeted with a tirade of profanity and abuse. "Shame on you to come here! Shame, shame, shame! You are a coward and a deserter!" The captain's aides tried to calm him, but he went out of control. "A deserter must be executed! I shall behead you myself!" He drew his *samurai* sword, and the lieutenant knelt in silent submission. But as Inouye raised the weapon, his aides wrested it from him. As they led the lieutenant away for treatment of his wounds, the captain burst into tears. "Suribachi has fallen," he lamented, "Suribachi has fallen."

Nights on the island were no longer as steadily illuminated as at first, since the Navy's recent economizing now extended to its star shells. The Marines, however, had their own supply of stars, which helped to compensate for the deficiency.

At dawn on February 24, D plus 5, Colonel Ikeda's lines protecting the second airfield became the object of the main thrust of the American effort. A breakthrough here in the center was bound to aid the advance of the troops on the right and left. This was a critical moment in the battle. A great part of the attack had been virtually stalled for the past two days, and the Marines had little to show for their terrible losses. The 21st formed with the 2nd Battalion on the left and the 3rd Battalion on the right. The latter, commanded by Lieutenant Colonel Wendell H. Duplantis, was fresh, having replaced the decimated 1st, and was the regiment's best hope. Said Duplantis to his company commanders: "We have got to take that field today." The word went down the line to the platoons, squads, and fire teams. It was the kind of order Marines do not take lightly.

Plans had been made to precede the attack with the strongest combination of naval gunfire, aerial bombardment, and artillery that could be mustered, and tanks from all three divisions had been assembled behind the center. The work began at 8 A.M. when the battleship *Idaho*, lying off the west coast, opened up with salvoes of 14-inch shells. Her fire was joined from the eastern waters by that of the heavy cruiser *Pensacola;* the scars from the hits she had suffered on D minus 2 made her no less effective. The big shells *ka-rumphed* into a low, fortified ridge just north of the airfield, nearly a thousand yards from the line occupied by Duplantis and his battalion. This was the area the 21st had to reach and hold in order to achieve its breakthrough. The bombardment raised the now-familiar smoke, dust, and debris, and the trembling of the earth was felt by the men in their holes. Behind all of the front-line regiments, from coast to coast, the artillery began firing at 8:45, the salvoes sizzling overhead and crashing not only north of the airport but along the entire Japanese front, this being a preparation for the general attack. At nine o'clock the naval bombardment lifted to make way for the carrier planes, which sped in firing rockets and dropping bombs, their strikes aimed at the airfield defenses.

By this time the concentration of tanks behind the 21st had started toward the front. The attack plan was largely dependent on the ability of these machines to escort the infantry through. The tanks approached the airfield on two taxiways leading up from the field already captured, but these handy routes were not only mined but also covered by antitank guns, for the Japanese had anticipated just such a move. The leading tank in the western lane hit a mine and was disabled. A tank that moved around it struck a buried aerial torpedo and was demolished, four of its crew killed. Other machines were stopped by antitank fire. In the eastern lane, mines were the chief menace. The whole advance ground to a halt. While the tank commanders struggled to get things rolling again, it became time for the infantry to move out.

Wendell Duplantis and his 3rd Battalion were about 800 yards south of the center of the airfield, the spot where its two runways crossed. The low ridge that was their objective lay on the other side of the junction. Even if the tanks had been on hand, many of the Marines would have considered the thousand-yard trip almost impossible to make. But when the order came for them to jump off without tanks, they obeyed it.

The battalion started forward with Companies I and K abreast, their front stretching about 400 yards. Many of the men had extra grenades in pockets and dangling from odd straps of their gear, and the riflemen were at fixed bayonet. Some of the machine gun squads were covering the advance by firing bursts from high spots near the jump-off point, while others were moving with the companies. Mortar shells sailed overhead and crashed into defenses being approached, the mortarmen planning to work their way up as the attack progressed. Artillery shells from farther back were pounding the defenses across the airfield.

As expected, the supporting weapons did not keep the enemy inactive. Sniper fire zipped through the air, and machine gun bullets skipped along the sand, throwing up tiny geysers, ricochets whining. The dreaded enemy mortars first pierced the sand, then spewed it high. Bullets thudded home and shell fragments took their ghastly courses. In response to urgent cries, crouching corpsmen hurried about the field, and stretcher teams came running up from the rear, becoming targets themselves.

The two companies kept going, assaulting some of the bunkers and pillboxes with grenades, flamethrowers, and demolitions, while bypassing others, their orders not to neutralize the ground but to get over it to the airfield. The din grew louder, the confusion intensified, and the trail of green-uniformed dead and wounded grew longer. At 10:13 the commander of K Company, Captain Rodney L. Heinze, was wounded by hand grenade fragments, the tosser popping up from a spider trap. A BAR man got the Japanese the next time he raised the lid, and the executive officer, First Lieutenant Raoul J. Archambault, took over the company. At 10:17 the commander of I Company, Captain Clayton S. Rockmore, was killed by a bullet through the throat. Within minutes afterward, the lieutenants commanding three platoons went down. The attack was maintained, and observers in the rear were reminded of what they had read about Pickett's charge at Gettysburg.

There was no letup in the enemy's fire. On the contrary, the mortar barrages had been joined by artillery bursts, with their terrible concussion and whizzing fragments. Nevertheless, by 11:45 a handful of K Company Marines, running forward in short spurts, had managed to plunk themselves on the southern edge of the airstrip. The whine of ricocheting bullets was strong here, and the lane was perfect for artillery fire. "This," thought Raoul Archambault, "is like fighting on a pool table." The lieutenant had won medals on Bougainville and Guam but had never been imperiled as he was now.

The race across the strip was led by the platoon under First Lieutenant Dominic Grossi. The unit had been reduced to the size of a squad—only twelve men hit their stomachs at the foot of the fifty-foot elevation that was the objective. Another depleted platoon made it across and the men joined forces, gritted their teeth, and started up the slope. Artillery shells began crashing in their faces. Heartbreakingly, it was friendly fire mistakenly dispatched. The Marines recoiled down the slope and had the fire called off. Then they started up again. This time they were pushed back by the Japanese, some of whom emerged to fight in the open. These were Ikeda's troops, and, like the Marines, they had a reputation to maintain. The Marines made a third attack and again were unsuccessful. Realizing they were taking enfilading fire because of their lack of flank support, they picked up their wounded and fell back across the airstrip to re-form with the other elements of the attack. The morning's gains were consolidated.

At 1:30 in the afternoon, after a second period of heavy preparation by naval gunfire, aircraft, and artillery, the two assault companies, badly hurt but reorganized, resumed their work. K Company, led by Raoul Archambault, was again first to reach the foot of the objective. Less than 200 in number, the men formed a line and began another ascent. As they neared the summit, a wave of Ikeda's troops, shouting fiercely, rose up from the other side and charged over at fixed bayonet, the officers flourishing swords. The Marines were not caught unaware, but the rifles of some were clogged with sand, while those of others were quickly emptied.

In the mad hand-to-hand fighting that ensued, the Americans augmented their weak rifle power with grenades, pistols, bayonets, knives, clubbed rifles, and even entrenching picks and shovels. Two Marines fought back-to-back against five of the enemy until comrades came to aid them. A sergeant struggling with an officer was approached from the rear by a second Japanese and was saved by an alert friend whose rifle was working. The two teamed up to dispatch the officer.

It was a fight in which men were throttled, skulls were cleft, and limbs were broken, and in which blood poured from a variety of punctures and gashes. The grenade bursts, gunfire, thumps, and thuds were accompanied by wild curses, grunts, gasps, shrieks of pain, and terminal moans. It was all over in a few minutes, the Marines the victors after suffering few losses. Around them, dead or dying, lay about fifty Japanese.

I Company was moving up abreast now, and the two units tied in securely. The vital ridge had been won, and the breakthrough was a fact. Colonel Duplantis was delighted with his battalion's work. Speaking of the attack as a whole, he said, "It was the most aggressive and inspiring spectacle I ever witnessed."

Lending support to the conquest were tanks now operating on the runways, firing at every defense in sight. They were not safe to be near, since they attracted antitank fire and mortar barrages. They were sustaining this opposition, however, and the alert crews were using machine guns to detonate the mines in their way.

The day also saw considerable progress made by the 26th Marines of the 5th Division, operating just to the left of the central zone. One battalion went about 800 yards. In the 26th was Corporal

Benjamin Parra, a Papago Indian from Arizona, who suffered a minor injury in a curious way: "I saw a Japanese soldier crawl into a spider trap. I approached cautiously, and when I was getting near he blew himself up. A large rock came flying at me, hitting my thigh and giving me a charley horse."

On the west coast the 27th was slowed by a well-defended valley. According to one Marine: "The Japs could look down on us from a jagged, rocky ridge full of caves and artillery. The valley itself held bunkers and pillboxes, most of them hidden." Casualties were high. When stretchers ran out, evacuations were made with ponchos. This was a difficult and clumsy process, but it worked. The ponchos being waterproof, blood sometimes gathered in a sloshing pool beneath the wounded man.

Photo by Lou Lowery

Poncho being used as a stretcher.

As for the 4th Division on the right, its coastal flank remained entangled in the extremely difficult terrain on the cliffs, but elements of the 24th Marines operating inland spent the day shooting, burning, and blasting their way toward Charlie-Dog Ridge, at the southeastern edge of the airfield. At one time the front held so many casualties lying in exposed places that white phosphorus mortar shells had to be used to screen their evacuation. The objective was reached, but among the afternoon's wounded was the commander of the 3rd Battalion, Lieutenant Colonel Alexander A. Vandegrift, Jr., son of the Commandant of the Marine Corps. Vandegrift was lucky; three men near him were killed.

Casualties for the entire landing force were now 7,758. Of these, 558 were cases of combat fatigue, a category that for obvious reasons was high in this campaign. The 4th Division's casualties were the worst, and its combat efficiency was down to about sixty percent. Things were not much better with the rest of the landing force. Among the front-line materiel losses were thirty-two tanks.

Casualties notwithstanding, the sixth day of the campaign was one of general encouragement for the Americans. Significant progress had been made at the front, and the operation as a whole had reached a good state of organization. A second regiment of the 3rd Division, the 9th Marines, had been landed to take its place with the 21st in the center. The 3rd Division's last regiment, the 3rd Marines, would not be called in. More than 50,000 Americans were now ashore. The replacement drafts were handy, working as beach parties until needed at the front. All three division commanders had landed and established headquarters, as had the corps commander, Harry Schmidt, and the top Seabee, Captain Robert C. Johnson. They had utilized the cover of knocked-out emplacements. The pillbox occupied by General Cates smelled strongly of enemy corpses that were hidden by rubble.

The southern third of the island was becoming a busy military city. Equipment and supplies were being unloaded in growing quantities, additional roads were being opened inland, and depots were burgeoning. Men were planting poles to raise the network of telephone lines off the sand. The makeshift medical facilities were being replaced with field hospitals, clusters of tents protected by sandbanks. The 4th Division's chief surgeon, Commander Richard Silvis, was proud of his two operating rooms, twin Japanese cisterns with concrete walls and floors, and roofed with canvas. Division cemeteries were being laid out, after designated areas were cleared of mines and then bulldozed level. In contrast to their surroundings, the

Marine officers conferring in captured Japanese dugout. Seated in center is
Lieutenant General Holland M. "Howlin' Mad" Smith.

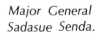

Major General
Sadasue Senda.

cemeteries were neat and orderly, the graves aligned in perfect rows, rows that kept lengthening. Each grave was marked with a white cross.

On this sixth day the Seabees began to reconstruct the southernmost airfield. The project was launched by crews who got down on hands and knees and crawled the full length of the runways looking for mines and shrapnel. The smallest pointed fragment would be a hazard to airplane tires. The men crawled and combed for most of the day. Never mind that tunnels beneath them still held live Japanese, that snipers were still sniping and shells were still coming down from the north. The renewal of the airfield was a highly important task, the first step in making Iwo Jima an American base.

When operations in the north resumed on the morning of February 25, D plus 6, the 5th Division, in its zone on the left, simply consolidated its gains of the previous day. Its front was about 400 yards ahead of that of the 3rd Division in the center, and it had to hold up until the 3rd came abreast. The 21st Regiment of the 3rd, after making its breakthrough across the center of the second airfield, had been relieved by the newly landed 9th Regiment, whose first assignment was to complete the field's capture.

On the regiment's right, the 4th Division was beginning its assault on a set of defenses harboring troops of Major General Sadasue Senda's 2nd Mixed Brigade, including elements of Baron Nishi's 26th Tank Regiment. This defense system, to become known as the "Meat Grinder," was comprised of Hill 382, a shallow bowl named the "Amphitheater," a bald rise called "Turkey Knob," and the village of Minami, its buildings smashed but its fortifications largely intact. Hill 382, its name indicating its height in feet, was the main objective.

On the east coast, other elements of the 4th continued their struggle with the cliff defenses. According to Captain Frederic Stott of the 1st Battalion, 24th Marines: "Neither on the lower flank [that on the beach] nor on the clifftop had we advanced anywhere more than a quarter of a mile. The strain had tired us, the casualties were steady, and moreover it was extremely disheartening to morale to strive so hard with so little apparent success."

When the men of the 3rd Division began their morning attack on the airport defenses, following the usual thunderous preparation by ships and planes and artillery, they were preceded by about twenty tanks of the 3rd Tank Battalion, commanded by Major Holly H.

Evans of Oil City, Texas. The Major relates: "We were hit by antitank weapons, machine gun cannon, five-inch guns, and 150-millimeter mortars, as well as mines of all descriptions. They knocked hell out of us for a while."

Struck in quick succession by an antitank gun were the three leading tanks, "Ateball," "Angel," and "Agony." The first remained operable, but the last two burst into flames, their crews tumbling out through the hatches. In the general scramble for cover, Corporal William R. Adamson was struck in the right leg by a machine gun bullet. Falling on his stomach, he tried to locate the sources of the enemy's fire, and soon spotted the flash of an antitank gun. His first move was to use the black smoke issuing from "Agony" as cover to attend to his wound, which was bleeding profusely. He tore a strip from one of his trouser legs and made a tourniquet for his thigh. Then he crawled over in front of "Ateball," the tank still in operation.

"So there he lay," the tank's driver said later, "right in the muzzle blast of our 75, and pointed out the antitank gun. We knocked it out."

Adamson next sighted the orange flame and wisping smoke of four machine gun nests scattered about among the rocks. He pointed them out, one by one, and the tank's 75 turned them into flying debris. Then the corporal spied a Japanese with a satchel charge trying to circle to the flank of "Ateball." This threat was removed by the tank's machine gun. But now about thirty of the enemy filed out of a cave about 200 yards away and, hunched over, moved down a trench toward "Ateball." Adamson soon noticed the movement, and the tank opened up with both its 75 and its machine gun. Half the party was cut down, and the other half dispersed.

"All this time," explains the tank's driver, "the Japs were pecking away at Adamson with machine guns and rifles. When we had blasted everything he showed us we pulled back, bringing him along."

Before the day was over, nine of Holly Evans's tanks were knocked out. But his support helped the 3rd Division's rifle companies, in spite of their own bitter losses, to obtain a firm hold on the high ground north of the airfield, except on the far right, where the northeast strip ran through and beyond the front lines. One of the day's special heroes was Pfc. Ralph H. Crouch of Arlington, Virginia, a runner for B Company, 9th Marines. Sent from headquarters with a message for one of the platoons, he got part of the way and then took a bullet through the stomach. Instead of lying where he fell, he crawled to the platoon and delivered the message, dying soon afterward.

The 4th Division made little progress against Hill 382 and the other components of the Meat Grinder, probably the best integrated and most powerful defense system on the island. According to the division's operations report for the day: "The combination of terrain skillfully employed to the best advantage by the enemy, terrain unsuited for tank employment, the locations of installations in areas which were defiladed from our artillery, and the stubborn fight-to-the-death attitude of the defenders had temporarily limited the advance. . . . But the division prepared to continue the attack." Mercifully unknown at the close of this costly and discouraging day was that the battle for the Meat Grinder had barely begun.

February 25 had been an unusual day for Lieutenant Harold Schrier and his men atop Suribachi. Equipped with powerful binoculars, they had an excellent view of the fighting in the north. Harold Keller interpreted the scene in simple terms: "The Japs had all the cover, and our men got clobbered." The detachment on the summit also did some mopping up, blowing shut additional caves. At the same time, Howard Snyder and Chick Robeson, using their entrenching tools, opened one that had been blown shut earlier. They were looking for souvenirs. Says Robeson: "It was the big cave where I had shot the Jap shortly after the first flag was raised, and where the second man had come running out waving part of a sword. The stench that met us was so foul we had to put on gas masks. We went in with a small flashlight and found the cave to have two sections. Dead Japs lay all about, so thick we had to tread on some. Many had killed themselves with hand grenades. We found souvenirs galore. I came out with several rifles, a canteen, and a bag full of smaller stuff, including a wristwatch. We also found some maps and other papers we turned over to Schrier. But we really caught hell for being so stupid, and the cave was blown shut a second time, so completely that no darned fools could try such a trick again."

Boots Thomas was gone from the summit—and from the island—for a few hours during the day. Holland Smith had summoned him out to the flagship *Eldorado* to tell of the fight for Suribachi and of the flag raising in a radio broadcast to the States. Suddenly drawn into the world of high brass and radio and newspaper people, the soft-spoken young platoon sergeant handled himself well, minimizing his own heroism and praising his platoon and the rest of Easy Company. Thomas was surprised to find Keith Wells on the *Eldorado*, and the two had much to talk about. Together they recounted the 3rd Platoon's story for a *Leatherneck* correspondent.

When he saw Thomas leave to go back to the island, Wells was more than ever determined to make his own return. He persuaded a doctor to give him a first aid kit filled with morphine and sulfa, and hitched a ride ashore in a press boat. Limping to Easy Company's headquarters near the base of Suribachi, he informed Dave Severance he was reporting for duty. The captain responded that he did not see how this was possible. The 3rd Platoon was on the summit, and Wells was in no condition to make the climb. The lieutenant solved this problem by phoning the summit and having two of the platoon's strongest men, Chuck Lindberg and Bob Goode, come down and get him. It was a long struggle, and the pair had to carry him much of the way, but the ascent was made. Wells enjoyed a warm reunion with the others, and, in spite of a fuming telephone protest from Chandler Johnson, he reassumed his command.

13

HEARTLESS IRON

On February 26 and 27, D plus 7 and D plus 8, the 3rd Division in the center and the 5th Division on the left made significant gains in the drive northward. The 3rd captured Hill Peter and Hill 199 Oboe, north of the second airfield, and the 5th fought its way about 700 yards farther up the west coast, reaching the approaches to Hill 362A.

The 4th Division on the right continued its debilitating struggle with the Meat Grinder, the direction of the attack having turned eastward. On February 26, elements of the 3rd Battalion, 23rd Marines, managed to reach Hill 382, an advance in which the efforts of a single man played a major part. Using a bazooka, Pfc. Douglas T. Jacobson knocked out sixteen positions and destroyed about seventy-five Japanese, a performance that earned him the Medal of Honor.

Several of the battalion's platoons succeeded in climbing the hill's first ridge, but when they reached the summit they were hit by mortar, machine gun, and rifle fire from front, flanks, and rear, some of it originating on Turkey Knob, about 500 yards to their right, which held a large blockhouse. The Marines were pinned down on the ridge for the next eight hours. Although its rugged surface provided considerable cover, there were many casualties, some from grenades coming over the opposite slope. A platoon of C Company lost half its number. The leader of one of I Company's platoons, First Lieutenant Harcourt E. Waller, Jr., tried to send a runner back to get help for the wounded, but the man had barely set out when he was killed.

Waller's men could see a Japanese command post in the valley beyond the ridge. Officers with swords at their sides hurried in and out of caves. Private Gilberto Mendez of San Antonio, Texas, in a fairly secure spot overlooking the post, decided to fill the harrowing hours by sniping with his Garand. His aim was unerring, and one by one a total of twenty enemy soldiers fell.

Other measures were tried. A bazooka man worked his way into a position that offered him a field of fire, but a sniper got him almost at once. Gunnery Sergeant Earl W. Griffith of C Company crawled forward with a demolitions charge and managed to blow up a 47-millimeter antitank gun, but he was killed coming back. A squad that moved against a machine gun nest was overcome in a hand-to-hand encounter.

Stretcher bearers could not get up the hill, and some of the wounded were cut off from the aid of corpsmen. In the end, the problem was not how to overcome the opposition but how to get back down the hill with the wounded. A smokescreen was called for, and soon the craggy ridge was covered with a white cloud. Even so, some of the wounded could not be reached. One lying within sight of his friends was heard to curse bitterly at his misfortune. All who could be gathered were taken down the hill, some conveyed in ponchos, others limping and hanging on to their helpers, and a few being half carried and half dragged. A corporal who saw the decimated and bloodstained platoons emerge from the smoke at the bottom of the hill found the scene suggestive of "something out of the movies."

Helping a disabled comrade to an aid station.

To be left lying helplessly wounded in terrain controlled by the enemy was the one thing Iwo's Marines dreaded most. In this case, some of the abandoned men were rescued the next morning. Chilling tales were related. Two Marines who were lying a few feet apart in the darkness heard a Japanese patrol approaching. They stretched out flat on their backs and covered themselves with their ponchos, heads included, and pretended to be dead. When the Japanese stooped over the first man and lifted his poncho he gave a start and was killed. The second Marine's situation was now worse than ever, for his own "death" was suspect. But he did not lose his head. He lay perfectly still, slowing his breathing to imperceptibility, and when his poncho was raised he looked truly dead. This was not enough for the enemy, however. One man reached for his chest to check for a heartbeat, and the Marine considered himself doomed, for his heart was beating wildly. But the Japanese felt his right side by mistake and became satisfied he was dead. Then the party searched through his pockets. Finding nothing of value, they carefully put everything back, covered him with the poncho, and went on their way. Three more groups found this Marine during the night. One man pricked his leg with a knife, but he did not flinch. His rescue was effected in the morning by Second Lieutenant William Turner, Jr., of Bonnyman, Kentucky, who was wounded in the process.

Getting away with pretending death in combat is usually not very difficult. It would seem that well-preserved enemy bodies lying around would be riddled with bullets each time they were spotted by new troops, to make certain no one was faking and was a possible threat. But this does not usually happen. Regardless of the abandon with which many soldiers maim the living, most seem to be averse to desecrating the dead.

The frustrating attack on Hill 382 was not entirely in vain, for its participants learned a great deal about the hill's defenses and the general layout of the other Meat Grinder systems. The line of 4th Division units facing the Meat Grinder had Hill 382 on their left, and the Amphitheater, Turkey Knob, and Minami Village in a cluster on their right. The Amphitheater was about 300 yards long and 200 wide, its far rim studded with pillboxes and caves, so that Marines trying to advance over the near rim were invariably met by a wall of fire coming across the shallow bowl. The blockhouse on Turkey Knob not only bristled with guns but was also an observation post and communications center. It seemed impervious to naval shells, aerial bombs, and artillery. Minami, once a village of houses, was now a village of pillboxes. As a whole, the Meat Grinder's mutually supporting defenses impressed the tired 4th Division Marines as being very nearly impregnable.

On the east coast, the 1st Battalion, 24th Marines, worn out by their struggles with the cliff defenses, had gone into reserve. Bothered by no more than an occasional sniper's bullet, they had a restful time of it and rapidly regained their strength and morale. Says Captain Frederic Stott: "We were plentifully supplied with water for washing, drinking, and even shaving, and with quantities of appetizing 10-in-1 rations." Some of the battalion's "chow hounds," still hungry when their portions were consumed, went down to the beach and tried to scrounge more. But the supply dumps were guarded by MPs, and the men were turned away. Corporal Franklin C. Robbins did not give up. He found a pencil and paper, and wrote: "Issue two cases of 10-in-1 rations to the bearer," and signed his name. Presenting the slip to a guard, Robbins was given the rations without question.

Had the Marines at the front known of a message Kuribayashi sent to Tokyo at this time, they would have been considerably encouraged. He reported that his defenses in general were weakening; that his front-line forces were down to about fifty percent of their original strength, with two-thirds of the officers gone; and that he had lost most of his machine guns and about sixty percent of his big guns.

On D plus 9, February 28, the 4th Division managed to win a precarious hold on Hill 382 of the Meat Grinder, and the 5th Division on the west coast began its assault on Hill 362A. Meanwhile, the 3rd Division in the center launched itself from Hills Peter and 199 Oboe, the 21st Regiment having replaced the 9th at the front. The general appearance of the Marines during this stage of the battle is described by a combat correspondent with the 21st, Sergeant Alvin M. Josephy, Jr.: "They were bearded and hunched over. Their clothes were dirty and torn, their eyes watery and distant, their hair matted, their lips puffed and black; and their mouths were open as if they were having trouble breathing."

Attacking on the right was Wendell Duplantis and his 3rd Battalion, the unit that had achieved the dramatic breakthrough across the center of the second airfield on February 24. The men of I Company, commanded by Captain Edward V. Stephenson, were soon involved in an eerie confrontation. They approached five mounds of earth that suddenly began to tremble and emit a throbbing noise. As the Marines stopped in their tracks, the mounds broke up, and out of them came five of Baron Nishi's tanks, with rocks, chunks of earth, and bits of shrubbery sliding off them, their guns booming. Confusion set in, and the American line was about to crumble when Captain Stephenson rushed to the front and directed a bazooka and flamethrower attack on the tanks. Three were knocked out, and as the other two turned and fled they were taken care of by 20-millimeter fire from planes that happened to be overhead at the time.

By the day's end the 3rd Battalion, vigorously supported by artillery, had gone about a thousand yards in a drive reminiscent of the breakthrough at the second airfield. The men were now entirely through the enemy's main cross-island defense line and had emerged on high ground overlooking the third airfield, which was in an unfinished state. The battalion had captured the fortified ruins of Motoyama Village, where the schoolchildren had greeted Kuribayashi when he arrived on the island the preceding June. As had been the case during its previous breakthrough, the 3rd bypassed many positions that required mopping up by other units, and left another long line of casualties. But division commander Erskine was pleased. These were the very tactics he had directed his unit leaders to use; they were, he thought, the key to the quickest victory at the lowest cost. When Colonel Hartnoll J. Withers, commander of the 21st Marines, radioed division headquarters in a light vein, "Shall we keep going?" he was answered in the same spirit: "Go ahead. We'll send an LCI around to the north shore so you won't have to walk back."

About half the island was now in American hands, and the past few days had brought other developments in the south. The first aircraft—Marine spotters from the fleet—came in to start using the airfield, and the Seabees and Marine engineers cheered as the little Grasshoppers touched down. A base for seaplanes—PBM flying boats from the Marianas—had been set up in the waters off Suribachi, and the western beaches had been prepared for unloading operations. Also on the west coast, Marine engineers had built the first water distillation plant; the supply of fresh water brought by the invasion force was running low. Near the east coast the 4th Division had established a post office designed to handle mail for all three divisions. A milestone was passed on D plus 8 when Major General

James E. Chaney of the U. S. Army came ashore with his staff. Chaney's forces, both infantry and air units, would garrison Iwo after the Marines won it.

Keith Wells, Boots Thomas, and their forty men were still on Suribachi's summit, the big flag waving above them. They divided their time between watching the remarkable show below and seeking

Post office established by 4th Division.

out Japanese hidden in obscure caves, war dogs having been sent up to help. Wells had trouble getting around, his haunches painful, the injuries infected, but he led the investigations. "Each day we thought we had them all," he explains, "and each night Jap signal flares would go up all around us and Colonel Johnson would phone to ask if we were losing the summit." The surviving Japanese were hungry and thirsty, and their will to fight had waned. One night a Marine awoke to see one of the enemy drinking from a canteen he had placed on the rim of his foxhole. No struggle developed; the Marine gave a shout and the Japanese fled to his hidden cave.

In the darkness, an occasional Japanese buzz bomb made a try for Suribachi's summit. Says Wells: "I would see little streaks of fire at the other end of the island and would light a cigarette and take several puffs before the bomb screeched overhead and into the sea. One night they lowered their aim and a bomb landed in the crater. The mountain shook like jelly. A portion of the crater caved in and exposed raw sulphur to the air. This caused a steam-like gas to billow upward, and we got a call from below asking whether the volcano was about to erupt. The buzz bomb threat was ended the next day when one of the Marine companies moving northward overran the position."

Dave Severance and the rest of Easy Company—in fact, all the Marines of the 28th Regiment—were encamped in foxholes scattered about Suribachi's base, still in corps reserve. Most did not expect to do any fighting in the north, convinced that the units operating there would soon secure the island. In the main, the days were restful. Good rations were abundant. But at first, according to Frank Crowe, the atmosphere was detrimental to gourmet eating: "Dead bodies of the enemy littered the area, with tens of thousands of huge green flies buzzing around. The odor was terrible. Then bulldozers moved in and plowed the corpses under." Crowe goes on to tell how the American dead were disposed of: "Men from 'graves registration' arrived with a big truck. Wearing heavy rubber gloves reaching to their armpits and also black rubber aprons, they respectfully raised their slain comrades and placed them on board. Of course, there was also a detached arm or leg here, a head there and half a torso somewhere else. These, too, were gathered and placed in the truck, and the whole load was taken to the 5th Division cemetery."

At night, the reserve area was hit by artillery fire from the north, the worst shellings Easy Company had yet undergone. Some of the missiles burst in the air, their shrapnel screeching horridly, while others blasted great holes in the sand. On the night the bombardments began, Dave Severance had his command post in a large crater probably made by a 16-inch American naval shell. The seemingly imperturbable captain said later: "This was my first experience with heavy artillery, and I was scared as hell. I crowded myself against the edge of the crater so hard that I gradually inched myself right over the top." The captain's reaction was hardly unique. Each shelling caused the men of Easy Company utter terror. During one of the aerial bombardments, Frank Crowe found his teeth chattering so badly he was sure their enamel was chipping. Miraculously, three nights of the enemy's fire cost the company only one man wounded, although packs, canteens, and other equipment, arranged around the rims of the sheltering holes, suffered various perforations.

It was on the last day of February that the 28th Marines received orders to prepare to move north and relieve the 27th Marines at the 5th Division front on the west coast. When Dave Severance called

Keith Wells and his men down from Suribachi, Wells ran into trouble. Chandler Johnson had told him in a phone call to the summit that he could not go along north, but Wells tried anyway. Says Chick Robeson: "Johnson caught him and really gave him hell. I'll always remember the way we marched off in a double column with Wells standing between us and grabbing each of us emotionally, almost in tears because he had to stay behind." Wells did not leave the island, but reported to the 5th Amphibious Corps field hospital on the east coast near Suribachi, where he was ordered to bed at once.

With Wells gone, Boots Thomas was again in charge of the 3rd Platoon. He was uneasy about the move north. He had gotten a good idea of the intensity of the fighting while watching it from the volcano, and he was heard to say, "My twenty-first birthday is coming up March 10, but I'll never see it."

Easy Company spent the night in its assigned assembly area behind the northern front. It was relatively quiet there, since the enemy was again shelling the south. Just after 2 A.M. the 5th Division's main ammunition dump was hit, setting off a wild mixture of explosions, and filling the night sky with flames, fountains of sparks, and vividly illuminated columns of smoke. In the confusion, both an air raid alarm and a gas alarm were sounded, and the confusion was compounded. The air raid alarm was not entirely unwarranted, for there was a Japanese torpedo bomber, probably from Chichi Jima, over the waters north of the island, and the destroyer *Terry* was nearly hit. As for the inferno ashore, several units were rallied to fight it, and squads rushed right up the edge of it to pull out containers of ammunition. A number of men were burned and others were knocked down by concussion, but no lives were lost. Engineers driving bulldozers pushed sand over the flames. It was dawn before the dangerous business was concluded, and a fourth of the division's ammunition had been lost. Kuribayashi had scored again.

Early that morning the destroyer *Terry*, which had escaped the aerial torpedo a few hours before, was cruising north of the island when she was shelled by six-inch shore batteries. The warship suffered thirty casualties, and was covered in her escape by the *Nevada* and the *Pensacola*. Extensively damaged, the destroyer was ordered to leave for Pearl Harbor, but first there was a solemn ceremony on deck as the dead were buried at sea.

The day was March 1, D plus 10, and it saw the 3rd Division continuing its drive through the center, its left wing capturing a part of the unfinished airfield and its right swinging eastward from Motoyama Village. The 4th Division made some progress against the Meat Grinder, strengthening the hold it had secured on Hill 382 the preceding day but at a cost that diminished its combat efficiency to fifty-five percent. According to Major F. E. Garretson, executive officer of the 2nd Battalion, 24th Marines: "Artillery and naval gunfire was paving the way out in front, but the resistance close in had to be dealt with as usual by the attacking companies employing hand grenades, rifles and automatic rifles, 60-millimeter mortars, flamethrowers, demolitions, and bazookas."

In the 5th Division zone on the west coast, the 28th Marines went back into action for the first time since the fall of Suribachi. The regiment attacked with all three of its battalions on line, the 3rd moving up the beach while the 1st (on the right) and 2nd (on the left) advanced against the ridge that held Hill 362A.

This was a costly day for the Marines of Easy Company, who moved over rough terrain against the ridge just to the left of its crowning elevation, 362A. The hill, the ridge, and the approaches abounded with caves, tunnels, and pockets harboring very active defenders. Dave Severance earned the Silver Star for "skillfully directing the assault against this strong enemy position despite stubborn resistance, and courageously leading his unit to the accomplishment of its mission."

Among the wounded was flamethrower operator Chuck Lindberg, one of the raisers of the first flag, who received a bullet through the forearm. Also hit was Robert Leader, who had helped provide the first flagpole. He was advancing on a bunker with a hand grenade, covered by Harold Keller and Chick Robeson, when a bullet, perhaps from a spider trap, went through his middle. Keller dragged him into a depression and called for a corpsman. Although the spot was a hot one, a corpsman came, but in his haste to do his job and get out of there he dressed only the wound in front where the bullet had entered, failing to notice the larger hole in Leader's back. Keller saw it: "Leader's guts had come out. I pushed them in and dressed that wound for him and got him started to the rear on a stretcher." Leader would have a tough time for several months, his body emaciating to about seventy pounds. But he survived to become a well-known professional artist and senior professor in the art department at the University of Notre Dame. He credited Keller with saving his life.

Not as lucky as Leader was Hank Hansen, who had also helped raise the first flag, and who had earlier been saved from death when Don Ruhl smothered a demolitions charge. Hansen was about to move around a huge boulder on his way forward when Art Stanton warned him that the enemy had that spot covered. Hansen responded with, "You worry too much," walked around the boulder, and was instantly killed by small-arms fire. Also killed during the day were Mike Strank and Harlon Block, two of the six men who had raised the second flag and were in Joe Rosenthal's photograph. These men died completely unaware of the fame their deed on Suribachi was to achieve.

The Japanese suffered, too. They were incinerated, ripped by hand grenade fragments, and shattered by demolitions. Corporal Bob Sinclair of the the 1st Platoon and leader of its assault squad says that "hundreds of pounds of C-2 were used effectively." One of Sinclair's men was I. J. Fuertsch, whose job was to blow cave entrances by running at them with charges while the others covered him with rifles and BARs. This was one of the most dangerous jobs on the island, and Fuertsch often saw bullets kicking up dust around him or heard them snapping past. "They made me run that much faster."

As usual, most of the Japanese the Marines destroyed were not visible. This was surely one of the strangest battlefields in history, with one side fighting wholly above the ground and the other operating almost wholly within it. Throughout the battle, American aerial observers marveled at the fact that one side of the field held thousands of figures, either milling about or in foxholes, while the other side seemed deserted. The strangest thing of all was that the two contestants sometimes made troop movements simultaneously in the same territory, one maneuvering on the surface and the other using tunnels beneath.

At least one Japanese rifleman encountered by Easy Company was not deeply concealed. He was about 200 yards to the right of the company in a niche near the top of Hill 362A, the ground falling away almost vertically below him. Enemy fire from several other places had stopped the company on the approaches to the ridge that was its objective, and this particular sniper had hit two or three men, one through the buttocks as he lay on his stomach. Dave Severance and Frank Crowe were on the scene, crouched along an embankment that gave them some cover but also allowed them to help scan the hill to locate the sniper's position.

At last Sergeant Angelo L. Romeo spotted the man's helmet and fired his Garand, but the bullet merely ricocheted off the edge of the niche. At that moment, to Easy Company's surprise, the commander of F Company, Captain Art Naylor, along with several of his men, appeared on the summit of the hill just above the sniper's position, obviously unaware he was there. These Marines had worked their way up the hill on a course not in Easy Company's sight. Frank Crowe jumped to his feet and began shouting and pointing, trying to get Naylor's attention, but was unsuccessful. Meanwhile, the enemy soldier, startled by Sergeant Romeo's shot, realized he had been spotted and decided to change his position. This move caught Naylor's eye, and he opened fire with his Thompson submachine gun. The impact knocked the Japanese off his ledge, and he tumbled down the steep hillside, landed among some rocks, and was still. In his excitement over the incident, Crowe, as he admitted later, "began jumping up and down like a high school cheerleader." Someone yelled "Get down, you damn fool; you'll be killed!" Crowe took the advice.

Moments like this were morale raisers, and the Marines of Easy Company needed such moments badly that day. By the time they were established on the ridge, thirty-eight men had become casualties—the Company's worst one-day toll since the break-through to the foot of Suribachi on February 21. In all, since D day, the company had lost about ninety men, forty percent of its original strength. The actual number of men hit was higher—about a dozen of those still in action wore bandages.

While Easy Company and the rest of the 2nd Battalion were being cut up in their zone on the left of 362A, the same thing was happening to the 1st Battalion on the right. One of those killed was Medal of Honor winner Tony Stein. Among the wounded was Corporal Bill Faulkner of Wesley Bates's platoon. (Bates himself, his broken arm badly in need of attention, had been evacuated after the fall of Suribachi.) Says Faulkner: "I got it in the right elbow. As I started for the rear, everybody seemed happy to see me go. They knew I was at least walking away from it."

Sergeant Al Eutsey of A Company was crawling forward when he was hit: "A grenade or mortar landed at my left side, a fragment cutting the thick strap on my pack and entering my left chest. My head was ringing, my side felt numb, and I was bleeding. In a few moments Corpsman Keith Hawkins was on the spot, giving me first aid. Mortars and grenades were pounding the area as he stuffed the hole in my chest with gauze. A team of stretcher bearers reached me, loaded me up, and started back. But now the Japs opened up on the stretcher bearers. The first thing I knew I had been dropped in a ditch as the team ran for cover. I believe one of the men was killed or wounded. I ended up with a different set of bearers, and I got dumped a couple more times due to enemy fire before they got me back to an ambulance jeep. It had stretcher racks, and I was put on facing the rear. The jeep was drawing fire and took off in a hurry. I lay and watched the shells bursting behind us as we moved. Our luck held, and we got back okay."

It angered the Americans to realize they were considered fair game by the enemy even after they were wounded and out of action. The story is told of a Marine who was being carried back on a stretcher, a bullet hole in his leg, when a second bullet grazed his chest. Raising himself on an elbow, he shook a fist at the concealed sniper and shouted, "God damn you, isn't once enough?"

Stretcher team evacuating a casualty.

Photo by Lou Lowery

Nightfall brought on the usual Japanese infiltrations, individually and in groups, all along the corps front from coast to coast. The 4th Division Marines on Hill 382 were kept especially busy, since they hadn't secured the hill but were sharing it with the enemy. This was another curious thing about the battle. In many cases—perhaps most—the front lines did not face each other, a no-man's-land between them; they were intermingled. And at night the Japanese called the tricks. They could sleep if they wished, feeling secure with the Marines all around. These men, they knew, were not likely to leave their foxholes. Japanese soldiers who felt aggressive or wanted to end their lives in an approved way could prowl among the Marines, using familiar routes through tunnels, passages in the rocks, antitank ditches, and trenches. For the Americans, every night at the front continued to be a terrible ordeal. If a man was not involved in an infiltration incident, he was apt to be kept on edge by hand grenade explosions, shots, and shouts from spots where infiltrations occurred. Usually the enemy approached quietly; the burst of his grenade was the first indication of his presence. But sometimes he jumped up a few yards away and rushed in screaming, "Marine, you die tonight!" On this particular night, two 4th Division Marines suffered saber cuts.

The next day, D plus 11, the division overran the whole of Hill 382 and carried the front lines 150 yards beyond it. The job was accomplished by the 2nd Battalion, 24th Marines, commanded by Lieutenant Colonel Richard Rothwell. The "overrunning," of course, was done slowly and painfully. The casualties of one unit, E Company, included five of its officers, two of whom were wounded fatally, while another had his right leg blown off below the knee.

In one incident during the day, Captain Walter Ridlon, commander of F Company, climbed atop a small, ordinary-looking knoll behind his front lines and sat down to direct operations. Suddenly the knoll rumbled and shook, and the captain was jarred off. A 75-millimeter fieldpiece within had opened up, not at Ridlon's men but at a target on the eastern beach. The captain and a couple of others found an aperture and reduced the bunker with hand grenades and a satchel charge.

The 4th Division units operating against the Amphitheater, Turkey Knob, and Minami Village had another discouraging day, shedding much blood but making no significant gains. The attack on the Turkey Knob blockhouse was supported by eight tanks, some equipped with flamethrowers. They poured in dozens of 75-millimeter shells and used a thousand gallons of flamethrower fuel. As long as this fury was maintained, the blockhouse was silent, its occupants having withdrawn to safety below. When the assault subsided, the blockhouse came back to life.

The rifle companies had plenty of other support during the day—from ships, aircraft, artillery, and the engineers with their demolitions teams—and many caves and other fortifications were blasted. But three parts of the Meat Grinder remained unsubdued. Even Hill 382 was going to need a great deal of mopping up. "It appears," said a 4th Division report, "that there are underground passageways leading into the defenses on Hill 382, and when one occupant of a pillbox is killed another one comes up to take his place."

One of the Marine spotter planes that operated over the Meat Grinder had a passenger with a unique mission: to take photographs. According to the official explanation, this had become necessary because "the sustained bombardment of Iwo Jima had so torn the face of the land that pre-D-day maps were by now of little use in terrain appreciation."

The 3rd Division spent the day continuing its work in the island's center, its left flank units advancing 500 yards toward Hill 362B, which was actually in the 5th Division's zone but had been causing the 3rd considerable trouble with its fire. Less successful were the units of the division's right wing, now attacking in an easterly direction, with the coast only about 1,500 yards away. In front of this wing was a sector soon to become known as Cushman's Pocket. The sector's most distinguished occupant was Baron Nishi.

Nishi had his headquarters in a large cave complex on three levels, now filled with wounded from the front. The air was hot and fetid. A curving passageway leading to the top level from the outside had about fifty blankets hanging from the ceiling, one behind the other, a curtain arrangment Nishi hoped would diminish the heat of a flamethrower attack. His compact personal room was illuminated by a single dim lamp. He had managed to keep himself supplied with liquor, and there was usually a bottle and glass on his small table.

Nishi had approached this stage of the battle with outward resolution but inward sadness. No Japanese on the island had more to live for. In addition to a wife and children, he had affluence, social stature, an international reputation. He was in his prime, and eager to continue his fulfilling way of life. Now it appeared that his beloved horse Uranus, though old, would survive him. He still carried the lock of mane in his breast pocket, a memento of days of glory. Like many educated Japanese, Nishi questioned the *Bushido* code even as he followed it to the letter. Fighting without quarter and to the death may have had its place on feudal battlefields, but in modern times victory in war depended as much on material superiority as on personal valor. Kuribayashi had summed it up when he said that he wasn't afraid of three Marine divisions but that no amount of Japanese dedication and sacrifice was going to triumph over America's ever-increasing number of ships, planes, tanks, and other armaments. One of Nishi's own lieutenants took issue with an ancient poem that proclaimed, *"Bushido* is to die." The lines, he admitted, had an inspirational ring, but the theme had no application to a place like Iwo Jima. Here, on the modern world's most dismal battlefield, the Japanese were facing "heartless iron."

But face it they did, and *Bushido* was kept, with the baron and his lieutenant showing as much courage as the most ardent believers. And the Marines of the 3rd Division's right wing would be occupied with the reduction of Cushman's Pocket for the next two weeks.

On the west coast, March 2 found the 5th Division moving slowly from the ridge that held Hill 362A toward Nishi Ridge, 300 yards farther on. "The trouble with this place," an officer complained, "is that there are too damned many ridges. You take one ridge, and then you've got to take another. There's always another ridge." To worsen matters, the ridges were really "jungles of stone," conglomerations of ravines, cuts, crevices, and piles of rubble. And the terrain between them wasn't much better. Concrete fortifications were fewer here; they weren't as necessary. In addition to the many cave and tunnel entrances, there were innumerable pockets, nooks, and crannies from which the enemy could fire. It was a hellish maze, and the advancing Marines never knew what they might encounter next. Fortunately, not all of the Japanese reacted as aggressively as they might have, some doubtless stunned and confused by the intensity of the bombardment that preceded each advance.

The Marines of the flag-raising company were picking their way along when BAR man Rolla Perry realized he had passed a cave. He went back and peered in, and saw a Japanese lying near the entrance. Perry was looking the man over, BAR poised and ready, when his attention was drawn to the base of a pole a little farther inside. In the half-light he saw the toes of a pair of sneakers extending from behind it. "I fired through the pole. As that Jap went down, the one on the ground jumped up, and I got him, too." Perry next stepped inside the cave and sat down on a wooden box. He watched the two men die, and scrutinized the dim interior for additional occupants. "It suddenly occurred to me that another Marine might come by and mistake me for a Jap and shoot me. I got up and started out of the cave. Then I got curious as to what I had been sitting on, and looked back. The wooden box, which was sealed, had a big red crab painted on its side. I figured it had to be a case of crab meat. I carried the box outside and pried off the top with my combat knife. Sure enough, the cans of crab meat were there. I opened one, and it looked and smelled delicious. I was going to have crab meat on Iwo Jima! But then I stopped. We had been told not to eat any Japanese food because it might be poisoned."

Perry's next move was to holler for his buddy, Pfc. Lowell B. Holly, a good-humored Texan the men called "L.B." Says Perry: "He and I had walked through hell together, and there was no better man on Iwo Jima." Holly came running, but on the way he stumbled into a ditch the Japanese had been using as a latrine. As he climbed out, surveying his soiled shoes and pants, his face reflected anything but good humor. When he reached Perry, he growled, "What the hell do you want?" Perry responded, "I found some Jap crab meat, and I'd like you to eat some to see if it's poisoned."

No one knows what would have happened next if it hadn't been for the intercession of the enemy. A third man was in the cave, and he came charging out. L.B. shot him from the hip. Then the two friends moved on, leaving the case of crab meat where it lay.

L. B. Holly was soon involved in another drama. His platoon was pinned down, and he became impatient, saying, "This is no way to run a railroad!" What followed is related by Art Stanton: "Holly took his M-1, got on his hands and knees, and crawled around a rocky corner. In a few minutes he came running back yelling, 'I need a bazooka! I need a bazooka!' He got hold of one, along with a few shells, and went around the corner again. Soon we heard two or three *ka-whams*. Then Holly came running and yelling, 'I need a flamethrower! I need a flamethrower!' In a couple of minutes he had one and had disappeared around the corner for a third time. Next we heard flames crackling, followed by some shooting. Then it was quiet. We waited, not sure what was happening. Holly was in the midst of the Japs that had us pinned down. Finally we heard a 'Ding, ding! Ding, ding! Ding, ding!' I said, 'Here comes the ice cream man.' It was Holly, riding around the corner on a bicycle, ringing its bell. He had found a cave with a steel door, had knocked down the door with the bazooka, and assaulted the cave with the flamethrower and a BAR. He had found the bicycle inside. He told us there were more bikes in there if we wanted them."

Easy Company was the first unit of the 28th Regiment to reach Nishi Ridge. The news went back to Chandler Johnson, and he was gratified. This hotheaded, rough-spoken, but frequently smiling man, with his chunky figure, jaunty fatigue cap, and the .45 pistol jammed into his hip pocket, was by this time firmly fixed in the affections of his troops. His visits to the front always raised morale. It was not only his cool contempt for Japanese shells and bullets that made an impression. He often stopped by the men's foxholes and inquired after their welfare. Was mail from home beginning to reach them? Were they getting enough to eat? He knew a good number of them by name.

The time was about 2 P.M. and things were temporarily quiet in Easy Company's zone on the ridge when Johnson was seen approaching. The Marines were scattered about in casual positions. Harold Keller and Chick Robeson were sitting with their backs to a rock. Art Stanton, who was opening a C ration, was perched on a low bluff with several others. Someone was riding around on L. B. Holly's bicycle and ringing the bell. A number of men were watching a 37-millimeter crew emplace its weapon, having just brought it up from the rear. One of the first to spot the colonel was Rolla Perry, and he watched the development of an interesting situation. Unaware, Johnson was walking directly toward a crater that held two dead Japanese. Would the fearless colonel, Perry wondered, be startled when he saw Japanese soldiers in a hole where he expected to find Marines? Johnson strode up to the crater, made an abrupt stop, and withdrew a step. Perry threw back his head and laughed. At that moment a heavy shell landed at the colonel's feet and blew him to pieces. Perry found himself gagging on a fragment of flesh.

The shell, which some witnesses believed to be a misplaced round from an American gun, killed and wounded others, devastating the 37-millimeter crew. Easy Company had one man killed and one or two wounded. The man who died was sitting on the bluff beside Art Stanton, having just accepted a cracker from his ration. The shell fragment, according to Stanton, "cut the top of his head off right above the eyes, all the way to the back of his neck, and the piece was hanging from his collar like a bucket lid."

Chandler Johnson's death stunned the 2nd Battalion, particularly the men of Easy Company, who had seen their esteemed leader practically vanish before their eyes. One second he was striding toward them in all his vigor; the next he was in pieces scattered over a wide area. Art Stanton and Rolla Perry were among those drawn to the scene. "The biggest piece we could find," says Perry, "was his rib cage." Stanton picked up a shirt collar, neatly cut off and free of blood. Someone else found a hand and wrist with a watch on it. The watch had not been harmed.

14

BATTLES IN THE DARKNESS

March 3, D plus 12, brought little change in the 4th Division lines embracing the Meat Grinder, except that the units which had overrun Hill 382 moved ahead about 200 yards and at the end of the day declared the hill secured at last. The Amphitheater, Turkey Knob, and Minami Village, though weakened by the pounding they were taking, continued to hold out. The combat efficiency of the 4th Division was now down to fifty percent, one report citing a depletion of leaders and the fact that the men were "very tired and listless." In the center of the island, the 3rd Division's right wing began to get a good idea of the strength of the pocket it was facing, and the knowledge was not welcome. The division's left wing, which had been relieved of its work against Hill 362B by the 26th Marines of the 5th Division, pushed on to Hill 357, about a thousand yards from the sea. The 5th, with the 26th on the right and the 28th on the left, pushed from 200 to 500 yards farther up the west coast, but at a fierce cost, losing 518 men, 135 of whom were killed.

About fifteen of the casualties were members of the flag-raising company. Bob Sinclair's assault squad suffered severely. Sinclair relates: "We were in a shallow depression when a tank came up on our right flank. This drew heavy mortar fire, and, along with others in my squad, I was hit hard. My kneecap was blown out and my femur was shattered, with my left foot hitting me in the face." While waiting for the arrival of a corpsman, Sinclair tried to stem the bleeding by putting a tourniquet on his thigh. Another man who took a serious leg wound was I. J. Fuertsch, who also had a hole torn in his side. He considered himself lucky: "I was making up a demolitions charge when the shell came, with the charge in my lap and a cap in my hand. Had that charge gone off it would have made me a part of the landscape." One man who was mortally wounded, with blood pouring

Fifth Division Marine advancing past dead Japanese during fighting on March 3, D plus 12.

from a hole in the side of his head, took out his cellophane-covered identification card and lay staring at it. Under the cellophane were a few strands of hair. They belonged to his girl back home, but were not from her head.

Easy Company lost two platoon sergeants that day. Joe McGarvey was wounded, and Boots Thomas was killed—a week before his twenty-first birthday. The 3rd Platoon was in a tight spot, and Thomas was phoning for tank support when he was shot through the head. Harold Keller was with him, and said later, "As was so often the case, there was no telling where the bullet came from." Thomas's death was especially tragic because he was a brilliant, personable youth who appeared destined for high achievement.

One of the cave areas in Easy Company's zone was the scene of another kind of tragedy. Second Lieutenant Leonard Sokol and several others were picking their way forward when a man who was well in the lead fell, wounded by a bullet. As the advance halted, two or three of the enemy darted out of a cave and dragged the Marine inside. Leonard Sokol started toward the spot, but drew up when narrowly missed by a shot from another cave. Taking a hand grenade and pulling its pin, the lieutenant turned toward the new threat. A second shot winged him and he fell on his armed grenade, which exploded and killed him. The captured Marine was found when the area was secured. He had been tortured and slain.

Easy Company had by this time lost over half its original number. Four of its seven officers had been hit. Its executive officer, Hal Schrier, had been transferred to D Company to replace its wounded commander. This left Easy Company in the hands of Dave Severance and Second Lieutenant Robert E. Schuelzky, while the platoons were led by sergeants. Keith Wells, back in the 5th Amphibious Corps hospital, was out of bed again, and Severance received a note from him: "They have been trying to evacuate me, but I have held them off. My wounds have lost their infection, and I would like very much to be with you. I think you might need me, and that's what I'm here for." The captain hastened to send word declining the offer, lest Wells suddenly appear at the front. The lieutenant would fight no more, but managed to stay on the island until it was secured. He thus became, at least technically, a veteran of the entire battle. After the war, this remarkable Texan earned a degree in petroleum geology and established a fine career as an independent oil man, devoting a great part of his spare time to working with youth.

The Marine landing force as a whole, now in control of two-thirds of the island, had sustained about 16,000 casualties, with more than 3,000 having been killed. General Kuribayashi, who had begun the fight with about 21,000 men, estimated that he had only about 3,500 effectives left. Undoubtedly, there were twice that many capable Japanese still alive, but communications were breaking down, along with organization. Hundreds of living Japanese had been absorbed by the American advance and were slipping from cave to cave, mainly during the night, in a search for food and water. Often during the day these men were tormented by the sight of Marines eating and drinking their fill. Some of the Japanese made successful raids on American supply dumps, and clothes were obtained by stripping the Marine dead. Not all of the wandering men had lost their fighting spirit. The Americans behind the lines continued to be subject to sniping by day and infiltration by night. There was still not a spot on the island where an American could feel truly safe.

So far the Marines had taken only about eighty prisoners, more than half of them Korean laborers. It was not easy for a Japanese soldier to surrender, even if he wanted to. Such a course could be expected to result in banishment by his nation and his family. Closer at hand, if his intent was perceived by his comrades they were apt to do all they could to thwart him. He might be executed by an enraged officer. On the other hand, he faced the possibility of being shot down by the Marines the moment he stepped into the open to surrender. Should he enter their hands alive, he would still be in danger. One Japanese who was captured in the north was turned over to three men for delivery by jeep to their regiment's headquarters. The route was rough and rocky, and the Marines, as the jeep bounced along, "accidentally" jostled the enemy soldier out onto the ground. They stopped and put him back in, only to have a similar "accident" occur a little farther on. The procedure was repeated at least once more before the trip ended. One of the Marines said later, "We got him back to headquarters alive, but he was a pretty sorry sight." The Japanese probably wasn't the least surprised by the brutality. This was the sort of thing you risked when taken prisoner. It was the way war was conducted.

The Seabees now had a thousand-yard strip of the lower airfield

A group of prisoners.

Photo by Lou Lowery

in operation, and March 3 saw the landing of the first two planes from the Marianas. The earliest was a hospital plane carrying medical supplies and mail. One of its passengers was a newswoman, Barbara Finch of Reuters, and as she stepped off the plane, with mortar shells from the north hitting the strip, an astonished Marine yelled, "How the hell did you get here?" She was pushed under a jeep and told to stay there. A half hour later the plane, with the woman on board, along with a dozen wounded Marines, was on its way back to Saipan. The second plane, a supply transport, brought in mortar ammunition, and left as soon as it was unloaded. Other transports from the Marianas appeared over the island that day, but their loads were parachuted down, a procedure begun some days earlier. The aerial activity was heartening to the Marines, since it symbolized success for their operation. Practically, it meant regular mail service, an expedient emergency supply line, and a quicker way of evacuating the wounded.

The next day, March 4, or D plus 13, was an even bigger day for the budding American air facilities on Iwo. "Dinah Might," a B-29 Superfort returning from Japan in a crippled condition, unable to get its reserve fuel flowing, sought the island and made a successful landing, though it used almost every inch of the runway. As the silver craft came to a stop at the northern end, shellfire began hitting near it. The Japanese wanted that first B-29 badly. But "Dinah Might" swung around and taxied out of range toward Suribachi. Hundreds of Seabees and Marines cheered their throats dry as the sixty-five-ton plane stopped and cut its engines. Easy Company's Frank Crowe was there, having come south from the front to have an eye infection treated. "The hatch opened," he relates, "and four or five members of the crew jumped down and fell to their hands and knees and kissed the runway. What a contrast! Here were men so glad to be on the island they were kissing it. A mile or two to the north were three Marine divisions who thought the place was hell on earth, its ground not even good enough to spit on."

The crew of "Dinah Might" soon had the faulty gas valve working, and, though invited to stay overnight while the airstrip was lengthened, decided to head for their Marianas base. The bomber had only about fifty feet of runway left when it became airborne, and the enemy in the north opened up with antiaircraft fire, but the departure was achieved and the trip home completed. Ten of the

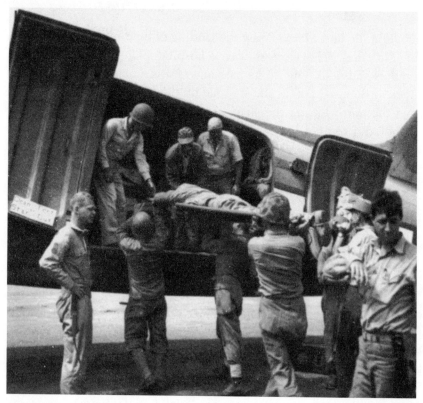

Evacuation of casualties by air.

eleven men saved by Iwo Jima that day were lost during later missions. But the island had begun to function as intended. This was what the battle was all about.

Kuribayashi believed that his garrison's defensive efforts were entering their final phase, and he radioed Tokyo: "Our strongpoints may be able to fight delaying actions for several more days. Even when the strongpoints fall, we hope the survivors will continue to fight to the end." The Americans, the general went on to say, had nearly achieved their main purpose, that of occupying the island, and he feared this would result in stepped-up air raids on Japan. "I can imagine the scenes of disaster in our empire. However, I comfort myself a little in seeing my officers and men die without regret after struggling in this inch-by-inch battle against an overwhelming enemy with many tanks, and being exposed to indescribable bombardments. Although my own death is near, I calmly pray to God for a good future for my mother country." His soul, he promised, would assault Japan's enemies and defend her lands forever.

Kuribayashi intended this message to be his final one, but the battle's end was not as near as he supposed. The strongpoints in the north were indeed strong, and the points in between were still deadly. Moreover, the combat efficiency of the Marines, due to casualties and fatigue, was continuing its decline. According to Frank Crowe, the men had begun to resemble zombies in a mechanical routine: "The artillery would open up each morning and bombard the enemy's positions. Then the infantry would move out and capture as much ground as possible. In the afternoon the artillery would bombard again, and again the infantry would advance. At dusk we would button up for the night by digging in or by flopping into a shell hole. The whole thing began again the next day." The Marines were now being required to perform in a way almost beyond human endurance, both physically and psychologically. History is filled with examples of high casualties in battle, but few armies with front-line losses of over fifty percent have been ordered to keep attacking, especially in the face of heavy fortifications. No troops with less *esprit de corps* than these Marines could have kept going.

Corps commander Harry Schmidt set aside March 5, D plus 14—the fifteenth day of the battle—for rest, reorganization, and resupply. The infantry made no attacks, except where brief actions were necessary to straighten the lines. Men napped in their foxholes. Some of those near the coasts bathed and swam in the sea, though the western waters were found to be sulphurous. A few of the luckier men received coffee and doughnuts from the rear, where a bakery was in operation. Fresh water was supplied in quantity; the Seabees had augmented the distillation work of the Marine engineers with six new systems.

All along the front, groups of replacements came marching in. Paradoxically, as much as the depleted rifle companies needed bolstering, these new men could not be expected to increase combat efficiency, and might even diminish it. In the first place, many were green. Youths not long out of boot camp were handed BARs and were not adept with them. A new man assigned to a machine gun crew was asked if he had any questions. "Yeah, one," he replied. "How do you operate this thing?" The veterans looked at the replacements and shook their heads. The first order of business would be to try to keep them alive. Even replacements with experience usually did not function well at the outset. Thrust among strangers and ordered to attack, they naturally felt isolated and bewildered. Green or experienced, only those men with a capacity for quick adjustment to difficult situations were likely to survive long enough to become a real part of the team.

A controversy had arisen over the failure of Admiral Turner and General Smith to land the 3rd Regiment of the 3rd Division, the last unit in floating reserve. Corps commander Harry Schmidt wanted the regiment badly, but Howlin' Mad told him that Turner believed the number of Marines on shore to be sufficient to take the island, and that another regiment would only add to the congestion. Actually, one area that wasn't congested was the front; the lines were thin. But Schmidt could not claim a dire emergency, the island being already two-thirds taken, so the 3rd Marines went back to Guam. This seems to have been a mistake. Every Marine ashore would have rejoiced to see a fresh regiment come in. Schmidt's operations officer, Colonel Edward A. Craig, said later: "Commitment of this well-trained and experienced regiment would have shortened the campaign and saved us casualties."

The day of rest was at no time completely quiet. In some parts of the front, tanks turned their 75s against caves and other defenses, and salvoes of artillery shells crashed in the regions beyond. The big naval guns were also heard, and carrier planes flew numerous missions. Although the enemy's riflemen were relatively inactive, the artillery and mortar crews bestirred themselves. By the end of the day of rest the Marines had suffered another 400 casualties.

Admiral Raymond Spruance, commander of the Fifth Fleet and Kelly Turner's superior, headed his flagship toward Guam that day. The Navy's role in the operation was tapering off. Some of the gunfire support vessels had left earlier, and so had the unloaded supply transports. Task Force 58 had not returned to Iwo after its second trip to Japan and its raid on Okinawa. As the Navy's work at Iwo diminished, the Army's grew. The Seabees were preparing to receive the island's air commander, Brigadier General Ernest C. Moore, who was bringing from the Marianas the first complement of fighter planes—twenty-eight P-51 Mustangs and twelve P-61 Black Widows. Already the Seabees had established a road system on southern Iwo, and now they prepared to take their bulldozers to Suribachi's summit, cutting a road for Army trucks with radar, weather, and navigation equipment. Watching with astonishment the pace of American progress on the island were the Japanese lurking in bypassed holes, and also the handful of prisoners in a barbed wire enclosure near the first airfield.

At the front, the night of March 5 was filled with the customary infiltration and shellfire worries. And, as usual, many of the Marines were chilly in their foxholes. Others, however, were quite comfortable, and had been so for the past few nights, thanks to their occupation of spots with subterranean heat. In the dawn light, a curious phenomenon was noted. Hanging in the cool air above the warm foxholes were ghostly columns of steam. The men in these spots even had warm rations, obtained by the simple expedient of burying the cans.

That morning the Marines went back to work. Although their attack was preceded by the battle's heaviest artillery preparation, along with the usual pounding by ships and planes, they made only very limited gains. Throughout the day the Japanese who were compressed into the last third of the island fought back fiercely. "General Kuribayashi," reported Robert Trumbull of the *New York Times*, "is conducting his now hopeless defense like a German field marshal, making the Marines pay as heavily as he can for every yard gained."

The Japanese commander, the Americans had come to realize, was "one smart bastard." Holland Smith found him to be the "most redoubtable" of all his Pacific adversaries: "Some Japanese island commanders were just names to us and disappeared into the anonymity of enemy corpses left for burial parties. Kuribayashi's personality was written deep in the underground defenses he devised for Iwo Jima." Said one of Smith's aides: "Let's hope the Japs don't have any more like him!"

Especially unhappy about the lack of progress in the March 6 attack was General Graves Erskine, commander of the 3rd Division. His men had been making some spectacular advances up the center of the island until their right wing hit Cushman's Pocket. Even so, the left wing had pushed abreast of the pocket and was within sight of the sea. Getting there was important, for it meant a division of the Japanese forces, the final disaster for their organization and communications. Erskine received permission from Harry Schmidt to try an attack in the darkness just before the next dawn, one with no heavy-weapons preparation to warn the enemy he was coming. This would be a departure from usual practice for the Marines, who had previously held to their holes until daylight. As a diversionary measure, the units on the right facing Cushman's Pocket were to move forward in the darkness about 200 yards. The main attack was to be made by a battalion on the left. From a position abreast of the pocket, this unit would swing to the right and move behind the pocket to Hill 362C.

Major General Graves B. Erskine discussing attack plans with subordinates.

Chosen for the main attack was the 3rd Battalion, 9th Marines, commanded by Lieutenant Colonel Harold C. Boehm. This battalion was not at the front that night but was in reserve, bedded down in the rear. The weather was overcast and rainy. When Boehm got word that his men were expected to pass through the lines of the 21st Marines in the misty darkness and attack with no visual knowledge of the enemy's positions, he protested. He was told to bring his company commanders to the front for a briefing, which he did. Under the light of a star shell, a high dark mass was pointed out as the objective, Hill 362C. It was only about 300 yards distant, and Boehm was surprised. He thought Hill 362C was farther away. His company commanders shot an azimuth to the hill. If they could not see it as they advanced, they would follow a compass course. Boehm was ordered to launch his attack at 5 A.M., use the front lines of the 21st Marines as his line of departure, maintain maximum secrecy and silence, and seize the hill. This was all to be done in complete darkness, star-shell fire to be called off.

Boehm's men began picking their way from their reserve area to the front at 3:20 A.M. as a light rain fell and illumination from the air continued. The units of the 9th Marines assigned to make the diversionary advance on the right, into the fringes of Cushman's Pocket, were already in position at the front. These were the 1st Battalion under Major William T. Glass and the 2nd Battalion under Lieutenant Colonel Robert E. Cushman, the man after whom the pocket was named.

A few minutes before the attack was scheduled to begin, the artillery sent over a concentration of white phosphorus shells as a smokescreen. This would not alarm any of the enemy who happened to be awake, since smoke shells had been used liberally in night harassment work. But at 5 A.M., with the attack about to jump off and darkness supposed to be absolute, a star shell from a destroyer burst overhead and came floating down under its parachute. Everyone froze while word was sent to the Navy to knock it off.

As the Marines began a slow advance into the enemy's defenses along a front of about a thousand yards, quiet was strictly maintained. The air was wet and the darkness nearly total. Men bruised their shins against rocks and stumbled into ditches, but nobody cursed. It was a time for prayers alone, and silent prayers at that. Past somber bunkers and pillboxes and the black mouths of caves and fissures the squads crept. Inside the defenses the enemy slept, never dreaming the Marines would try such a thing. If a few Japanese were awake and heard men passing, they doubtless assumed them to be their own comrades.

The silence lasted half an hour, and the Marines were deep among the defenses when a Japanese machine gun opened up on the far left of Harold Boehm's battalion, which was swinging toward the hill. A blast from a flamethrower pierced the darkness, and the shooting stopped. Soon the Japanese in other spots along Boehm's line began to realize what was happening, but their resistance remained manageable, many being incinerated or shot before they could begin to function effectively. By six o'clock Boehm was reporting to the rear that his battalion had taken the hill. Then, with daylight coming, the colonel took a look at his maps and aerial photographs. His men were on the hill that had been pointed out to him but it was the wrong one! Hill 362C was 250 yards farther ahead.

Meanwhile, grave trouble had overtaken the two battalions making the diversionary advance on the right. Following their orders, they had quietly penetrated 200 yards into the pocket that had held them off for days. Just before dawn the enemy began coming to life, and the Marines took cover. At daylight they discovered that they were in the midst of a tangle of caves, pillboxes, emplaced tanks, stone walls, and trenches, The system was manned by the crack troops of Baron Nishi's 26th Tank Regiment. Cut off from retreat, the Marines found themselves under heavy fire from all directions. Robert Cushman's units, operating on the left, were pinned down. Forty-one men of F Company, led into the pocket by First Lieutenant Wilcie A. O'Bannon of Levelland, Texas, crouched in a spot that was covered by Japanese with hand grenades and by machine gun fire from both the front and the rear. As explained by O'Bannon: "Half my men were hit. There was nothing the rest of us could do. We couldn't see anything from our foxholes. Sticking your head up meant losing it." O'Bannon himself was well equipped with hand grenades, and presently he was able to start lobbing them at the rear machine gun, which was close to his hole. He eventually knocked it out, but the firing was taken up by snipers. On the other battalion's front, to the right, the situation was not much better. Everywhere along the two-battalion line the Marines who could move were fighting desperately, not to win enemy territory but to save their lives. Nishi's men taunted them with such cries as "Hey, Marine!", "*Banzai!*", and "Charge!" Says O'Bannon: "Luckily they didn't charge. It would have been curtains for all of us."

Over on Harold Boehm's front, a bold decision was made. The Marines on the wrong hill, though now under stiff fire, were ordered to press on to the true objective, Hill 362C. Following a ten-minute artillery preparation, the new attack jumped off at 7:15 A.M. Progress was slow as the Marines assaulted the caves and other defenses one by one, but by 2 P.M. the crucial hill had been taken. The rest of the day was spent consolidating the position. "Most notable in the night attack," asserts Boehm, "was the fact that, although nearly all the basic dope was bad, the strategy proved very sound."

But the diversionary advance had resulted in the sacrifice of many good men. The two battalions spent the day of Boehm's success entangled in Cushman's Pocket. By noon William Glass's companies had recovered sufficiently to try an attack, but it was unsuccessful. All efforts were then focused on an attempt to extricate the Marines who remained pinned down. Tanks were unable to make it all the way to the front, but their fire relieved some of the pressure. At dusk Glass ordered B Company, isolated on a forward ridge, to attempt a withdrawal. Twenty-three of its members had been killed, twenty others wounded. The survivors were reluctant to leave their holes. The company commander, Second Lieutenant John H. Leims, later said: "I told them I was afraid we'd be massacred if we stayed. They saw it my way. They would have followed an order, but this called for more than following orders." Covered by mortar fire from the rear, the company came out through the darkness with only twenty-two men unhurt, some carrying wounded comrades on their backs. John Leims earned the Medal of Honor for getting the company out and then making two trips back in to rescue wounded men left behind. Of Colonel Cushman's companies, two were still in there in the darkness, surrounded by the enemy. They were the men under Wilcie O'Bannon and those under Captain Maynard Schmidt. The few survivors, O'Bannon included, were rescued the next day.

Despite the sacrificial losses, General Erskine was well satisfied. His pre-dawn attack had succeeded, and another significant gain had been made. Baron Nishi and his tank regiment were still in full control of the pocket, but Boehm's battalion had gotten around behind it, and the entire leftward three-quarters of the 3rd Division front was now only about 800 yards from the sea.

On the west coast, roughly abreast of Erskine's lines, the 5th Division had spent March 7 driving to within 1,500 yards of Kitano Point, the island's extreme northern tip. At one time during the advance a large number of Marines were assembled on a ridge when the enemy blew it up. The blast was one of the loudest that had been heard on the island. A sheet of flame and tons of debris rose high, and some of the Marines tumbled along as charred corpses. The smoking crater that resulted was big enough to have held a large apartment building. Men who saw friends vanish in the explosion and were themselves rocked by the concussion could hardly credit what had occurred. Some turned away in a daze, while others called out names of the missing and began to dig in the edges of the rubble. At least one Marine vomited at the sight of what he uncovered. The blast had killed or maimed forty-three men.

Example of terrain encountered during drive toward Kitano Point.

In the 4th Division zone, March 7 had seen nothing spectacular happen, but the strength of the remaining Meat Grinder defenses was ebbing and the division was preparing its own assault to the sea. During the two weeks in which the right flank was inching its way through the impossible terrain north of the coastal cliffs, the rest of the division was using this flank as a kind of hinge, the attack moving first northward and then eastward. It was like the swinging of a great door, and now the door, with about 1,500 yards to go, was about to crush the remaining Japanese against the east coast.

The Japanese commanders in this narrowing strip were the army's General Sadasue Senda and the navy's Captain Samaji Inouye, both strict adherents to the ancient traditions. Captain Inouye was the officer who had tried to execute the lieutenant who came north from Suribachi and who had cried at the news of the volcano's fall. Considered a colorful personality by his subordinates, he liked to boast of his prowess as a fighter, swordsman, lover, and drinker. Now he had about a thousand men left, and General Senda had even fewer, but the two men planned an attack. It was to be a very ambitious one. They were to break through the American lines and head southward, first blowing up the American planes on the first airfield and then going on to recapture Suribachi and replace the Stars and Stripes with the Rising Sun. On a more realistic level, the attack order stated: "Every unit will advance toward Mount Suribachi to the last." General Senda radioed word of the plan to Kuribayashi, in his headquarters bunker near Kitano Point at the island's northern end. Furious at the news of so futile a scheme, the commander radioed back: "Cancel your *banzai* charge." But the order was not heeded.

On the evening of March 8, sad ceremonies were performed in the Japanese lines. Cups of water were passed around for sipping, and the men said, "Let us meet again at the Yasukuni Shrine in Tokyo." Sadder still were the scenes among the hundreds of helpless wounded lying in hot, foul-smelling caves. General Senda had told his subordinate officers to go among these men and pass out hand grenades for mass suicides, to be performed as the officers watched. Few could go through with this. Most simply gave each wounded man a grenade and explained that the healthy men were about to leave to make an attack and did not expect to return. Says Lieutenant K. Musashino of his visit to a group of wounded: "When they received the hand grenades, tears came out on their faces in the candlelight. I pitied them more than the healthy soldiers. In the shelter, there was no longer rice or water. As I stepped outside, I faced toward my shrine in Kyushu, Japan, and prayed to my God to help the wounded."

On the American side, it was realized at dusk that something unusual was happening in the Japanese lines. Columns of men were seen winding in and out of concealment among the rocks and ridges, the movements accompanied by low but animated voices. While the Marines were trying to fathom the enemy's intent, rockets and artillery and mortar shells began bursting up and down their positions. This seemed to portend an attack, and they took a firmer grip on their weapons. The officers phoned to the rear for maximum star-shell illumination.

At first only minor infiltrations disturbed the front. There was much confusion among the forming Japanese; perhaps 1,500 men milled about, many uncertain of their place in the attack. Weapons ranged from bamboo spears to light machine guns, of which there were few. Rifles, too, were thinly distributed, but hand grenades were not, and some of the men carried their portion in a small tub or a sack. Also plentiful were demolitions, and there were attackers who had strapped charges to their bodies, turning themselves into human bombs. The officers carried their traditional swords.

The infiltrations increased until, half an hour before midnight, the star shells showed the Japanese wriggling forward in such numbers as to constitute a full-scale counterattack. Although spread over a front of several thousand yards, the enemy appeared in heaviest concentration before the 2nd Battalion, 23rd Marines, commanded by Lieutenant Colonel Edward J. Dillon. The Americans responded with a furious barrage of artillery, mortar, machine gun, and rifle fire, the show a colorful one under the parachuting lights. The shells burst in reds and yellows that turned instantly to puffs of smoke, and the machine gun tracers crisscrossed with dazzling speed, many ricocheting off rocks. From the Japanese side came rockets that left trails of golden sparks. Some of these missiles were faulty, and hit the Marine lines with nothing more than a muffled thump.

The Japanese died by dozens, by scores, and, before the night was over, by hundreds. Sections of the front were carpeted with torn and riddled corpses, the ground beneath them saturated with blood. Among the remains were those of true *Bushido* stalwarts, but the majority of the bodies were those of men who only a short time before had entertained wistful thoughts of their homes and families, had looked at pictures and fondled keepsakes, had expressed a willingness to die for the Emperor but had never really given up the hope that they might somehow remain alive. The field's carnage was not the product of American fire alone. Many of the badly wounded, either following the *Bushido* code or fearing capture, killed themselves by holding grenades to their stomachs.

Numbers of the attackers reached the Marine lines, the officers flourishing their swords and shouting in Japanese such orders as "Follow me!" and "Keep going!" One Marine dodged out of the path of a charging officer and shot him in the side with a .45 pistol. Some of the enemy enlisted men employed the ruse of running up dragging stretchers and calling out in English, "Corpsman! Corpsman!" Deceiving no one, they were shot down. Grenadiers with their sacks and tubs jumped into empty shell holes and began throwing their missiles right and left, and Marines were heard crying, "I'm hit!" Others dodged the bursts and began tossing grenades of their own. The duels were long and deadly, and one company expended 500 grenades. A Marine who happened to hit a man rigged as a bomb was astonished at the explosion, which killed several other Japanese in the same hole.

With the approach of dawn, the jarring sounds and flaring lights of the action receded. Both sides were exhausted. Dazed and leaderless, many bloody with wounds, the Japanese who hadn't been cut off among the Americans began falling back toward their warrens near the east coast. About 800 of their comrades were dead on the field. Included in this total was the dashing Captain Inouye, who was killed leading a charge. A member of the captain's command who lived said after the battle, "It's a pity he could not reach the American position for a full display of his final swordsmanship." It was believed by some survivors that General Senda, too, had perished, but he remained alive to continue his defense of the coastal terrain. However, his forces were now so depleted that not much of a defense was possible. This was exactly the sort of thing that Kuribayashi did not want to happen. The casualties inflicted on the Marines—perhaps two or three hundred—could have been doubled or trebled if all of these Japanese had fought to the death in their fortifications.

15
ON TO THE BITTER END

In the south, Army units were coming ashore from newly arrived transports and were setting up tent camps. Army aircraft flying from the lower field were replacing the carrier planes helping the Marines. Many of the remaining naval support vessels were leaving, Kelly Turner with them, his attention turning to the forthcoming invasion of Okinawa. A modest force under Admiral Harry Hill would continue at Iwo.

The heavy cruiser *Salt Lake City* was one of the vessels staying. The seagoing Marines serving on the cruiser had begun the campaign fretting about not being on the beach with the infrantry, where they felt they belonged. Then one day some wounded were delivered on board, among them a very young Marine with an unbandaged red stump where his right hand should have been. This sobered the cruiser's Marines. After that, Lieutenant Robert West noted, they were more inclined to be satisfied with the contribution they were making from their shipboard stations.

On March 9, D plus 18, elements of the 3rd Division broke through to the sea, despite the fact that part of the division's right wing was still heavily engaged with Baron Nishi's command in Cushman's Pocket more than a thousand yards to the rear. First to make it to the water, in the early afternoon, were twenty-eight men of A Company, 1st Battalion, 21st Marines, under First Lieutenant Paul M. Connally. They slid down a long rocky slope thick with pillboxes and cave entrances that had been blasted by the Navy. It was quiet as the party reached the beach. One man stooped and dipped his hands in the surf, saying he wanted "to wash off the smell of dead Japs." Several others removed their shoes and socks for the first time in a couple of weeks and waded in the cool salt water. "We all felt good," asserts Pharmacist's Mate 2nd Class Richard E. Pogue, a corpsman who was present, "at being the first outfit to reach the coast."

The good feeling lasted about ten minutes. Then the enemy hit the shoreline with a mortar barrage. As the waders splashed out of the surf and everyone began scrambling off the beach, seven men were hit, three seriously. "It was hellish," says Corpsman Pogue, who decided that the Japanese must have been watching all the time, delayed in reacting only as long as it took them to set up their mortar tubes and judge the range. Carrying the wounded, the party made it back up to the top of the slope, where other Marines were setting up a line.

By nightfall the 3rd Division was holding about 800 yards of bluffs overlooking the coast, and the defenses on northern Iwo were cut in two. A canteen filled with salt water was sent back through channels to division headquarters, and then on to the corps commander, Harry Schmidt. Attached was a note that read: "Forwarded for inspection, not consumption." There was rejoicing wherever the token went. This was the 3rd Division's greatest moment. The grip on the coast, however, still had to be consolidated, and Cushman's Pocket remained to be reduced.

That night the United States launched the first of its great fire raids against Japan. Well over 300 B-29s from the Marianas hit Tokyo with 1,665 tons of incendiary bombs, destroying sixteen square miles of buildings and killing at least 72,500 people, some estimates placing the figure as high as 130,000. The crews in the last waves of bombers, passing through the rising smoke, could smell the bodies burning, and some of the men, unused to such blatant evidence of the slaughter they were wreaking, grew sick. This raid was by far the most destructive single raid of the war, in any theater, up to that time. The tail gunners in the retiring planes could still see the flames when they were 150 miles away. Two damaged B-29s landed on Iwo Jima.

March 10, D plus 19, was a red-letter day for General Cates and the 4th Division. The Amphitheater, Turkey Knob, and Minami Village, which had been holding up a section of the front for nearly two weeks, were finally subdued and left behind. The whole front now linked up for a drive toward the east coast. Due largely to the shattering of the Japanese during their night attack on March 8, the day's gains were excellent. Some units advanced as far as 700 yards, which placed them little more than 300 yards from the sea. Patrols descended ravines to the beach, returning to report that no resistance had been met. The "door" was about to close, though the division's right wing had another pocket to reduce, the one holding General Senda, before the latch could be clicked.

During the past three days the 5th Division had continued its drive up the west coast toward Kitano Point. For these Marines, resistance was not diminishing but growing stiffer, for they were approaching the headquarters of General Kuribayashi himself. Everywhere were Japanese who fought to the death. Sometimes their efforts were almost superhuman. In one case, a Marine using a flamethrower sent a heavy stream into the rear entrance of a pillbox. A shriek was heard, and a man came running out, his clothing in flames and the sticky napalm burning on his arms and face and scalp. He had a grenade in each hand, and he threw both even as his blistered skin was turning black and he was falling into a crisp, smoking heap.

The 2nd Battalion, 28th Marines, took a prisoner on March 9. The man stepped out of a cave and surrendered to Sergeant Howard Snyder of the flag-raising company. Receiving the news at his headquarters just to the rear, Dave Severance sent Frank Crowe forward to bring the Japanese back. Says Crowe: "He was wearing nothing more than a loincloth, and appeared to have burn marks all over his legs and had great difficulty standing up. I called to him in Japanese to come, and he hobbled to me. Snyder ordered one of his men to accompany us back to the command post. Subsequently, battalion headquarters sent up an interpreter to take the Nip back for interrogation and incarceration."

Ironically, Howard Snyder, who had chosen to spare this Japanese, died shortly afterward, shot through the head from another cave. Snyder had been one of the first men to reach Suribachi's summit on the day the flag was raised. As for his capture of the Japanese, it gained Easy Company the congratulations of regimental headquarters. In the first place, the company would have been thought justified if it had killed the man without mercy, since one of its members had been tortured to death a few days earlier. In the second place, the man proved a valuable source of information about the defenses the 5th Division was approaching.

The capture and the congratulations became a part of the record. But the record was to remain blank concerning something that happened the following day. Several men of Easy Company, using their few Japanese phrases, coaxed a Japanese from a large cave believed to be holding a good number. The man was turned over to Art Stanton to guard while the party tried to persuade others to come out. Stanton was surprised to find his prisoner able to speak excellent English. It turned out that he had been educated in the United States. His *Bushido* spirit was not strong, and he had little of the usual Japanese fear of receiving rough treatment at American hands. He was obviously happy to have saved his life.

The Marines at the cave entrance had no success in getting any more Japanese to come out. What did come out was a rifle bullet, and it hit one of the Americans in the upper left arm, smashing the bone. Instead of succumbing to fear as a result of this serious wound, the Marine became furious. With a .45 pistol in his right hand, he approached Art Stanton and his prisoner, and almost snarled as he

Marines trying to persuade cave occupants to surrender.

said, "I'm taking this man to the rear." Stanton watched the pair go around a boulder, the frightened Japanese ahead, his back covered by the .45. The Marine's left arm hung useless, blood dripping from the fingertips. The two men were barely out of sight when Stanton heard the pistol shot. In a moment the wounded Marine was back, saying, "That dumb son of a bitch tried to escape." This Marine had more of an excuse for his wrath than he knew. He would lose his left arm at the shoulder, and some years later he drowned, unable to swim when his boat tipped over during a fishing trip.

The Marines of the 5th Division were now nearing the Gorge, or Death Valley, as it also came to be known. It was about 500 yards south of Kitano Point, the island's northern extremity, and it extended from its mouth on the western coast to a spot about 700 yards inland. From 200 to 500 yards wide, it was a jumble of ravines, gullies, and jagged outcrops, and was honeycombed with caves and tunnels, most with multiple entrances. If a heavy aerial bomb happened to hit an entrance, smoke would puff out of other entrances, sometimes an astonishing distance away. In and around the Gorge were about 1,500 Japanese under the direct control of Kuribayashi, Admiral Ichimaru, and Colonel Ikeda. Kuribayashi's huge headquarters blockhouse was near the inland end of the Gorge. Even when he laid out the island's defenses, the general had foreseen how the American attack would develop and had intended to use this region to make his last stand. From the point of view of the exhausted and depleted American troops, the whole thing appeared to have been planned with diabolical cunning.

At this time the Americans were making the most of their support weapons, since their use would have to be restricted when the infantry entered the Gorge. On March 10 Kuribayashi reported to Tokyo that "the enemy's bombardments . . . are very severe, especially the bombing and machine gun fire against division headquarters from thirty fighters and bombers, so fierce that I cannot express or write it here. Before American forces landed on Iwo Jima, there were many trees around my headquarters, but now there is not even a wisp of grass remaining. The surface of the earth has changed completely." But everywhere in the district, the general asserted, the Japanese troops were "still fighting bravely and holding their positions thoroughly." This was almost literally true, for the 5th Division's advances toward the Gorge were measured more often by feet than by yards.

Corporal Wilbur Young, who had begun the battle in charge of a shore party helping to unload ships but was now at the front with the 28th Marines, was amazed at the enemy's talent for concealment: "We would fight all day, rarely seeing a Jap, and it seemed that as many Marines were being shot from the rear as from the front." On March 11, Young was out ahead of the lines and had just tossed a grenade that finished off a machine gun emplacement when a rifle bullet hit him in the upper right arm, knocking him down. "I lay there wondering where the shot had come from. In a few moments a Jap stepped from behind some boulders about thirty yards from me, his rifle trained on me in case I moved. I didn't. It was somewhat of a surprise to see him dressed in one of our Marine Corps uniforms and aiming an M-1 rifle at me. When he returned to his cover behind the boulders I got up and started running in a zigzag path back to where I had left my men, my shattered arm flapping. While I was being given first aid, some of the enemy appeared on a ledge above us. A burst of BAR fire eradicated that menace."

Front-line scene on March 11, D plus 20.

When the time came for Young to be evacuated, he found he had lost so much blood he was too weak to walk, and he had to wait for stretcher bearers from the rear. A pair soon arrived. "To our mutual surprise," Young explains, "they happened to be men I had helped to train as a drill instructor at San Diego." Tears began running down the bearers' faces, and one said, "We hated your guts in boot camp, but we have given thanks many times on this island that you were tough and demanding." They took Young out under small-arms fire, apologizing for the need to run and cause him pain with the jostling. Bullets were still snapping about as they put him aboard a jeep ambulance, but no hits were scored. Young was soon on a hospital plane on his way to Hawaii.

While the Marines of the 5th Division were fighting near the southern rim of the Gorge, those of the 3rd were slowly reducing Cushman's Pocket, and those of the 4th were closing around the survivors under General Senda. American units in all zones were now only shadows of their former strength, bearing no resemblance to the smart appearance they had once presented on the parade ground. Uniforms were dirty, threadbare, and bloodstained, some composed of pieces borrowed from the Navy or the Seabees, and some improvised partly out of Japanese items rifled from captured caves. Combat efficiency was probably nowhere greater than forty percent, in some places considerably less. Experienced personnel were scarce; replacements made up a great part of the corps. Cooks and bakers and other specialized troops had become front-line riflemen. Junior officers were commanding companies, and corporals and first class privates had become platoon leaders. Some of the companies were hardly larger than platoons. The Marines were now like weary prizefighters, barely able to keep up their guard and throw an occasional blow. Many were so physically and mentally numb they were becoming careless about enemy fire. Gunshot wounds were being rivaled by dysentery and other illnesses as a source of casualties. There were men like Corporal Philip H. Haake, one of the few Hawaiian Islanders on Iwo, who had spent the battle worrying about getting hit but who now had the added concern that his extremely sore feet might not make it. Like thousands of others, Haake had not changed his socks since D day.

The high brass of both the Navy and Marines had grown impatient to bring the battle to at least an official conclusion. It had dragged on beyond all estimates of the time it would take, and the casualties were far higher than expected. Back in the United States, people were protesting. One woman wrote the Navy Department: "Please, for God's sake, stop sending our finest youth to be murdered on places like Iwo Jima." There was a flag-raising ceremony at Harry Schmidt's headquarters on March 14, D plus 23, though the island was not at that time declared secured. The bugler had to compete with the sounds of combat involving the last three pockets of resistance, the firing of American artillery pieces shaking the very ground around the flagpole. Moved to tears by the ceremony, Holland Smith turned to an aide and said, "This was the toughest yet." He was speaking not only of World War II but of the entire history of the Marine Corps.

About the same time the Stars and Stripes made this triumphal ascent, Colonel Ikeda, in one of the caves of the Gorge, was trying to decide what to do with the proud emblem of the 145th Infantry Regiment, then close to extinction. Kuribayashi advised him to burn the flag at the last moment to keep it from falling into American hands.

Bombardments notwithstanding, Kuribayashi was safe, at least for the moment, in his headquarters blockhouse. No American ground forces had reached the spot. Still in radio contact with Japan, the general experienced a poignant moment on March 14 when the schoolchildren of Tokyo made a special broadcast dedicated to the surviving defenders. They sang "The Song of Iwo Jima," which began:

> Where dark tides billow in the ocean,
> A wing-shaped isle of mighty fame
> Guards the gateway to our empire:
> Iwo Jima is its name. . . .

The song went on to glorify, in the name of the Emperor and the nation, the hardships and sacrifices necessary to the defense, and the final verse spoke of relegating "the hated Anglo-Saxons" to a place in the dust. The program closed with the children praying for victory. Kuribayashi radioed back his appreciation to the Japanese people.

Both the 3rd and the 4th Divisions completed their work on March 16, D plus 25. The 3rd, in the center of the island, extended its hold on the north coast leftward to Kitano Point as an assist to the 5th, which was unable to get there because the Gorge stood in its way. More importantly, the 3rd took Cushman's Pocket, where Baron

Nishi had held out for so long. Meanwhile, the 4th Division overran the pocket near the east coast held by General Senda. The general killed himself, but Nishi remained alive in his three-tiered headquarters cave. Its entrance, however, had been assaulted by the Marines as they went by. According to one of the baron's lieutenants: "Colonel Nishi suffered burns in his eyes. He had no trouble walking, but after that his adjutant was always with him."

Late in the afternoon of this day of American successes Kuribayashi radioed Tokyo: "The battle is approaching its end. Since the enemy's landing, even the gods would weep at the bravery of the officers and men under my command." The general added that these troops had "carried out a series of desperate fights against an enemy possessing overwhelming superiority on land, sea, and air," but that the survivors were running out of ammunition and water. He had no regrets about his own fate, for he owed his country "a debt of gratitude." Attached to the report was what Kuribayashi called one of his "poor poems." It expressed his deep sadness about having lost the battle, and closed with the line, "I worry over what Japan's future will be when weeds cover this island."

That evening the top American commanders declared Iwo Jima secured. This news astonished the Marines of the 5th Division, who had barely begun their work against the Gorge. In a day or two Admiral Nimitz would issue a communiqué from Pearl Harbor that included these words: "Among the Americans who served on Iwo Island, uncommon valor was a common virtue." The praise was in the past tense, and the communiqué even included a final casualty report. The Americans at home heaved a great sigh of relief. There was really nothing dishonest about all of this. It was the way things were done. Even Kuribayashi considered the battle to be about over. As he had reported, his surviving forces were running out of ammunition and water. Unfortunately for the 5th Division, there was enough of both in the Gorge to enable the Japanese to continue killing and maiming Marines in considerable numbers for another ten days.

Iwo Jima's importance as an American base was increasing rapidly. The Seabees had the second airfield in operation, which provided extra room for fighter planes, and daily strikes were being made against Chichi Jima, Haha Jima, and the shipping of the area. As the fire bombings of Japan continued, more crippled B-29s were landing on Iwo. Flight Surgeon Ernest F. Kish was with one of the crews. "After a mission against Kobe, we could not get our bomb bay doors closed and used up so much of our precious gas we had to head for Iwo to refuel. We landed on the morning of Saint Patrick's Day, March 17. There were still numerous ships offshore, and signs of heavy fighting on the island, with many Americans moving around. Smoke and gas with a sulphurous odor rose from the volcanic ashes and crevices. It was a scene somewhat reminiscent of Dante's Inferno. I was happy when, having refueled, we made a successful departure from Iwo and Mount Suribachi about noon."

Before the end of the war a total of 2,251 distressed Superforts carrying 24,761 crewmen would land on Iwo. What the island meant to the Army Air Force was explained in its wartime journal *Impact*: "Located about midway between Guam and Japan, Iwo broke the long stretch, both going and coming. If you had engine trouble, you held out for Iwo. If you were shot up over Japan and had wounded aboard, you held out for Iwo. If the weather was rough, you held out for Iwo. Formations assembled over Iwo and gassed up at Iwo for extra-long missions. If you needed fighter escort, it usually came from Iwo. If you had to ditch or bail out, you knew that air-sea rescue units were sent from Iwo. Even if you never used Iwo as an emergency base, it was a psychological benefit. It was there to fall back on."

General Kuribayashi's defeat was announced in Japan on the evening of March 17. Speaking by radio, Prime Minister Kuniaki Koiso called the battle's outcome "the most unfortunate thing in the whole war situation." But he hastened to add that there would be no unconditional surrender. As long as one Japanese remained alive, the nation must fight "to shatter the enemy's ambitions." Koiso had more to say in the same vein, but few of his hearers could have been heartened.

Even as the prime minister was making his broadcast, a curious drama was being enacted on Iwo Jima, deep below the surface of the Gorge in Admiral Ichimaru's cave headquarters. The survivors of the admiral's command, no more than fifty or sixty men, were assembled there in the lamplight, all faces solemn. "The loss of this island," said Ichimaru, "means that Yankee military boots will soon be treading upon our motherland." But in spite of this unhappy knowledge, he went on, all survivors must retain their fighting spirit to the end. They were urged to "kill as many of the enemy as possible" and to strive for their "seventh life." As he finished talking, the admiral signaled with his hand, and his senior staff officer stepped to a spot near one of the lamps and began reading from a sheet of paper: "Rear Admiral T. Ichimaru sends this note to Roosevelt. I have one word to give you at the termination of this battle. . . ."

The American president was accused of calling Japan "a yellow peril, a bloodthirsty nation, and a protoplasm of the military clique." The message continued: "Though you may use the surprise attack on Pearl Harbor as your primary material for propaganda, I believe that you, of all persons, know best that you left Nippon no other method to save herself from destruction. . . . The white races—especially you Anglo-Saxons—are, at the expense of the colored races, monopolizing the fruits of the world. . . . Why is it that you, an already flourishing nation, nip in the bud the movement for the freedom of the suppressed nations of the East? All we want is for you to return to the East that which belongs to the East. . . ." The admiral had something to say about America's choice of allies: "It is beyond my imagination how you can slander Hitler's program and at the same time cooperate with Stalin's Soviet Russia, which has as its principal aim the socialization of the world. . . ." In its conclusion, the message predicted eventual failure for the "barbaric world monopoly" the United States was establishing. Ichimaru's letter was penned in two versions, one in Japanese and one in English. It was the admiral's hope that the English version would be found by the Americans.

Iwo's radio contact with Tokyo was maintained by means of a relay station on Chichi Jima, and late at night on March 17 Major Horie, on Chichi, received orders from Imperial Headquarters to notify Kuribayashi that he had been promoted to full general. "I wanted to reach him in his lifetime," states Horie, "but unfortunately there was no answer from the Iwo Jima radio station." Having issued orders for a general attack to take place that night, Kuribayashi had left his headquarters blockhouse near the eastern end of the Gorge and placed himself at the head of perhaps 500 of his men. There was no attack, however. The general presumably had overcome the temptation to violate his own rule and waste his final strength. He simply took the men to another cave system farther down the Gorge toward the western sea. It had become an urgent necessity for him to do this, for the Gorge was now surrounded, except at its mouth on the west coast, and the Marines in the east had begun driving down its length and were closing in on the blockhouse and its cave complex. Kuribayashi's move did not cut him off from all radio contact with Chichi Jima, as Major Horie was to learn a few days later.

Iwo was the setting for a bizarre interlude on the evening of March 18. A bored American radioman invented a report that the war in Europe had ended (it still had nearly two months to go), and within ten minutes the false news was all over the island. In celebration, troops in the rear areas sent up flares and opened fire with antiaircraft guns, rifles, carbines, and pistols. Ships near the beaches joined in with similar demonstrations. On land and sea, bottles of booze were broken out. The shooting, drinking, and whooping went on for nearly an hour, stopping only when corps headquarters put out its own false report, setting "Condition Red—enemy planes in the area." The celebration added several names to the battle's casualty list.

Up to this point Baron Nishi had remained in his bypassed cave complex in Cushman's Pocket. No other officers of high rank were with him; all who remained alive were with Kuribayashi in the Gorge. Nishi was not even in contact with these men. On the night of March 18 the baron decided to lead the few score survivors of his command in a final attack, his scorched eyes notwithstanding. The badly wounded soldiers lying in the caves were given pistols and hand grenades and a three-day supply of bread, but no water. "We took much time," one man said later, "in saying goodbye to them."

At last all of the troops still on their feet, some of them walking wounded, went out into the night. Nishi had to rely on his adjutant to guide him over the stygian terrain. The baron was taking the pathetic little force northward to attack the Marine lines on the coast. As they neared the objective, the Japanese were pinned down by mortar and small-arms fire, and at dawn a deluge of hand grenades was added. Nishi ordered the survivors to assemble, and those who were able to crawl to him were told to take refuge in caves along the beach.

The baron's last moments are not a matter of record. His wife had believed him to be dead when Iwo's fall was announced in Japan. That night she had stood holding the hand of their youngest daughter on the beach facing the island, looking out over the water with tears running down her cheeks. Later she pieced together what she learned from survivors, added to this what she knew of her husband, and concluded that he had killed himself with his pistol while facing the sea. He had once told her that *hari-kari* with a knife was slow and uncertain, and that the best way to kill oneself was by means of a bullet in the ear. Since the body was never found amid Iwo's rubble, the baroness chose to believe it had been claimed by the clean surf.

On March 19 the remnants of the 4th Marine Division left the island, sailing for the unit's camp in the Hawaiian Islands. The 4th had now completed four campaigns in thirteen and a half months, ending with the most devastating. On Iwo, elements of the 3rd Division took over the occupation of the vacated zone, and were joined on March 20 by the 147th Infantry Regiment of the U.S. Army, which would garrison the island and continue mopping up when all of the Marines were gone.

In the 5th Division zone, the chief accomplishment on March 19 and 20 was the reduction of Kuribayashi's blockhouse and its cave complex near the eastern end of the Gorge. Blowing the blockhouse required four tons of explosives, divided into five charges. On succeeding days, the work against the Gorge was wearily pressed. Some of the Marines held a position along the southern rim, others moved from the blockhouse area westward toward the sea, and still others, already near the sea just to the north, made their way down over this rim. The Japanese were daily squeezed into a smaller compass. Tank dozers cut paths through the rocks and corrugated earth for the regular tanks to use. Flame tanks did some of their best work here. "This was the one weapon," said a 5th Division action report, "that caused the Japs to leave their caves and rock crevices and run. On many occasions the Japs attempted to charge our flame tanks with shaped charges and other explosives. Few of these attempts were successful." A demolitions-bearing Japanese who ran at one of the tank dozers was stopped when the operator raised the heavy blade in the air and dropped it, cutting the man in two.

If the Japanese failed against the tanks, they continued to punish the infantry, keeping busy with mortars, machine guns, rifles, and hand grenades. They fought especially well because they were in the presence of their highest officers. Kuribayashi was composing radio messages that were not sent immediately but saved for bulk transmission at the last opportune moment. On March 21 he wrote: "We are still fighting. The strength under my command is now about 400. . . . Tanks are attacking us. The enemy suggested we surrender through a loudspeaker, but our officers and men just laughed and paid no attention." The next day the general recorded that food and water were gone. "But our fighting spirit is still running high. We are going to fight resolutely to the end."

The Marines, too, were going to fight to the end. But their resolution and fighting spirit, far from running high, were kept alive by sheer willpower. The average battalion, which had landed with 36 officers and 885 enlisted men, was down to about 16 officers and 300 enlisted men, and this included the hundreds of replacements that had been brought up from the rear. According to a report issued by Chandler Johnson's 2nd Battalion of the 28th Marines, commanded since Johnson's death by Major Thomas B. Pearce, Jr., the companies had been reduced from their original strength of about 250 men to 45 to 85 men each, over half of which were replacements. "Casualties kept mounting daily," the report added. "The men were unable to get the proper food and sleep they needed. Enemy activity in front and behind them led to unsanitary conditions. The nervous systems of many were unable to stand the strain, resulting in numerous mental casualties. Not one officer platoon leader was available. Many platoons had PFCs in charge."

The flag-raising company had landed with about 235 officers and men, and had received about 70 replacements. By March 23, D plus 32, according to records kept by First Sergeant John A. Daskalakis, the company had suffered 240 casualties, more than a hundred percent of its original number. In addition, numerous men were hurt but still in action. Dave Severance was the only one of the company's officers left, for Robert Schuelzky had been killed on March 17.

After many narrow escapes following his burn injury from a mortar blast at the base of Suribachi, BAR man Art Stanton fell victim to another mortar shell on March 18. Rolla Perry witnessed the explosion: "I saw Stanton fly out of his hole, and when he landed his one foot was gone and the other was dangling. It was very sad to see him walking without feet, trying to reach his BAR so he could keep supporting his platoon, even though most of the original men were no longer there. Stanton and I had fought side by side, each depending on the other, and I had always felt safe when he was firing near me, for he was the best. Now, when a stretcher team loaded him up and started for the rear, I heard him say, 'You can't take me away. My old buddy Perry needs me.' "

Only a very few of the men associated with the two flag raisings were still in action. Chick Robeson, who had helped cover the first raising with his BAR, had been shot in the right hand. Franklin Sousley, who appeared in the famous photograph, had joined the dead, the third man of the six in the photo to die. John Bradley, the Navy medical corpsman in the picture, had been hit hard in the legs after three weeks of heroic attention to Easy Company's wounded. Rolla Perry saw the corpsman immediately after he was hit: "I was passing a big hole, and there sat Bradley with both legs bleeding, with five other Marines around him that he was treating, giving no thought to himself." Bradley was evacuated from the island by air the next day, and was recommended for the Navy Cross.

Jim Michels, the man with the carbine in the foreground of the first photo, would make it through the battle. So would Rene Gagnon, who had carried the second flag up the volcano and helped raise it, and Ira "Chief" Hayes, the Pima Indian, rearmost figure in the great photo. Hayes was to die an alcoholic ten years after the war, a nice guy who was never able to cope with the fame thrust upon him. For one thing, he felt guilty about being called a hero for having done nothing more than help replace the original flag. But, according to Rolla Perry, the Indian was one of Iwo Jima's real heroes: "Near the end of the battle, I saw to my right a Marine from another company coming up the line. As he passed in front of me, I was astonished to notice that he had an unexploded shell lodged in his left arm. It was about eight inches long and three inches around. The man went on to pass in front of Hayes, and the Chief ran out to him, put his left arm around his body, and with his right hand pulled the shell out and threw it as far as he could. It exploded when it hit the ground." This action probably saved the stranger's life, and perhaps even the lives of a couple of medical men.

During the last part of the battle, Easy Company's platoons, now only two in number and both small, were among the units that held a more or less stationary line along the southern rim of the Gorge. This was by no means an inactive zone; the Marines fought concealed troops all around them. Although few, the Japanese were deadly with their sniper fire, and many victims were shot through the head. There were countless "close shaves," such as the one experienced by Pfc. Jim Buchanan when a bullet cut the chin strap of his helmet. These last-ditch defenders were especially active at night, prowling everywhere and keeping the Americans in constant fear of their hand grenades and satchel charges. For the few Marines who had managed to escape death or serious injury since D day and were in the middle of their fifth week of this special hell, these were some of the worst moments of all, every man hoping desperately to stay lucky just a few more days. Pfc. H. C. Hisey, Jr., of the 28th Regiment's Headquarters and Service Company, complained in a letter: "It makes me mad when I think that the people back home believe this island was secured a week ago and that all the Marines have left. These people would think differently if they saw the wounded still being brought in."

The bodies of Americans and Japanese littered the front. According to Jim Buchanan: "The odor and the number of flies were unbelievable. We called for jeeps to take the bodies away but were refused. We offered to drive the jeeps ourselves but were told, 'Can't risk the jeeps.'"

Among the Easy Company dead by this time was Kenneth "Katie" Midkiff, felled by small-arms fire. Midkiff was the sergeant who had fretted wryly in training about being one of Keith Wells's "fifty men who aren't afraid to die." Not only a capable leader but also one of the best-humored and most popular men in the company, Katie was sorely missed.

The company command posts of the stationary front were located in clusters of holes just behind the lines, and all headquarters personnel had their moments of peril. During one of the last nights, six of the enemy were killed trying to infiltrate the Easy Company CP under Dave Severance. The daylight hours were somewhat calmer. Dave's radioman, Pfc. Leonard J. Mooney of Hackettstown, New Jersey, found time to carve in the soft rock of his foxhole: "L. Mooney, N. J., D day, Co. E, 2d Btn., 28th Marines." This inscription was discovered a few weeks later by a correspondent of the *New York Herald-Tribune*, and the result was a moment of fame for Mooney in his hometown.

Dave Severance had more idle time now that the battle was winding down, and he had much to think about. He was certain his company's performance on Iwo Jima had been second to none, and there were already indications that the unit would be remembered by history. Letters the men received from home bore the news that Rosenthal's photo was appearing in more and more newspapers and magazines, was becoming an inspiration to a nation grown weary of war, and was being compared with such classic patriotic paintings as "The Spirit of '76" and "Washington Crossing the Delaware." Already Admiral Spruance had suggested that the scene captured in the photo be made into a bronze statue. If there was injustice in the fact that the men of Keith Wells's 3rd Platoon who raised the first flag were being relegated to obscurity, there was no doubt that the famous picture was good for Easy Company, and was a great thing for the Corps and America.

But the captain wasn't thinking much about glory. Like other surviving company commanders he was greatly fatigued and depressed about the fact that he had lost so many men. Reviewing the weeks of fighting, he wondered whether he could have done anything to prevent this, whether he could have committed his platoons in a better way. He concluded that nothing he could have done would have changed what happened. To the wonderment of Frank Crowe, who had spent the entire campaign with him, Severance had never for a moment lost his image of imperturbability. One evening during the final days, Crowe was present at a meeting of the captain and the surviving noncommissioned officers commanding the platoons and squads. "They were murmuring about the losses and the inability to finish off the enemy, and intimated that they and their men were at the end of their rope. The captain listened to their lamentations, then quietly gave orders for the next day's fighting. His calm and confident manner had a strong effect, and everyone seemed to decide that the situation was not as critical as it appeared. The feeling of hopelessness changed to one of quiet resolve."

March 23 was the captain's worst day. First he received a letter from home that added heavily to his burdens: His wife had given birth to a baby boy who had not survived. As it happened, there was another "Dave" in Easy Company who was awaiting news from home concerning the arrival of a baby. He was Corporal David C. Bowman, who was commanding one of the platoons and doing a fine job of it. In this arena of death, both Severance and Bowman had found consolation in the knowledge that their wives were about to create life; it was a bond between them. Dave Bowman and his platoon were due to be relieved of front-line duty that day, and Severance was at the front when the new platoon, from another company, came forward. The captain was glad for Bowman, who was about to go back and who would probably not be needed at the front again. He was going to make it. Then, as Bowman was briefing the new platoon leader on conditions in the sector, he was shot dead. Badly shaken beneath his calm exterior, Dave Severance returned to his command post. Soon a new batch of mail arrived. Among the letters was one from Dave Bowman's wife, obviously the one he had been waiting for. Dave Severance finally lost his iron control. "I went off to an area all by myself and cried. I eventually regained my composure and continued on."

March 23 also was the day the final reports composed by General Kuribayashi were radioed to Chichi Jima. The messages were repeated several times, and then the receiver fell silent. Says Major Horie: "I could not stop weeping as I thought of the radioman sending these messages just before his death." About five o'clock in the afternoon the receiver crackled again: "All officers and men of Chichi Jima, goodbye." Major Horie, weeping anew, ordered the radioman to stand by, just in case something further came through. "But," Horie laments, "there were no more messages from Iwo Jima. Ah!"

Two days later, March 25, D plus 34, the 5th Division completed its capture of the Gorge. Remnants of all three regiments, with some of the men actually staggering, teamed up to overcome the last flurries of resistance. It was in this manner that the battle that had been expected to take ten days ended its fifth week. Even now, Iwo Jima held about 3,000 living Japanese, and General Kuribayashi and Admiral Ichimaru were alive somewhere in the Gorge. But every part of the island's seven and half square miles had been overrun. The Marines could finally claim the accomplishment of their mission.

But as if to mock them, a force of several hundred Japanese, many of them officers, formed near the northernmost airfield in the darkness of the early morning hours of March 26, picked their way through the Marine lines to the western sea, moved southward along the coast over a trail known only to them, and, before dawn, quietly infiltrated a cluster of tent camps housing Army Air Force units, Seabees, and Marine pioneers and shore-party personnel. A number of the airmen had their throats cut in their sleep before the alarm was raised. The ensuing battle, which lasted into the daylight hours, was confused and wild, with hand grenades exploding, rifles and machine guns crashing, and men on both sides shouting and cursing and lamenting in pain and terror. The Seabees employed their training as infantrymen, the Army brought up flame tanks, and the Marines first formed a defense line and then counterattacked. With the Marines was a shore-party unit made up of blacks who had seen no previous action, and they performed splendidly. In the end, more than 250 of the enemy lay dead and 18 had been taken alive. The rest melted back into the earth. The Americans had lost some 50 killed and well over 100 wounded.

One of the slain Marines was First Lieutenant Harry L. Martin, who earned the Medal of Honor that morning, the last of twenty-seven to be won at Iwo Jima—an incredible number considering the size of the island, the number of participants, and the duration of the battle. Sixteen of the medals were won by the 5th Division, which had traveled the longest route, from Suribachi to Kitano Point. This division also suffered the heaviest casualties.

As the fight in the south against the diehard Japanese infiltrators was sputtering to an end during the morning of March 26, the last of the 5th Division Marines were coming down from the northern hills to prepare to sail for Hawaii. The 3rd Division had assumed responsibility in the western zone as it had in the eastern zone on the departure of the 4th. Soon the Army would be assuming responsibility for the entire island, and the last units of the 3rd would sail for their camp on Guam.

The strained, bloodshot eyes of the Marines of the 5th brightened somewhat during the march southward as the men stared in amazement at all the changes they saw: the two large airfields with their myriad planes, among them damaged B-29s; the tent camps, Quonset huts, and other structures; the massive supply depots; the road systems over the once-treacherous sand, all busy with Seabee and Army traffic; and, most remarkable of all, the two-lane highway winding to the summit of Suribachi.

The Marines stopped at the 5th Division cemetery for a memorial service. Frank Crowe looked around at the men of Easy Company, standing with helmets off and heads bowed. Including replacements, they numbered one officer and sixty men. About thirty-five, some of them walking wounded, were all that remained of the original company. "My dear God," Crowe murmured to himself, "what happened to the other two hundred?"

The Marines of Easy Company traveled by small boat to the side of a large troop transport, and had to climb a cargo net to get on board. "We were so weak by the time we reached the top," explains Len Mooney, "that the sailors had to reach over the rail and pull us on deck." The transport provided the Marines with showers, clean clothes, good food. But stomachs had shrunk. Says Dave Severance: "I'll never forget how hungry I was and how little I could eat." That night the men had clean and comfortable bunks, but, according to the captain, their sleep was fitful: "During the night I received a head wound. I heard a noise, and, not realizing I was safely aboard ship, I jumped up and struck my head on the bunk above me. In the morning I learned that a great many other Marines had had the same experience."

With the Atomic Age dawning and World War II nearly over,

Fifth Division cemetery with Mount Suribachi as backdrop. Newly cut road winds to American installations on summit.

Easy Company would see no further combat, but it participated in the occupation of Japan. Dave Severance, a career Marine, soon left the infantry and became a fighter pilot. He served in the Korean War, and again managed to come through safely. Flying sixty-two missions, he won the Distinguished Flying Cross and four Air Medals. He retired with the rank of colonel in 1968.

On the morning that Severance rose from his shipboard bunk with a bruised head, a dismal drama occurred in the Gorge on Iwo Jima. General Kuribayashi, sitting in a cave with a number of his officers and men, decided it was time to end his life. Limping from a leg wound acquired during the fighting in the Gorge, he went to the mouth of the cave and faced north toward the Imperial Palace. Kneeling down, he bowed three times, then plunged a knife into his abdomen. Colonel Kaneji Nakane was standing over him with a sword, and brought it down hard on the back of his neck. The general died worrying about the future of his country and his family. He had no way of knowing that Japan would soon prosper in a friendship with America; that his son, Taro, whose strength of character he had fretted about, would become a respected architect under the new regime; and that his wife, Yoshii, would live a long life, once meeting with Iwo Jima Marines to accept a symbolic stone from Suribachi, and from time to time providing photographs to illustrate American writings about him.

The other remaining top Japanese officers on Iwo died on the same day as Kuribayashi. Admiral Ichimaru presumably was cut down by machine gun fire while leading the few surviving navy men in an attack. Found by the Marines in the cave where it had been left was the English version of Ichimaru's letter to Roosevelt. This would come to rest in the museum of the U. S. Naval Academy at Annapolis, to be read by Americans for generations. The admiral could hardly have asked for more.

During its mopping up, the 147th Infantry Regiment of the U. S. Army killed 1,602 Japanese and took 867 prisoners. As late as May 17, when Donald C. Palmer, a Navy aviation radioman, arrived for duty on Iwo, the work was continuing. "There was a story going around that Jap officers were still sneaking out of caves at night and using their swords to cut up Americans right through the sides of tents. I put my cot in the middle of the tent and slept with my .38 under my pillow."

By this time most of the Japanese survivors were concerned only with staying alive. They slept in their caves by day and traveled in search of food and water by night, often stealing them from the Americans. Friends would meet during these wanderings, pause to discuss the hopelessness of the situation, then go on. "On moonlit nights," one Japanese wrote later, "I was particularly sad. Watching the moon, I counted the age of my son or thought of my wife's face."

In all, only 1,083 of the defenders were captured. About 20,000 died violently or perished in the caves. The final casualty figures on the American side were 6,821 dead (those buried on the island being slated for removal to the States after the war), 19,217 wounded, and 2,648 cases of combat fatigue, a total of 28,686. Newsmen began calling the battle "the worst since Gettysburg."

It is doubtful that anyone regretted the losses more than Holland Smith, yet the old general found in them a positive military lesson. "Iwo Jima," he said, "proved the falsity of the theory that regiments or battalions that are decimated can never win battles."

EPILOGUE

It seemed ironic to American veterans of Iwo Jima that the island should be returned to Japan, as it was in 1968. The final irony came ten years later, when newspapers broke the story that Iwo was to be remilitarized. "When the project has been completed," a release explained, "the island will serve as a key strategic base for Japan's national defense. . . ."

Said one aging ex-Marine: "By hell, I'll run off to Canada before I help take it again!"

BIBLIOGRAPHY

Aurthur, Robert A., and Kenneth Cohlmia. *The Third Marine Division.* Washington, D.C.: Infantry Journal Press, 1948.

Bartley, Whitman S. *Iwo Jima: Amphibious Epic.* Washington, D.C.: Historical Division, Headquarters U. S. Marine Corps, 1954.

Chapin, John C. *The Fifth Marine Division in World War II.* Washington, D.C.: Historical Division, Headquarters U. S. Marine Corps, 1945.

Commager, Henry Steele, ed. *The Pocket History of the Second World War.* New York: Pocket Books, Inc., 1945.

Conner, Howard M. *The Spearhead: The World War II History of the Fifth Marine Division.* Washington, D.C.: Infantry Journal Press, 1950.

Fane, Francis Douglas, and Don Moore. *The Naked Warriors.* New York: Appleton-Century-Crofts, Inc., 1956.

Garand, George W., and Truman R. Strobridge. *Western Pacific Operations: History of U. S. Marine Corps Operations in World War II.* Vol. 4. Washington, D.C.: Historical Division, Headquarters U. S. Marine Corps, 1971.

Hashimoto, Mochitsura. *Sunk: The Story of the Japanese Submarine Fleet, 1941–1945.* Translated by E. H. M. Colegrave. New York: Henry Holt and Company, 1954.

Henri, Raymond. *Iwo Jima: Springboard to Final Victory.* New York: U. S. Camera Publishing Corporation, 1945.

Henri, Raymond, Jim G. Lucas, W. Keyes Beech, David K. Dempsey, and Alvin M. Josephy, Jr. *The U. S. Marines on Iwo Jima.* Washington, D.C.: Infantry Journal, 1945.

Horie, Yoshitaka. "Fighting Spirit: Iwo Jima." Manuscript account.

Howard, Clive, and Joe Whitley. *One Damned Island After Another.* Chapel Hill: University of North Carolina Press, 1946.

Huie, William Bradford. *From Omaha to Okinawa: The Story of the Seabees.* New York: E. P. Dutton & Company, Inc., 1945.

———. *The Hero of Iwo Jima and Other Stories.* New York: Signet Books, 1962.

Josephy, Alvin M., Jr. *The Long and the Short and the Tall.* New York: Alfred A. Knopf, 1946.

Leatherneck magazine. Issues of May and June, 1945, and of September, 1947.

Lovell, Stanley P. *Of Spies and Stratagems.* Englewood Cliffs, N.J.: Prentice-Hall, Inc., 1963.

Millot, Bernard. *The Life and Death of the Kamikazes.* New York: The McCall Publishing Company, 1971.

Nalty, Bernard C. *The United States Marines on Iwo Jima: The Battle and the Flag Raising.* Washington, D.C.: Historical Division, Headquarters U. S. Marine Corps, 1970.

Newcomb, Richard F. *Iwo Jima.* New York, Chicago, and San Francisco: Holt, Rinehart and Winston, 1965.

Proehl, Carl W., ed. *The Fourth Marine Division in World War II.* Narrative by David Dempsey. Washington, D.C.: Infantry Journal Press, 1946.

Rosenthal, Joe, and W. C. Heintz. "The Picture That Will Live Forever." Fifth Marine Division reunion journal. Capistrano Beach, Calif.: Gallant/Charger Publications, 1978.

Russell, Michael. *Iwo Jima.* New York: Ballantine Books, 1974.

Sherrod, Robert. *History of Marine Corps Aviation in World War II.* Washington, D.C.: Combat Forces Press, 1952.

———. *On to Westward.* New York: Duell, Sloan and Pearce, 1945.

Smith, Holland M., and Percy Finch. *Coral and Brass.* New York: Charles Scribner's Sons, 1949.

Smith, S. E., ed. *The United States Marine Corps in World War II.* New York: Random House, 1969.

Toland, John. *The Rising Sun.* 2 vols. New York: Random House, 1970.

Wheeler, Keith. *We Are the Wounded.* New York: E. P. Dutton & Company, Inc., 1945.

Wheeler, Richard. *The Bloody Battle for Suribachi.* New York: Thomas Y. Crowell Company, 1965.

Yukota, Yutaka, and Joseph D. Harrington. *Suicide Submarine!* New York: Ballantine Books, 1962.

INDEX

Page numbers in italics refer to illustrations.

Adamson, William R., 176
Admiralty Islands, 6
Adrian, Louie, 56, 136
"Agony" (tank), 176
"Angel" (tank), 176
Archambault, Raoul J., 170–71
Arkansas, 66
"Ateball" (tank), 176
Atsuchi, Kanehiko, 87, 92, 121, 146

Basilone, John "Manila John," 86
Bates, Wesley C., 88–89, 126, 189
Bellamy, Wayne, 162
Benard, Alphenix J., 98–99
Berard, Louis, 75, 112, 131
Bismarck Islands, 6–7
Bismarck Sea, 145
Blandy, William H. P., 64–66, 70–71
Blankenberger, Edward O., 140–41
Blevins, Robert L., 134
Block, Harlon H., 162, *164*, 188
Bloom, Wilfred A., 35
Boehm, Harold C., 206–8
Bougainville (Solomon Islands), 47, 55
Bowman, David C., 230
Bradley, John H., 114, 138, 141, 162, *164*, 227–28
Bradley, Paul, 82
Buchanan, James C., 55–56, 143, 228–29
Bushido code, 10, 20, 193, 212, 217
Butterfield, Jackson B., 132
Butts, John C., Jr., 98

Campbell, Bob, 163
casualties, Japanese, 182, 199, 212, 215, 231, 234

casualties, U.S., 108, 144–45, 157, 173, 191, 197, 199, 213, 227, 231, 234
Cates, Clifton B., 47, 85, 173
Chambers, Justice M. "Jumpin' Joe," 85, 107, 125, 151–52
Chaney, James E., 184
Charlo, Louis C., 157
Chester, 66
Chichi Jima, 16, 17, 20–22, 30, 41
Clark, Joseph J., 11, 12
Cobia, 22
Cole, Darrell S., 86
Collyer, Robert L., 58, 112, 131
Connally, Paul M., 214
Coral Sea, 7
correspondents, war, 103, 104
Craig, Edward A., 204
Crouch, Ralph H., 176–77
Crowe, Frank L., 57, 140–41, 185, 188–89, 201, 203, 216, 230, 232
Cushman, Robert E., 207–8
Cushman's Pocket, 192–93, 205, 207, 209, 214, 221, 225

Daskalakis, John A., 227
Dillon, Edward J., 211
Dollins, Raymond W., 78–79
Dooley, Raymond A., 78, 111
Duplantis, Wendell H., 168–69, 171, 182

Easy Company, *see* U. S. Marines, 5th Division, 28th Regiment, 2nd Battalion, E Company
Eberhardt, Fred C., 111
Ehrenhaft, Eugene J., 52
Eldorado, 63, 146, 163, 177

239

Emery, Gregory, 84
Erskine, Graves B., 47, 183, 205, *206*, 209
Estes, 70
Eutsey, Al C., 88, 125, 189–90
Evans, Holly H., 176

Faulkner, Bill B., 77, 89–90, 126, 150, 189
Finch, Barbara, 201
Forrestal, James V., 63, 163
Fredotovich, John J., 92
Freedman, Bert M., 92
Friday, Daniel, 56, 140
frogmen (underwater demolition teams), 67–71
Fuertsch, Isadore J., 52, 142, 188, 197
Fuji, Nosaro, 77

Gagnon, Rene A., 161–62, *164*, 228
Gandy, Douglas W., 66
Garretson, F. E., 187
gas warfare, 13
Genaust, Bill, 163
Gilbert Islands, 6, 7
Glass, William T., 207–9
Goode, Robert D., 138–39, 178
Gorge (Death Valley), 218, 222, 224, 226, 231
Griffith, Earl W., 180
Grossi, Dominic, 170
Guadalcanal, 7, 39, 47
Guam (Marianas Islands), 6, 7, 47, 204

Haake, Philip H., 220
Haas, Ralph, 111
hachimaki, 40
Hack, Chester B., 60, 65, 153, 154, 159
Haha Jima, 21, 30, 41
Hansen, Henry O., 135–37, 157, *158*, 188
Harbin, Kealer, 26
Hathaway, Wayne C., 137
Hawkins, Keith, 190
Hayes, Ira "Chief," 56, 162, *164*, 228
Headley, James C., 152
Hebert, Gordon A., 130, 152, 159
Heinze, Rodney L., 170
Helm, Jack R., 58
Herring, Rufus G., 69

Hill, Harry, 214
Hill 199 Oboe, 179, 182
Hill 357, 197
Hill 362A, 179, 182, 187, 188, 189, 193
Hill 362B, 192, 197
Hill 362C, 206–9
Hill 382, 175, 177, 179, 181–82, 187, 191–92, 197
Hill Peter, 179, 182
Hirakawa, Kiyomi, 74
Hirohito, Emperor of Japan, 10
Hisey, H. C., Jr., 228–29
Holly, Lowell B., 194–95
Hong Kong, 6, 10
Horie, Yoshitaka, 13, *14*, 15, 16, 20–22, 31, 224, 231
hospital ships, 117–18

Ichimaru, Toshinosuke, 23, *24*, 26, 36, 167, 218, 223–24, 234
Idaho, 66, 168
Ikeda, Masuo, 151, 165, 168, 170–71, 218, 221
Inouye, Samaji, 167–68, 210, 212
Iwo Jima: description of, 5–6; strategic importance of, 30, 222–23

Jacobson, Douglas T., 179
Japanese Armed Forces: Iwo Jima Naval Guard Force, 26; 23rd Army, 10; 26th Tank Regiment, 22, 175, 208; 109th Infantry Division, 26; 2nd Mixed Brigade, 26, 175; 17th Mixed Infantry Regiment, 3rd Battalion, 26; 145th Infantry Regiment, 26, 151; 204th Naval Construction Battalion, 26; 309th Independent Infantry Battalion, 77
Jarvis, William O., 123
Johnson, Chandler W., 51–55, 92, 122, 132, 138, 142, 148, 155, 156, 161, 178, 186, 195–96
Johnson, Robert C., 173
Josephy, Alvin M., Jr., 182
Junker, Curt, 72

Kalen, John J., 85
Kalen, Robert L., 85
kamikaze, 145–46
Keller, Harold P., 55, 93, 136, 156–57, 167, 177, 187–88, 195, 198

Kintzele, Arthur J., 139–40
Kish, Ernest F., 222–23
Kitano Point, 209, 216, 218, 221
Koiso, Kuniaki, 223
Koizumi, T., 81–82, 114–15, 128
Krisik, Edward, 137
Kurelik, Edward S., 114
Kuribayashi, Tadamichi, 8, 9, 10, 12–15, 20, 23, 26, 27, 28, 29, 33, 34, 37, 38, 39, 42–43, 65–66, 68, 78, 80, 87, 100, 112, 136, 144, 147, 160, 182, 193, 202–3, 205, 210, 218, 221–22, 224, 226, 230, 233–34; Takako (his daughter), 12; Taro (his son), 29, 37, 43, 234; Yohko (his daughter), 37; Yoshii (his wife), 10, 12, 29, 37–38, 42–43, 234

Lane, Robert M., 136
Langley, Clifford R., 135
Leader, Robert A., 57, 93, 139, 157, 164, 187–88
Lee, John P., 165
Leims, John H., 209
Lindberg, Charles W. "Chuck," 93, 137–39, 157, *158*, 178, 187
Liversedge, Harry B. "Harry the Horse," 94, 148, 150, 155
Lowery, Louis R., 155, 158, 161
Lucas, Jacklyn H., 123–24

MacArthur, Douglas, 7, 31
Marianas Islands (Guam, Saipan, Tinian), 1, 7, 19, 24, 30, 35, 46
Mariedas, James P., 102
Marines, *see* U. S. Marines
Marshall Islands, 7, 46, 61
Martin, Harry L., 231
McCarthy, Daniel J., 148
McGarvey, Joseph, 137, 198
McRoberts, Eual D., 91
Mears, Dwayne E., 88
"Meat Grinder" (Hill 382, "Amphitheater," "Turkey Knob," Minami Village), 175, 177, 179, 181–82, 187, 191–92, 197, 215
Meiji, Emperor of Japan, 43
Mendez, Gilberto, 179
Michels, James R., *158*, 228

Midkiff, Kenneth D. "Katie," 54, 136, 229
Midway, Battle of, 7
Missoula, 75, 112, 131, 155
Mitscher, Marc A., 64–65
Miura, Kanzo, 17–18
Mooney, Leonard J., 229, 232
Moore, Ernest C., 204
Mosely, George V. H., 10
Mosher, James R., 25–26
Motoyama Village, 183
Mount Suribachi, *see* Suribachi
Mowrey, Harry L. "Hap," 89, 125, 126
Musashino, K., 211
Musashino, Nakajima airplane-engine plant at, 34

Nakane, Kaneji, 33, 37, 233
Nanpo Shoto island chain, 5
Naylor, Arthur H., 189
Netherlands East Indies, 6
Nevada, 66, 186
New Britain, 6
New Guinea, 6, 7
New Ireland, 6
New York, 66
Nimitz, Chester W., 7, 46, 222
Nishi, Takeichi, 22–23, 34, 36, 192–93, 222, 225
Nishi Ridge, 195
Nishu Maru, 22
North Carolina, 74

O'Bannon, Wilcie A., 208–9
Okinawa, 30, 154
Olivier, Leonce "Frenchy," 82
Olympic Games, Los Angeles (1932), 22

Paljavcsick, Paul P., 133
Palmer, Donald C., 234
Parra, Benjamin, 172
Pearce, Thomas B., Jr., 227
Pearl Harbor, 6, 58–59
Pennell, Edward S., 94, 134, 137–38, 142
Pensacola, 66–67, 168, 186
Perry, Rolla E., 56, 193–96, 227–28
Philippine Islands, 7, 31
Philippine Sea, 15–16
Pogue, Richard E., 215

Queeney, Martin J., 89

Rice, Harold E., 88
Ridlon, Walter, 191
Roach, Phil E., 88
Robbins, Franklin C., 182
Robeson, James A. "Chick," 56, 136, 148, 157, 159, 167, 177, 186–87, 195, 227
Rockey, Keller E., 47
Rockmore, Clayton S., 170
Rodabaugh, Delmer, 98
Roi-Namur (Marshall Islands), 47
Romeo, Angelo L., 189
Roosevelt, Eleanor, 47–48
Roosevelt, Franklin D., 13, 47
Roselle, Benjamin F., Jr., 99, 100
Rosenthal, Joe, 163
Rothwell, Richard, 191
Rozek, Leo, 93, 136, 157
Ruhl, Donald J., 56, 105–7, 116, 135–36, 188
Rybiski, Benjamin J., 125–26

Saipan (Marianas Islands), 7, 11, 17, 47, 61, 64, 155
Salt Lake City, 32, 40, 66, 214
Samurai, 8–10
Sandstrom, Eric "Mom," 165–66
Saratoga, 145, *146*
Savory, Nathanial, family of, 16–17
Scheperle, John G., 92
Schmidt, Harry, 46, 63, 173, 203–5, 215, 221
Schmidt, Maynard, 209
Schrier, Harold G., 52, 155–57, *158*, 159, 161–62, 177, 199
Schuelzky, Robert E., 199, 227
Scott, George S., Jr., 52
Seabees (Naval Construction Battalions), 50–51, 98–99, 204–5
Senda, Sadasue, *174*, 210–12, 222
sennimbari, 40
Severance, Dave E., 51–52, 92, 94, 104, 114, 134, 138–39, 142–43, 148, 155, 178, 185, 187–88, 199, 216, 227, 229–30, 232–33
Shaker, Conrad F., 89–90

Shepard, Charles E., 132, 143
Sherrod, Robert, 46, 103–4, 111, 115, 128
Shintoism, 6, 10
Sibley, 58, 112, 117–18, 131
Silvis, Richard, 173
Sinclair, Robert D., 52–53, 139, 140, 188, 197
Singapore, 6
Smith, Holland M. "Howlin' Mad," 46, 63–64, 67, 72, 112, 118, 146, 163, *174*, 177, 204–5, 221, 234
Snyder, Howard, 136, 157, 160, 177, 216
Sokol, Leonard, 141, 198
Solomon Islands, 6, 7
"The Song of Iwo Jima," 34, 43, 221
Sousley, Franklin R., 162, *164*, 227
Spearfish, 35
Spruance, Raymond A., 63, 204, 229
Stanton, Arthur J., 56, 137, 144, 188, 194–96, 217–18, 227
Stein, Tony, 90–91, 189
Stephenson, Edward V., 182–83
Stoddard, George E., 52, 62, 94, 114, 133
Stolieckas, George C., 139–40
Stone, Carey A., 25
Stott, Frederic A., 125, 175, 182
Strahm, Raymond A., 134
Strank, Michael, 55, 142, 161, 162, *164*, 188
Suribachi, 5, 15, 19, 35, 48, 52, *81*, 86–91 (attack on), 92, 94–95, 121, 133–34, 142, 147, 155–59 (captured, flag planted), 163 (second flag raising photographed), 177, 184, *233*
Suver, Father Charles F., 164

Tachibana, Yosio, 21
tanks, *97*, 121, 140, 169, 183, *see* "Ateball," "Angel," and "Agony"
Tarawa, 46, 47, 64, 82
Temple, Bernard, 25
Tennessee, 66–67
Terry, 186
Texas, 66
Thomas, Ernest I. "Boots," 55, 141–43, 155, 157, *158*, 177–78, 184, 186, 198
Thostenson, Thorborn M., 90

Tinian (Marianas Islands), 7, 47, 61–62, 63
Tojo, Hideki, 8
Tokyo, 7, 34, 37
Tokyo Rose, 48, 58, 72
Turner, Richmond Kelly, 63, 71, 119, 145–46, 164, 204, 214
Turner, William, Jr., 181
Tuscaloosa, 66
Tuttle, A. Theodore, 161

U. S. Air Force: B-24 bombers (Liberators), 24–25, 28; B-29 bombers (Superforts), 31, 34–35, 201–2, 215
U. S. Army, 184; Seventh Air Force, 24, 36; 28th Photo Reconnaissance Squadron, 17
U. S. Marines: training, 44–46, 48–51; disparaging remarks about, 47–48; 5th Amphibious Corps (VAC), 46–57; 3rd Division, 47, 64; 3rd Regiment, 118, 204; 9th Regiment, 118, 173, 175; 1st Battalion, 207–8; 2nd Battalion, 207–8; 3rd Battalion, 206–8; 21st Regiment, 118, 126–27, 150, 165, 168, 175; 1st Battalion, 214; I Company, 169–70; K Company, 169–70; 4th Division, 47, 58, 64, 108, 124–25; 14th Regiment, 127; 23rd Regiment, 77, 118; 1st Battalion, 85, 111; 2nd Battalion, 85, 211; 3rd Battalion (K Company), 101–3; 24th Regiment, 118, 182; 2nd Battalion, 191; 25th Regiment, 77, 118; 1st Battalion, 85; 3rd Battalion, 84-85, 107, 108, 151; 5th Division, 47, 48, 58–59, 64, 108, 122; 13th Regiment, 113, 122; 26th Regiment, 118, 171; 27th Regiment, 77, 113, 118, 172; 1st Battalion, 86–87;
2nd Battalion, 86; 28th Regiment, 77, 118, 187; 1st Battalion, 86, 104–6, 113, 121, 125, 132; A Company, 90; B Company, 87–90; C Company, 87–91; 2nd Battalion, 86, 121, 132, 144; D Company, 92; E Company, 51–57, 92–95, 104–7, 114, 132–44, 148, 155–60, 185–87, 189, 195, 216–17, 228, 232; F Company, 92; 3rd Battalion, 121, 132, 143
U. S. Navy: medical teams, 82; Task Force 58, 63, 154

Vandegrift, Alexander A., Jr., 173
Vessey, William T., 122
Vicksburg, 66

Wachi, Tsuenezo, 8
Wagner, LaVerne, 101–3
Wake Island, 6
Waller, Harcourt E., Jr., 179
Washington, 74, 128
Weller, Donald M., 70
Wells, George G., 155
Wells, J. Keith, 53–55, 92–94, 104–7, 116, 134–38, 141–42, 146, 155, 178, 184, 186, 199
Wells, Robert, 150
West, Robert K., 33, 40, 159, 214
Wheeler, Keith, 104
Henry A. Wiley, 129
Williams, Robert, 121
Withers, Hartnoll J., 183
Wood, Alan S., 161
Wright, Frank J., 88

Young, Wilbur A., 152–53, 219–20

Zurlinden, Cyril P. "Pete," 110